Chewing Gum in
America, 1850–1920

I0025132

SELECTED OTHER WORKS BY KERRY SEGRAVE
AND FROM MCFARLAND

Wiretapping and Electronic Surveillance in America, 1862–1920 (2014)

Beware the Masher: Sexual Harassment in American
Public Places, 1880–1930 (2014)

Policewomen: A History, 2d ed. (2014)

Extras of Early Hollywood: A History of the Crowd, 1913–1945 (2013)

Parking Cars in America, 1910–1945: A History (2012)

Begging in America, 1850–1940: The Needy, the Frauds,
the Charities and the Law (2011)

Vision Aids in America: A Social History of Eyewear
and Sight Correction Since 1900 (2011)

Lynchings of Women in the United States: The Recorded Cases, 1851–1946 (2010)

America Brushes Up: The Use and Marketing of Toothpaste and
Toothbrushes in the Twentieth Century (2010)

Film Actors Organize: Union Formation Efforts in America, 1912–1937 (2009)

Parricide in the United States, 1840–1899 (2009)

Actors Organize: A History of Union Formation
Efforts in America, 1880–1919 (2008)

Obesity in America, 1850–1939: A History of Social Attitudes and Treatment (2008)

Women and Capital Punishment in America, 1840–1899: Death Sentences
and Executions in the United States and Canada (2008)

Women Swindlers in America, 1860–1920 (2007)

Ticket Scalping: An American History, 1850–2005 (2007)

America on Foot: Walking and Pedestrianism in the 20th Century (2006)

Suntanning in 20th Century America (2005)

Endorsements in Advertising: A Social History (2005)

Women and Smoking in America, 1880 to 1950 (2005)

Foreign Films in America: A History (2004)

Lie Detectors: A Social History (2004)

Product Placement in Hollywood Films: A History (2004)

Piracy in the Motion Picture Industry (2003)

Jukeboxes: An American Social History (2002)

Vending Machines: An American Social History (2002)

Age Discrimination by Employers (2001)

Shoplifting: A Social History (2001)

Chewing Gum in America, 1850–1920

The Rise of an Industry

KERRY SEGRAVE

McFarland & Company, Inc., Publishers

Jefferson, North Carolina

LIBRARY OF CONGRESS CATALOGUING-IN-PUBLICATION DATA

Segrave, Kerry, 1944–
    Chewing gum in America, 1850–1920 : the rise of an
industry / Kerry Segrave.
        p.   cm.
    Includes bibliographical references and index.

    ISBN 978-0-7864-9845-1 (softcover : acid free paper) ∞
    ISBN 978-1-4766-1981-1 (ebook)

    1. Chewing gum industry—United States—History.
    2. Chewing gum—United States—History.   I. Title.

    HD9970.5.C453U674 2015
    338.4'76646—dc23   2015001174

BRITISH LIBRARY CATALOGUING DATA ARE AVAILABLE

© 2015 Kerry Segrave. All rights reserved

*No part of this book may be reproduced or transmitted in any form
or by any means, electronic or mechanical, including photocopying
or recording, or by any information storage and retrieval system,
without permission in writing from the publisher.*

On the front cover: Advertisment for Adams California Fruit Gum
American Chicle Company with Virginia Pearson, Circa 1919 (CTG
Publishing)

Printed in the United States of America

McFarland & Company, Inc., Publishers
    Box 611, Jefferson, North Carolina 28640
    www.mcfarlandpub.com

Table of Contents

Preface

This book looks at chewing gum in America over the period 1850 to 1920, the beginning of the commercial production, distribution and retailing of the product in a substantial way. While people chewed gum in various parts of the United States before 1850, it was mainly done on an individual basis. A person went into the woods, scraped off exudations from trees, and consumed them. Some chewing gum was commercially produced before 1850 but in an apparently very limited way.

By 1920 the industry came to be dominated by chicle-based product that banished its rivals almost completely. Those rivals were the products based on the exudations from native trees, with spruce and balsam being the most widely used. The other rival was the petroleum-based gum, often called waxes or paraffins.

For the most part this book looks at the reality and perception of the users of the product, and attacks on the product from newspaper editors, reformers, and religious leaders, as found in the pages of the popular newspapers and magazines of the time period covered.

Research was conducted in Vancouver, British Columbia, at the University of British Columbia, Simon Fraser University and the Vancouver Public Library. Sources used were indexes such as *Readers' Guide to Periodical Literature* and online databases such as Proquest historical newspapers databases and newspaperarchive.com.

Introduction

Americans began chewing gum long before 1850, but it was mostly on a small and personal scale. Someone wandered into the woods in, say, New England, scraped some material off spruce trees, took it home and perhaps cleaned it of impurities such as bits of bark and insects, and chewed the gum. Commercially-made chewing gum was available, apparently, but on an extremely limited basis.

Chapter 1 looks at the origins of the pervasive commercial chewing gum industry. During the middle of the period the three main types of chewing gum emerged and battled for domination of the field. Type one was the exudation from native American trees such as spruce and balsam, among others. These products were the so-called natural gums, which were the sole commercially available item during the 1850s and into the 1870s. Type two was the oil-based gum, often referred to as waxes or paraffins, with the raw material being a slab from a Pennsylvania oil refinery. By the 1890s paraffin gum was rapidly declining in popularity and gone entirely by 1920. Natural gum was disappearing. Type three was chicle-based; it was a natural latex product harvested from trees not native to the United States. After its arrival in the 1870s, chicle-based gum came quickly to outperform its rivals, and by 1920 it was mostly alone in the field.

Chapter 2 explores the idea that it was only women and children who consumed gum and the response and reaction to this idea, which held sway for several decades. Chapters 3 and 4 look at the popularity and spread of chewing gum, who the users were and where they were.

Chapter 5 discusses the reaction (almost entirely negative) to the chewing gum habit from newspaper editorial writers, other opinion leaders and shapers, reformists, and religious figures. Chapter 6 examines the effects of chewing gum from the physical to the mental. Some of these effects were grounded at least a little in fact or common sense, some were not; some were bizarre. Employment and the courts are the subjects of Chapter 7; that is, how employers reacted to staff who chewed and how the courts responded to those with the gum habit.

Chapter 8 looks briefly at the attempts by the United States to export the habit worldwide. These efforts were unsuccessful. It was a singularly American habit. It traveled poorly or not at all. Chapter 9 is devoted to wads (what happened to gum after the user was finished chewing) and novelties such as the "casket" to wear like a locket around the neck and wherein the user could store, instead of a photo, a favorite gum wad for later use.

1

The Business of Gum

People in the United States have been chewing gum for a long time prior to the period covered by this book. And prior to 1850 it was virtually all "natural" gum they chewed—that is, the exudation from various types of trees. Many trees were used for that purpose, including peach, pear, balsam, and spruce trees. The first gum produced commercially in America was spruce gum almost in its natural state. Initially, no addition was made to the naturally occurring spruce tree exudation. Items such as sugar and flavoring would come later. About all that was done at first was to wash the spruce exudations to get rid of at least some of the impurities that could sometimes be found in it and, of course, to process it to a consistent size and shape for the retail market. While exudations from various trees were used by people as natural gum they were not equal in popularity. Balsam gum may have been produced commercially—one or two vague references suggest it could have been in a limited way and only in certain locations. By far the most popular natural gum was the exudation from the spruce tree. And it dominated the chewing gum market into the 1880s. During that decade it was supplanted by chicle-based gum, which soon became the only chewing gum one could easily buy.

Chewing gum was also a singularly American institution. According to one reporter, "savages and backwoodsmen" from every climate and age had chewed the gum that exuded from any number of different trees, but the United States was first to make gum chewing a commercial enterprise and an "innocuous vice."[1]

A journalist stated, in an 1886 article, that most of the people involved then in the chewing gum business did not know where the practice started. However, it was reported that a majority of researchers were disposed to trace the practice to the "barbaric tribes" of Africa, whose women gathered the resinous gum that the tropical sun caused to exude from the trees, and chewed it. It was probable, thought the reporter, that the custom was introduced into the Southern states by the African slaves brought over who found the pine trees of the south as prolific in exuding gum as the trees of their native forests. The white women of this part of the nation, at this time, were said to be almost entirely given "to the nauseating habit of 'dipping snuff'"—that is, rubbing it over their gums with the frayed ends of a pine stick. In time they adopted the supposedly cleaner and healthier custom of their slaves, and the gum of the pine tree became their favorite, largely superseding snuff dipping. An observant Yankee traveling through the South in antebellum days noticed the feminine gum habit and saw a prospective fortune in manufacturing an artificial gum of superior flavor to that gathered in the woods. A little rancid tallow, a trifle of gum arabic mixed together and hardened, then cut into small cubes and wrapped in colored paper constituted the chewing gum of 20 years earlier, thought the journalist. That mixture found a ready sale among Southern women and in time the demand reached into the cities of the North. Gum-chewing in a few years spread rapidly among the females of the East, and finally crossed the Alleghenies and "swept over the West like wildfire."[2]

Two years later a different reporter spoke briefly about the origins of gum chewing by remarking that children in the United States began to chew the exudation from different trees such as peach, plum, pine, spruce, and sweet gum, thus giving somebody the idea to make an artificial gum. It was first made of beeswax, gutta-percha, and other rubbery and sticky substances which, he said, "were perfectly pure and harmless," and not costly in preparation. But then, around 1885, some "inventive genius" discovered that by boiling some of the baser elements of petroleum and mixing in a small amount of beeswax, a similar gum could be produced that was "quite susceptible to flavors and trifling in cost." By the use of scents and large quantities of sugar (the principal item used in the composition of any gum), the disagreeable odor and taste of petroleum was completely eliminated. Around that same time a gum called "balsam tolu" was produced, which found a ready market, especially among children. However, soon the paraffin and white gums (balsam tolu) found their time was over, as the chicle-based product arrived and dominated the field.[3]

1. The Business of Gum

Reportedly, the first gum maker of importance in the United States bore the name of Curtis. He founded an establishment to make spruce gum in Portland, Maine, in 1836, and his children, under the name of Curtis and Sons Company, still turned out a large amount of the old-fashioned spruce gum, at least through 1902.[4]

In the period covered by this book, chewing gum was produced from three different base ingredients. First were the so-called natural gums—predominantly spruce—that dominated the market until roughly the 1880s. Included in this group was balsam tolu and exudations from various other trees native to America. From the 1880s onward such gums lost popularity to the chicle-based product. Such gum was, of course, also a natural (latex) product but from a tree not native to the United States. In the middle of this period, roughly from the 1870s to the 1890s, gum produced from a petroleum byproduct (waxes, paraffin, and the like) enjoyed a brief period of popularity. By all accounts it was a somewhat foul product and faded from view fairly quickly. Thus, for a period of time around the 1880s all three types of gum were competing in the marketplace.

An early reference to gum of some sort appeared in a Maryland newspaper in March 1831. It told, briefly, the story of a child, the son of a dentist, who met his death that month in Philadelphia in an "extraordinary" manner. At school one day the teacher discovered that many of his students were chewing what was called in the news account "Gum Elastic (Indian Rubber)." The teacher began to verbally berate those he detected chewing. The boy in question, having a piece of the substance in his mouth, swallowed it to avoid detection and escape the teacher's wrath. However, the substance swelled up inside the boy's body with such rapidity, said the account, he died within a few hours.[5]

Early in 1851 a Milwaukee newspaper reported that the manufacture and sale of chewing gum had lately got to be quite a "spruce" business. Hundreds of tons of the product were made down East, where the trees were tall and abundant, and sent out yearly to keep the jaws of the nation in motion. "Everywhere folks are chewing, chewing, chewing—men, women and children have always a mouthful of gum," said the reporter. "The ladies chew it over their sewing, the children chew it at school, those religiously disposed chew it in meetings.... At least it is so in Milwaukee." That reporter and a friend set out to do their own observations of the spruce-gum users in Milwaukee, and out of 350 people they noticed in the course of a day, 294 were chewing spruce gum. Lately a wholesaler brought 400 boxes of the article to Milwaukee. Each box contained 416 sticks—175,400 sticks in total—and each stick sold for one cent. With an estimated 5,000 people being gum chewers in Milwaukee, this would keep those chewers supplied for three to four months. The assumptions made were that each user would get 35 sticks and that a stick of the spruce gum lasted on average three days.[6]

An ad placed in a Janesville, Wisconsin, newspaper in September 1851 by Holden, Kemp and Company outlined some of the benefits of their product. That firm was a Janesville company and agents and importers of spruce gum into their town. That ad read: "A superior preparation of Spruce Chewing Gum, for cleansing and preserving the Teeth, a most desirable article for sweetening the breath, imparting a delicious fragrance to it, and leaving the Teeth and Gums in a healthy state." Maker of the product was Curtis and Perkins, druggists in Bangor, Maine. The advertisement went on to caution the public against counterfeits and imitations of the article, specifically naming as supposed miscreants the Curtis and Brother, and the C. H. Hammond firms. "All of these are base imitations of our article and probably do not contain a particle of Spruce Gum," continued the ad. "We shall prosecute both makers and vendors of all spurious articles, we having secured the right of putting up the article in full as above described."[7]

By the summer of 1860 it was reported there were then established in various parts of the United States "immense factories with steam power and multitudes of hands, to manufacture chewing gum." It was said to have grown to be an immense business with a lot of capital invested and the ingenuity of man taxed to invent machines that would turn out the article of mastication in quantities sufficient to meet the demand. Said the reporter, "This chewing gum is supposed to be the natural ooze of the spruce tree, and such indeed may have been the original article introduced into the market. But the increase of rumination has caused the manufacturers to substitute a preparation of Burgundy pitch and resin, in which preparation the latter (resin) and cheaper compounds of course predominate." The reporter was worried that, to that point, *Hall's Journal of Health* had not officially condemned chewing gum. Nor had the newspapers said anything about the item containing deleterious substances. And that amounted to a serious shortcoming, in the view of the reporter.[8]

In 1882 the spruce gum trade of Maine was reported to be $10,000 per year. It was said there was not a city or town in the state in which it was not sold, and it was estimated that more was sent out of Maine than was used within that state. Best sales took place in communities where there were factory girls. Large quantities were sold in the communities of Lewiston, Biddeford, Lawrence, and Lowell.[9]

Another newspaper carried a story similar to the above, but in expanded form. This article mentioned factory girls and the same four towns, but declared that $40,000 worth of spruce chewing gum was gathered in the state of Maine every year. In Oxford County a man bought seven to nine tons of the product every year from the individuals who went out into the woods to collect the exudations. The gum was found chiefly in the region around Umbagog Lake and around the Rangely Lakes. A number of men did nothing else in the winter in Maine except collect gum. With snowshoes, axes, and sleds on which they packed the gum, they spent days and nights in the woods. The clear, pure lumps of gum were sold in their native state with the best bringing $1 a pound (the best lumps were those with the least amount of impurities such as bits of bark). Gum not immediately saleable was refined by the individual collectors. Sieve-like boxes were covered with spruce boughs, on which was placed the gum. Steam was then introduced underneath. The gum was melted, was strained by the boughs and then passed into warm water, where it was kept from hardening until the collector took it out, drew it into sticks, and wrapped it into tissue paper, making it ready for market. In the lumbering camps of Maine it was said gum was used as a means of extending hospitality. Clear lumps of spruce gum were placed before the visitor and he

A STRICTLY PURE ARTICLE.

A MOST DELICIOUS CHEWING GUM.

A VALUABLE SPECIFIC FOR LUNG & THROAT TROUBLES

Made by Curtis &Son. Portland, Me.

This is a simple and straightforward 1893 ad from a pioneer company for its very basic spruce gum.

was asked to take a chew. This account commented also on the problem of adulteration: "Spruce gum is adulterated and those who adulterate take the trouble to fashion the pieces of gum to appear like those taken in a pure state from the trees. The ingredient of adulteration is supposed to be the gum of the pine tree."[10]

In 1884 it was reported that it cost $2,000 a year to keep Augusta, Maine, citizens in spruce chewing gum, and, "Young ladies, especially those in school, are proverbial gum chewers." On a day in May in 1884 an unnamed Frenchman arrived in Augusta and marketed 125 pounds of the spruce article. One druggist alone took 75 pounds, which cost in the neighborhood of $1 a pound. It was described as prime gum that was white, free from imperfection, in lumps, and that had been carefully scraped from the trees and cleansed. The Frenchman, having apparently sold all he had brought to town, said he had another 200 pounds of the item at home that he planned to market. Gum from young spruce trees was said to be the best quality, being of a lighter color and of a better flavor than that taken from old trees, which was of a darker shade and had a "rank" taste. It was noted that there were men who made gum gathering a business and derived a good income from that source. But a warning was sounded that even then, in 1884, the spruce forests from which the gum was gathered were failing and the day was said to be not far distant when there would be a "famine" in the genuine gum. Lumber companies were making inroads into the ranks of trees and the spruce worm had injured or killed thousands of trees.[11]

Reportedly, in 1885 two or three firms in Maine had bought large quantities of spruce gum, just as it was hacked from the crotches of old trees, from the lumbermen and individual collectors for the purpose of refining it. It was said that refining consisted of adulteration of the item with resin. First, the refiners threw the spruce gum into a big kettle, bark and all, and boiled it until it reached the approximate consistency of thick molasses, skimming the impurities off as they rose to the surface. Then, if the refiner wished to adulterate the item, he added some lard or grease, in some cases a little sugar, and a lot of resin. The mixture then became thicker and, after more stirring, was poured out on a slab where, while it was still hot, it was rolled out in a sheet about one quarter of an inch thick, and then chopped with a steel die into pieces half an inch wide and three-quarters of an inch long. Then those individual pieces were wrapped in tissue paper and packed in wooden boxes, each box holding 200 pieces. Some refiners processed the spruce gum in the same fashion but without any adulteration. According to this piece, the best quality spruce gum always came from the biggest spruce trees.[12]

A New York chewing gum manufacturer took exception to an article in a New York City newspaper in 1887 that petroleum-based gum had driven all other products in that line out of the market. That New York maker said the supply of natural gum was still very large and would be still larger were it not for the fact that the spruce forests from where it was obtained had been so thinned out by the inroads of lumber firms that the gum collector could not obtain the quantities he had gathered in former years. One of the principal occupations in Bennington, Vermont, declared the New York manufacturer, was the dealing in spruce gum, also the case in Belfast and Augusta in Maine. Spruce gum was said herein to be worth $1 a pound in cash to the collector. Dealers in Augusta said the retail trade in spruce gum in that city alone ran to over $5,000 a year. The largest spruce gum dealer in the world was said to be based in Bennington, where he handled between 15,000 and 20,000 pounds of spruce gum per year. He employed not less than 75 people to collect gum for him in the season, which ran from October to June. Hot weather gathering was not possible, as the gum ran together and formed masses that caused it to deteriorate in value.[13]

Spruce gum was then obtained in the forests of Canada, Maine, New Hampshire, and Vermont. Each collector went out into the woods by himself and stayed there until he gathered 100 pounds of the item. Then he carried it to his home, where the women and children cleansed the gum of all its impurities such as bark, twigs, and other foreign substances. Then the family sorted the gum into its different grades, all of which were said to be "known even to the youngest child in the business." It was a big day's work for a woman to clean and sort 10 pounds of spruce gum.

As the collector went through the woods he looked for virgin spruce trees. When the gum that formed on the outside of the tree was once removed, the tree, it was said, would never again yield enough to make it worthwhile for the collector to visit it again. So he had to constantly move around, hunting out the spruce trees that had escaped the notice of all other collectors during all the years the woods had been searched by them. Each collector, as he went about gathering the gum, carried a stout pole that was in sections, like a fishing rod. At one end of the pole was a chisel fitted snugly to the wood. Beneath the chisel was a cup holding probably half a pint. When the collector discovered a mass of gum on a tree, no matter how high it might be, he ran his chisel up against it and cut it off, whereupon it fell into the waiting cup. Then it was placed in an oil bag that was slung across the collector's back. The process was so slow the collector considered himself lucky if he gathered 100 pounds in a month. The newspaper article claimed that Boston consumed more spruce gum than any other place in the United States, with Chicago in second place.[14]

A report late in 1888 that first appeared in the *Chicago Tribune* declared, "It is quite the fad at the present time to chew spruce gum. It, at least, is pure from all adulterations which are now so common. Dealers in gum say that until within a few years its use was almost exclusively confined to children, but at the present time the demand among adults is continually increasing." Of course, spruce gum was not free of adulteration and it was, in fact, sharply declining in popularity.[15]

A New York City journalist was exploring the topic of chewing gum in 1896 in his city with a small-scale manufacturer and wholesaler of gum. That wholesaler told the reporter that 25 years earlier (around 1871) there were only two kinds of gum available, the regularly made spruce gum sold in the stores and shoemaker's wax, which the boys used to beg or steal. Then white paraffin gum—coal oil gum, the children called it—came out and was a ladies' favorite from the start. "It was soft and did not tire jaws like the tough, unyielding spruce. Besides, it would not dislodge a set of false teeth, was cleansing and could be used in emergencies to cover over black, decayed spots in the natural teeth," explained the wholesaler. That was followed by "taffy tolu" and "snappy wax," both of which acted as pioneers for the trade, inducing by their sweetness and flavors a far more general use by adults.[16]

An article about a young couple who spent the husband's month-long vacation (from mid–February to mid–March) in the woods of New England gathering spruce gum appeared in the *Washington Post* in January 1911, at a time when spruce chewing gum barely existed after a rapid decline in popularity. The couple profiled (unnamed) were amateurs, not regular collectors. They sold the first grade spruce gum they gathered for $1.30 a pound, while the second grade material brought them 75 cents a pound. After deducting their expenses they reckoned they made a profit of $7.75 a day. The woman said that before going to the North Woods she had always believed spruce gum to be the best of all for chewing: "Now I take what the native of Maine call patented gum, patented meaning adulterated. The truth about pure spruce chewing gum is that it is next to impossible to get it." That was because before the gum was put on the market it was boiled or melted. After all the impurities were removed, a quantity of paraffin and resin and a little sugar was added. "This is the gum as it reaches the market. Any one who has attempted to chew the gum as it comes from the trees, the really pure gum, will tell you that the preparation is a great improvement," the article concluded.[17]

Stories about the manufacture of gum sometimes included a lurid account of how the item was likely tainted. One such story was published in the fall of 1867. It started by remarking that a great many American girls had acquired the "particularly disagreeable habit" of chewing gum. This account told how the product was made at an establishment in Podunk, Massachusetts, a manufacturer described as the "greatest" in the land and one whose fame was "in the mouth of all the world." Reportedly, one of its employees had recently been fired and had come forward to reveal to the newspaper how the product was made. It was said the product was made of certain parts of gum arabic, gum tragacanth, and a small quantity of resin and fat. The fat used was not lard, that being too expensive, but it was "a substance expressed from the dead hogs, cats, dogs and other animals found on the commons of our city." And, said the article, that was not the worst of it. "After the various ingredients are melted in a huge kettle, a certain kind of alkali is put in for the purpose of whitening the gum. This alkali is the same that is used by dyers with indigo to give a deep and permanent blue to flannels."[18]

It was an idea that did not easily go away. Eight years later the same type of story was published in a newspaper in a different state. It was identical in the sense it told of fat taken from dead dogs and cats and so forth, and told of the use of a certain kind of alkali.[19]

At the start of 1879 a newspaper in Utah stated there was then just one chewing gum factory located in New York City, with the few others in New England, other New York State communities, Ohio, Illinois, and

Tennessee. Also noted was that chewing gum was sold by druggists, grocers, and confectioners in cities, and the country grocery store that did not stock the item was considered incomplete. Gum from spruce trees, continued the account, had been exclusively used to produce the product until recently, when it found a rival in gum mastic, a white and attractive article made from paraffin, which was sweetened. Consumption of that rival form of chewing gum in the United States was estimated at about 30 tons yearly. As well, there was a gum made in Tennessee from balsam tolu and sold in just the southern United States. Consumption of that article was estimated at 20 tons annually. Both, of course, took a back seat to spruce gum. Additionally, it was noted that lately a new material was being used to produce chewing gum; it was styled as "rubber gum." (This was perhaps the first mention of what would soon be referred to as chicle.) According to the piece, the material was the sap of the sapota tree of South and Central America. The sap, like that of the India rubber tree, had a milky look. That gum had first been imported into the U.S. with the view of melting it with India rubber in order to produce a cheaper article than the latter—that is, to adulterate pure rubber. However, it was found to be less pliable than necessary and therefore useless for its intended purpose. It had long been chewed by the South and Central American Indians and found useful in allaying thirst. Therefore, experiments were conducted in the United States for purifying the item for chewing, experiments that proved successful. It was reported to be tasteless and had the merit of lasting longer than other gum, which more quickly dissolved and crumbled in the mouth. So great was the ductility of this new material that a piece half an inch long, after being heated in the mouth, could be stretched into a thread 100 feet long. Its consumption was estimated at about 50 tons a year.[20]

The beginnings of the American chicle-based chewing gum industry went back to the close of the Civil War. In 1866, Thomas Adams, Jr., happened to be visiting at the home of a friend at Sailor's Snug Harbor, Staten Island, New York, and there was introduced to Antonio Lopez de Santa Anna, the exiled military dictator of Mexico. Adams went to the room that was occupied by Santa Anna to hear something of his life and see the relics he had brought with him from Old Mexico. During the course of their conversation Santa Anna went to a drawer in a bureau in his room and took out a light brown substance and began to chew it.

Adams asked him what it was and the Mexican said it was chicle, the gum of the Sapota tree, which grew abundantly in Mexico. He offered some of the substance to Adams, who accepted it and began to chew it. To Adams it seemed to belong to the rubber family, tasteless but not unpalatable even in its crude natural state. Immediately, Adams was interested in the gum because he had made a study of rubber and he felt that he might have discovered something of commercial value. He asked Santa Anna to give him a larger piece to use for experimental purposes and the Mexican willingly wrapped a portion about the size of a man's fist in a piece of paper and gave it to Adams.

Over the following few days Adams took the substance to a chemist in New York, and after telling him about its origins and how he had come by it, suggested the chemist make an analysis of the gum and see if it was not possible to vulcanize it and produce hard rubber. For more than a year the chemist and Adams experimented along those lines but it was finally decided that it was impossible to vulcanize the substance. Still, Adams did not lose interest. While talking with his son Thomas, the idea to develop it into chewing gum was conceived. On a total investment of $35 the elder Adams and his sons Thomas and John D. started the manufacture of the first chicle gum. It was marketed under the name Adams New York Chewing Gum, later changed to Adams Pepsin Gum when pepsin was added to the product.[21]

A different account of Adams' entry into gum manufacturing said he began to experiment with chicle in 1867. He had hoped, it said here, to adulterate rubber with chicle and thus lower the costs of rubber. After he had tried and failed to use the product as rubber, or in rubber, Adams conducted other experiments, such as adapting it to cable purposes and making glue. All of those other efforts also ended in failure. Then Adams tried to sell his still large stock of the product, but as it had no known uses there were no takers. He even considered just throwing his chicle away, as it cost him for storage fees. (In this account he obviously had much more chicle to work with than the first account implied.) Then one day he was in a confectioner's store when a little girl came in to ask for a penny's worth of mastic chewing gum. Instantly the idea flashed through his mind, why could chicle not be made into a chewing gum? Then Adams began a new set of experiments and after months of trial and error and many disappointments he succeeded. When the manipulation of the chicle was developed to the point where it was a pure, white substance, he applied for a patent and became the sole proprietor of a new gum business.[22]

When a reporter interviewed Thomas Adams, Jr., in 1884, he asked the gum maker how it all started. Adams said, "Seventeen years ago [1867], when Gen. Santa Ana was in this country, his secretary had with him a piece of this chicle. I saw the stuff and believed I could use it as a substitute for caoutchouc [rubber] or India-rubber. I spent $30,000 trying to vulcanize it, and then gave it up. Meanwhile, I had learned that the natives chewed the gum. I concluded that I would begin the manufacture of chewing gum.... We call the manufactured article 'rubber chewing-gum' or rather that name was promptly given it as soon as we put it on the market. It won't wear out like spruce or paraffin gum. It tastes like rubber, and to people who want to chew gum it is just as satisfactory as any other kind."[23]

One year later, at the start of 1880, a lengthy article outlined the different ways that chewing gum was then produced. Spruce received a brief bit of attention, but only a line to say the time was when the fragrant spruce furnished the most common material for this purpose "but this is no longer the case." As an opening remark, the reporter wondered who would suspect that chewing gum was often from a refined production of petroleum. The process of refining coal oil—the thick, brown liquid that came from the earth—at one stage of its manufacture was by straining it through heavy linen cloths. The residue left after that operation was a dirty brownish yellow wax that "smells abominably." That substance, after being melted, bleached, deodorized and prepared for commerce, appeared in masses that weighed about 100 pounds, resembling oblong blocks of clouded ice. It then had no odor and no taste except what belonged to any wax in its purest state; it could be used for many purposes.

Manufacturers of chewing gum purchased those blocks and at once melted them down. To each block of 100 pounds of wax the maker added about 30 pounds of sugar and gave the mixture a flavor by the use of some essential oils such as lemon or vanilla, and perhaps added some coloring matter. Mr. Riggs of Riggs and Company (the only chewing gum maker in Cincinnati) said it was rare for any dangerous drug to be used in the process of coloring. Chewing gum was then usually white, or tinged simply red or yellow. After all the ingredients had been combined, the melted mass was poured onto a clean marble slab and cut into the various shapes "known to masticators" and in favor at the time with the makers. Different brand names such as Motto Gum, Shoo Fly Gum and Base Ball Gum, said the reporter, did not indicate any marked difference in the quality of the product. Motto Gum was said to be quite a favorite with the young ladies in boarding schools while Base Ball Gum was coveted by the boys before they got out of short pants. The paper in which Base Ball Gum was wrapped bore a picture of a player about to strike a ball, or something similar. Ice Cream Gum was so called because it had a yellowish tinge.[24]

Also mentioned in the 1880 account was a substance obtained from a different South American tree, not chicle. In any event it was likely very short-lived. Balsam of tolu, a resin, reportedly from South America, was at first in an almost fluid condition. It was a product of a tree known as "myraspermium toluiferum." That balsam was boiled by the maker until it reached the consistency whereby it could be run through rollers. It came out in the shape of a little slender rod, of a brownish yellow color, which was cut into pieces, each about 2 to 2½ inches long. Sometimes the balsam was mixed with a less costly wax. Lastly, chicle-based gum was briefly mentioned. According to the reporter, the balsam from the "chicle tree" from Central America was used in making what was known as snapping gum. It was very ductile when worked and moistened, and the process of making it was similar to that of pulling taffy.[25]

A New York chewing gum manufacturer told a reporter in 1882 that natural gum was then almost unknown. There used to be a trade in spruce gum, he explained, and still was in New England, but nowhere else. Commercially-made chewing gum, he declared, was nearly all paraffin wax. There was one maker in New York City, though, who used what was described herein as "a species of India rubber; gum chikley is its trade name." For this manufacturer the adding of sweetening was the only difficulty involved in the making of chewing gum because, for example, you could not boil paraffin wax with sugar, as the two ingredients would separate. The sugar syrup had to be worked in cold by pressure. He felt that if there was any staple chewing gum it was what was known as White Mountain Gum, made in Maine. It was a paraffin wax with a natural white color, but very sweet.[26]

In the fall of 1883 it was reported there were 25 to 30 factories in the United States devoted exclusively to the manufacture of chewing gum. Tolu was said to be the most popular in the West, made from the gum of the South American balsam and sweetened. Spruce gum was still gathered in Maine and exported from Portland. Most of the gum sold, however, was made from paraffin obtained from the Pennsylvania petroleum refineries and constituted the cheaper grades.[27]

Later in 1883 a chewing gum manufacturer in New York City told a reporter that nearly 75 percent of all the chewing gum sold in the United States was then made from petroleum. He showed the reporter a lump of petroleum he had just received—one of those large oblong blocks that resembled a piece of marble—and explained that a few days earlier it had come out of the ground in Pennsylvania "a dirty, greenish-brown fluid, with a smell that could knock an ox down." The oil refiners took it and put it through a lot of chemical processes that he, the maker, knew nothing about, and after taking out a large percentage of kerosene, a good deal of naphtha, considerable benzene, "a cart-load or so of tar, and a number of other things with names longer than the alphabet, left was this mass of nice clean wax. There isn't any taste to it, and no more smell to it than there is to a china plate." Then the manufacturer explained the process he used to turn the block of wax into individual pieces of gum. It was the same as explained above. Reportedly, that lump of wax produced 10,000 penny pieces of gum and the manufacturer used one such block every week, as did dozens of other manufacturers.[28]

Some months later when another newspaper ran a recap of this story, it added a sarcastic editorial comment: "Chewing gum is now made principally by crude petroleum. This is quite a step in advance. The chewing gum that used to be made of glue factory refuse was hardly the thing for the cultured Vassar taste."[29]

By 1884 the chicle-based product was coming to dominate the chewing gum field. The Adams factory in New York then was said to be importing 200,000 pounds of chicle a year, all for its gum factories. Asked how the gum was made with chicle, the maker explained, "It is a simple process. The chicle is thoroughly steamed so that all the impurities are worked out of it. Then, when in a semi-liquid state, it is run into the molds." The reporter asked if the chewing gum produced at the plant was pure chicle and nothing more. The answer: "Nothing more.

We put up a kind which we recommend for colds. That contains a little licorice. When that is extracted pure chicle alone remains."[30]

Another manufacturer explained, also in 1884, that he imported a gum from Mexico called chicle that was the sap of a tree like spruce, and was not injurious. His plant manufactured the product in various ways and sold it to grocers, confectioners, notion houses, and druggists in parcels that ranged in size from $300 to $500 worth. As well, he sold to jobbers, in lots as small as $5 to $25 worth and those jobbers sold, in turn, to other retailers. Product from his plant sold all over the United States and was exported to a number of foreign nations. Asked how the gum was prepared and presented to the public, this maker said it was produced in "various shapes and flavors. There is some in round sticks folded in tinfoil. There is some in square cakes flavored in aniseed." Asked who his customers were, he replied: "Our trade is supported chiefly by women and girls. Men very often use gum in order to break off from the habit of chewing tobacco."[31]

As of late 1884 it was reported that the fruit of the tree from which the chicle was exuded was called sapodilla. It was about the size of an apple had an appealing flavor, and was widely used in Mexico as food. The chicle was collected by tapping the trees in the same way Americans tapped maple trees. Chicle ran out freely then and was molded into cakes near the trees and left in the sun there to harden. Hardened chicle cakes were brought to market on pack mules with each animal carrying about 300 pounds.[32]

Meanwhile, the gum made from coal tar continued to enjoy a brief period of popularity. As of 1885 it meant that most of the coal-tar derived base for the product came from Pittsburgh, with many of the major oil refineries located there; Standard Oil was the biggest. After petroleum had been refined into coal oil the refineries took the residue from the crude oil refining process and worked it in an agitator, producing a certain grade of paraffin, a wax-like substance. That was sent on to one of two firms (one located in Boston, the other in New York) who put it through another refining process, cut the material up into small pieces, and sent it on to gum makers. The wax as loaded on the rail cars at Pittsburgh was worth 17 cents a pound, but when put through the second refining process its cost was 30 cents a pound. One pound of refined paraffin would make 500 pieces of chewing gum, retailing at one to two cents a piece. According to this article, 25 barrels of paraffin were shipped out of Pittsburgh each week, to eventually be turned into chewing gum. In total, though, about 50 barrels a week were shipped out of Pittsburgh. The rest of it was bound for other uses such as finishing up the insulation of telegraph and telephone wires, or for making fancy candles. However, the "best grades" of the paraffin were destined to be used for making chewing gum.[33]

When a gum manufacturer in Brooklyn spoke to a journalist late in 1887, one of the things he said was that sales of his product were seasonal, his busiest time of the year beginning in March and ending in about October. He believed the quantity of gum consumed in America was then at least 3,000,000 pounds annually. When exports were included he felt the manufacture of chewing gum in the United States was at least 6,000,000 boxes a year, with each box containing an average of 150 pieces of gum.

Explaining how it was made, he said the base ingredient was the sap from the tree known as "chico zapote," which grew in South America, and more specifically in the Yucatan area of Mexico. Native Indians were the ones who tapped the trees, collected the sap, formed it into cakes, hardened the material, and then put it on pack mules bound for markets that could be as much as 300 miles distant. They sold the chicle for cash to the agents of the American gum manufacturers. After the chicle reached the United States, he explained, it was first melted in a furnace, and then refined, after which flavoring and sugar were mixed with it. At that stage the material was ready to be rolled flat and cut up into pieces. Prior to being cut into pieces the rolled out material was spread out on tables and allowed to dry for about two days in the sun. All of the cutting was done automatically by machinery. For rolling the product and wrapping it in tinfoil, this plant employed 250 people, all but 50 of whom were girls.[34]

An explanation of how chicle was made into gum, in 1890, was slightly different from that just described. By this account, chicle was first heated until it became pliable or juicy. Then it was washed and the foreign particles taken out of it. Then it was worked up like dough. Ingredients that might be then worked into it were items such as the essence of barley, sugar, and flavoring extracts. Machinery described herein as "improvised" did most of the work.[35]

20

1. The Business of Gum

High profits for the chewing gum industry were reported in November 1890. A statement from a New York druggist said that the tolu gum that sold for five cents a package (five sticks) cost less than one-half cent to manufacture, and even when the tinfoil and other wrapping was included the total cost of a package of gum did not reach one cent. Three kinds of chewing gum, it was said, were then manufactured—flavored tolu, spruce gum, and the small white sticks that were popular with schoolchildren some 25 years earlier. Spruce gum was the most expensive, white gum was the cheapest. A druggist said, "There is really no such thing nowadays in trade as pure spruce gum." The manufactured spruce article sold in the cities was adulterated by a mixture of glucose and licorice "with precious little of the original spruce gum" contained therein. The genuine spruce gum article was too expensive, explained the druggist, and the supply was not equal to the demand. That white gum he mentioned was made with paraffin as a base, with glucose and a little bit of cheap gum thrown in. According to this source the gum that was in general use was made of tolu or chicle with licorice and glucose and some flavoring extract. It was boiled and rolled out in great heaps and cut into blocks by machinery. Gum arabic was used formerly to give it consistency, but little of it was then employed because it was too expensive. Instead, gum of turpentine was substituted.[36]

A reporter remarked in 1892 that ordinary chewing gum was made of gum chicle, sugar and a variety of flavors, with gum chicle being merely a form of India rubber. After it had been chewed for a while the sugar and flavor were entirely gone and what remained was the rubber-like product, which was chicle gum nearly pure. That gum was the sap of the sapodilla (or sapota or zapota), a Mexican tree. It was collected like India rubber sap, by cutting incisions in the bark, between the months of November and April.[37]

A lawsuit over trademark infringement brought in 1892 by one chewing gum manufacturer against another one brought to light certain information that normally would not have been publicized. The Beeman Chemical Company, maker of Beeman's Pepsin Chewing Gum, sued the F. J. Banta firm, claiming the latter had started to copy the Beeman gum sometime in 1891. Prior to that the Banta company produced gum under various brand names, including, "Sweet Clover Gum," "Florida Fruit," "Banana," "Blood Orange," and "Cream Fruit." During the court case

Beeman told the court that it spent $25,000 to $30,000 annually to advertise its gum and place it before the public.[38]

A brief news item in 1895 stated that 90 percent of the gum consumed in America was made of chicle, the gum of the sapodilla tree. The other 10 percent was comprised of spruce gum and white, or paraffin, gum, the latter a product of petroleum, mixed with sugar and flavoring essence.[39]

One of the major figures in the gum industry was William Wrigley. By dint of years of hard work he had gotten his chewing gum fairly well introduced and in moderate demand. But he lacked a leader, a dominant product. Then, just before Christmas in 1886 it occurred to him that as peppermint candy was a general favorite with children, why shouldn't a peppermint flavored chewing gum enjoy a similar success? Wrigley experimented and produced such a gum, and when he sent a box of the new item to one of the local newspapers as a Christmas present, he was rewarded by being given a free advertisement for the item in the paper. So successful was the new item that in just two years Wrigley was able to erect a large, new factory, quadruple his work force, and increase his orders to the point where he was from three weeks to three months behind in filling those orders.[40]

Reportedly, in 1895, approximately four million pounds of chicle, valued at $1.5 million, was imported into the United States. A walk through a leading chewing gum manufacturing plant revealed a facility where over one billion pieces of gum were produced each year, for home consumption and for export; 300 employees worked there. As a first step the chicle was gathered in Mexico and exported to the U.S. in bales of 150 pounds each. Once those bales reached the American factory, each one was chopped into small pieces and extraneous matter such as tree bark and wood chips were removed by picking and steaming. Then the remaining material, the chicle, was ground in mills. That ground gum was then subjected to a continuous heat of 110 degrees F. in drying rooms. Next, the gum was sent to the "white aproned cook" who added sugar and cream, granulated pepsin, other flavorings, and any other ingredients, and then cooked the mixture in a steam-jacketed cauldron until it had assumed the consistency of bread dough. At that point the "dough boys" took over the material and kneaded into it a finely powdered sugar, passing it to the "idlers" until it was of the proper thickness and was next sent off to the "markers"—steel-knifed rollers that left their impression (like perforations) on the long sheets of gum. Then it went on to the "seasoning room" where it was broken on the lines left by the markers. From there the gum was moved on to the wrapping room, where 150 female employees used waxed paper, tinfoil and outer wrapping material to envelop the gum. Finally, the "packers" received the wrapped pieces of gum and packed them into boxes to await shipment out of the plant to wholesalers and direct to retailers.[41]

The largest chewing gum factory in the world was said to be in Cleveland, as of 1897. Only a few years earlier its owner was described as a "poor man," making his gum in the basement of an old building, offering in vain his whole business for sale for $100, and with his wife as his sole assistant and employee. As of 1897, though, his 300 employees made him profits for a millionaire. When a reporter described how the chicle-based chewing gum was made, he outlined the process related directly above, with some additions and extra details. Under the steam rollers the gum was reduced to thin strips about 18 inches wide and a yard long. A grooved roller cut it into squares, which were laid on a trays and left for 24 hours. After that day of drying another grooved roller marked the material into the shape in which it would be sold, whereupon it was broken into those shapes and wrapped and packed in boxes. Finally, the boxes of chewing gum were sent to an inspection room where each box was opened, examined, and passed. Every broken scrap of gum that appeared along the way was saved and returned to the melting kettle.

That Cleveland factory was described as being complete in itself and containing many departments. The top floor was given over to the manufacture of pasteboard boxes for the gum, while the basement functioned as a printing plant. A railroad spur line allowed for the loading and unloading of everything at the factory door. Six brands of gum were made in the building. One brand of gum alone—Yucatan—had sales over the previous 10 years that had totaled 50,900 "miles" of gum. In each day of that previous 10 years that meant that the average sale of Yucatan gum had been 13.5 miles.[42]

A 1905 report said the chicle tree, herein the "chico zapote" tree, grew in abundance in very few places. Therefore the price of chicle was on the rise. Reportedly, there was one part of one province of Mexico, namely Yucatan, where the chico zapote grew in great quantities. Collecting chicle was called the "simplest" thing in the world. The Indian collectors merely had to spear the bark and a milky sap issued forth, which was collected very much as maple syrup or rubber was collected; then it was boiled down until the watery part was expelled, packed in leaves, and delivered to the port of export where it was weighed and the collectors paid. Other names often used for the chicle tree were "sapota," "sapodilla," and "naseberry."[43]

Herbert R. Wright, Iowa state drug and pure food commissioner, had been devoting his attention, in 1907, to the purity of sausages, maple sugar, vinegar, and other commodities under his purview that were thought likely to be adulterated in some way. All of that came in the wake of Upton Sinclair's now justly famous novel *The Jungle.* Although Sinclair had hoped to focus public attention on the plight of the industrial workers in America involved in the meat packing industry he, instead, found the public had focused its attention on the unhealthy and

GROWTH OF W. V. MOSER'S BUSINESS

What Enterprise, Good Goods and Low Prices Have Accomplished.

The Canton Gum Co.,
Manufacturers of the
Famous Pepsin Chewing Gum

"Try Me" and "Canton Pride"

30 employes. Occupying the whole block up-stairs.

Flavors of Orange, Lemon, Pineapple, Strawberry, Peppermint, Wintergreen and Tula.

Dealers who received Gum from the old firm that was not perfect are requested to return same to their jobber or to us direct and receive new in return.

In 1896 W. V. Moser commenced business on Corner Brown and West Tuscarawas Streets in one floor of one room, the total capital at his command was $46. The store room and dwelling was all on one floor. Today he owns the whole block in which his business is located, (a cut of which is herewith given). Two and one-half year ago he purchased the building and 3 months ago Mr. Moser purchased the business of the Southern Gum Company, manufacturers of Chewing Gum.

This business is now in full operation in Mr. Moser's Block, under the name of THE CANTON GUM COMPANY.

This 1904 ad related how a Mr. Moser had expanded his business and taken over the Southern Gum Company, renaming it the Canton Gum Company.

unappealing industrial processes that led to the meat America placed upon its tables. Thus, Wright, and people like him in every state, began to intensely study and investigate how food and drugs were prepared for American consumption.

At this time Wright in Iowa began to turn some of his attention to chewing gum; he had fears that adulteration could be found in the product, especially in some of the cheaper grades. Wright believed he had

This fairly wordy 1904 ad touted the virtues of Chiclets candy-coated chewing gum.

In 1905 this Wrigley ad touted Nips, chewing gum with a candy jacket. It was, obviously, aimed at Chiclets users.

found a new and dangerous adulterant in the product, namely talc, which was a grade of soapstone. As a result he had been going from store to store in Iowa buying gum in a search for impure chicle. Said a reporter, "The announcement that much of the chewing gum used is believed to be impure and permeated with the white earth product which develops soreness of the mouth and gums will be received with much concern by many young women and young men whose chief recreation is chewing gum in public places to the lasting disgust of those with whom they come in contact." Commissioner Wright declared, "But if the girls must chew gum let it be pure stuff."[44]

With Commissioner Wright hot on the heels of the gum makers in Iowa, C. H. Behring of St. Louis, a representative of one of the largest chewing gum manufacturers in the United States, was interviewed by a reporter while the sales agent was staying at an Iowa hotel. "Mr. Wright says that he has found that a number of different brands of gum contain soapstone, and I don't doubt his word in the least," said Behring. "I know that some of the cheaper brands of gum contain ingredients that would make those of the fair sex who are addicted to the habit gasp with astonishment and know that henceforth they would buy the best or let their jaws rest." Moving on to a different aspect of gum, the traveling salesman observed that chewing gum never grew smaller from chewing. After a stick of gum had been chewed for a while the glucose and flavoring gradually worked out of it. After it was chewed for a certain time nothing was left but the chicle and that was harmless. However, there was little or no taste to it. He felt the durability of gum would limit its sale were it not discarded soon after it lost its sweetness and fresh flavor. Then, too, a "treasured" wad was often misplaced: "Who could estimate the number of millions of these that are even now sticking to the underside of tables, mantles, chairs, and on the headboards of beds."[45]

Within a week of the first reports on Wright and his crusade against gum in Iowa, the whole campaign came to an abrupt end with one reporter declaring, "Turns out there is no protection for the women who persist in chewing gum." Soapstone or talc may indeed have been included in the composition of the chicle but the Iowa pure food department was helpless to act, as it was determined that chewing gum did not come within the jurisdiction of the pure food law. Wright explained that chewing gum did not come under the definition of a food, or a drink, or a confection. Not falling within any of those three categories meant that Wright had no jurisdiction over the item.[46]

As of the summer of 1908 there were three main chewing gum manufacturers in the United States—American Chicle Company, Wrigley Gum Company, and the Colgan Gum Company. They dominated the market in the U.S. and Canada. During the six months ending June 30, 1908, the Wrigley firm produced a little over 500,000 boxes of one brand of gum alone. Each box contained 100 sticks, for a total of 50,000,000 pieces of gum. The market price of the liquid flavoring spearmint had been $1.40 a pound prior to its use in chewing gum. Once it was used as a flavoring for gum the immense quantities of the spearmint flavoring demanded by the gum maker for this single brand ran the price of spearmint up to $9 a pound.[47]

Journalist Frederic Haskin reported that nearly three billion sticks of chewing gum were manufactured in the United States in 1910. He also noted that a report from the U.S. Department of Commerce declared the second cleanest factory of any kind inspected by that department was one where chewing gum was made (although it was not named). As well, Haskin remarked that repeated attempts had been made to mix or adulterate chicle or to find a substitute for it, but there seemed to be no substitute for it. (Presumably, manufacturers had undertaken such searches in the hopes of lowering their costs to produce the product.) Chicle was then imported into the United States to the extent of five million pounds a year, valued at about $2 million annually. A chicle tree could be tapped profitably for 25 years. Planted 400 trees to the acre, each tree yielded some 2,000 pounds of gum annually. An import duty of 10 cents a pound of chicle was then in place and had been imposed only after a struggle in the United States Congress that led to the inclusion of chicle, along with other items, that were to have import duties imposed on them.[48]

Russell Millward produced a 1910 article that delved more deeply into chicle than did most others. According to Millward, chicle was known in the 15th century to Spanish explorers, who reported that the Indians used the gum from the trees to quench thirst and relieve exhaustion. But the universal use of the chicle gum could not be said to have begun until as late as 1876. Prior to 1888 chicle sold for seven cents to eight cents a pound; in 1896 it sold for 36 cents a pound; and in 1910 it went for $2 a pound. The tree, "achas sapota," from which the chicle was obtained, was indigenous to northern South American countries, Central America, and in the Mexican states of Yucatan, Campeche, Tabasco, Chiapas, Veracruz, Oaxaca, Puebla, Jalisco, and San Luis Potosi. As yet, said Millward, the systematic cultivation of achas sapota had not been carried out, but experiments had shown that trees planted at a distance of 10 feet apart, or 400 to the acre, would yield from five to six pounds of chicle gum when from eight to 10 years old and from 12 to 15 inches in diameter. In its wild state the tree was usually found in groups, often growing to a height of 40 to 50 feet. The wood was a reddish color, closely resembling mahogany. It was quite hard, heavy, and compact in texture and fine grained. The wood was in demand by cabinet makers who used it in the manufacture of high grade furniture and household fittings.[49]

Millward explained that the tapping of the trees was done by chicle gatherers or "chicleros." It was possible for a collector to gather 10 to 15 pounds of sap per day, for which he was paid a contract price of 10 cents to 15 cents per pound. In some cases trees had been tapped for 25 years, although after that time they produced much less sap, from one-half to two pounds of sap. However, if those older trees were allowed to remain untapped for a period of from five to six years, they would then be able to produce more sap, from three to five pounds of gum. The average height of one of these trees was from 25 to 40 feet and maturity was reached at from 40 to 50 years. A tree that was 25 years old and producing from 20 to 25 pounds of chicle each year would measure from 25 to 30 feet in height and would be about 22 inches in diameter. After the sap was gathered the collectors carried it to the boiling sheds and by the use of a "rather primitive" boiling procedure, the gum was brought to the proper consistency—that is, like "loaves." Much of the chicle was shipped in rough, uneven loaves to the United States via Canada. While it was in Canada the material was further refined and dried out to half of its original weight, thereby saving 50 percent of the duty when it finally entered the United States. Under the American tax code prior to 1897, chicle gum was admitted free of duty to the U.S., but in accordance with the tariff-revision act of 1897 a duty of 10 cents a pound was fixed, which remained the rate in 1910. For the fiscal year ending June 30, 1909, there was imported into the United States 5,450,139 pounds of chicle, valued at $1,987,112, as compared with 929,959 pounds valued at $156,402 in 1885.[50]

Chicle imports continued to increase dramatically. During the calendar year 1913, America imported 13,401,316 pounds of chicle valued at $5,119,500.[51]

The Liggett and Myers Tobacco Company signed a contract with the Wrigley Chewing Gum company in 1914 whereby Wrigley would manufacture several brands of gum exclusively for the tobacco firm. Liggett and Myers planned to sell those brands of gum through the same channels that then handled the tobacco brands for the tobacco manufacturer. At the time that contract was signed it was estimated that the Wrigley Chewing Gum Company had about 60 percent of all the chewing gum business in the United States.[52]

A report in 1920 about the sapota or sapodilla tree remarked that it was a pear tree but that the steady tapping of the trees for chicle gum had so reduced the size of the pears that they no longer were sold in Latin American markets. Chicle was the name given to the juice of that tree by the ancient Aztecs, who may have been the original gum chewers.[53]

Only a few reports ever surfaced about labor trouble in the chewing gum industry, and those few episodes were brief. A "near strike" took place in March 1888 at the Adams chewing gum factory located at Sands and Bridge Streets in Brooklyn, New York. Reportedly, that plant was the largest chewing gum factory in the world. Over 100 girls were employed there just in the wrapping and packing of the gum into boxes for shipment. On March 17, about 40 of those girls stopped work. There had been, apparently, a pay reduction. A reporter spoke to 39 of them in a group and expressed amazement that not one of them was chewing gum. He had "never before seen thirty-nine pretty girls assembled together without finding the jaws of at least half the number working with clockwork regularity. But then these girls knew how the gum was made."

One of those striking women explained the situation to the reporter. Adams used to pay them four cents a box for packing the brand of gum called Tampico, which enabled the women to earn from $4 to $5.50 a week. But management had suddenly reduced that piece rate payment to two cents a box.

Later on the same day they stopped work, a delegation of three of those strikers, Jennie Watson, Jessie McLean, and Mamie Combs, was appointed to visit Adams and negotiate. They returned a little later to tell the rest of the strikers that Adams had agreed to pay three cents a box. All of the striking females except 12 accepted that offer and returned to work, still on March 17. Adams explained to the press that competition in the chewing gum industry had made it necessary for him to stop tying up the packages of gum with fancy ribbons and to substitute much cheaper rubber bands. "This is much less trouble for the girls who do the packing, and we thought it right to reduce the rate from four cents to two, said Adams. "But to avoid any more bother we have promised to give them three cents, although it is more than the work is worth."[54]

A decade later another strike was reported at the same Adams factory in Brooklyn, on April 14, 1898. Once again the strikers were those who wrapped and packed the gum, but the account declared that 300 employees were involved this time. Reportedly, those girls had been earning from $9 to $10 a week until a short time earlier, when the Adams firm arranged to put on the market a cheaper brand of gum, intended to sustain U.S. soldiers and sailors in the coming war with Spain, and which the Adams firm planned to christen the "Untied States Brawn and Muscle" brand of gum. "In spite of the laudable object for which the new brand was introduced the patriotism of the girls did not rise paramount to a concurrent cut in pay which came with the cheaper gum," said a reporter. "So they struck. At the works it was said that they would all be replaced by more patriotic girls and that the chewing gum industry will suffer no serious setback."[55]

A different newspaper's account of the strike said that in the face of war with Spain the U.S. Navy should be provided with a specialty cheap brand of tutti frutti to be called "Navy Brand," or something like that. It was to be so cheap that Adams did not want to pay his packers the usual rate—herein it said they had been earning $6 to $9 a week—so he cut the pay for the new gum. Thus the girls struck but a compromise was reached and they returned to work the next day. Under the compromise each packer would spend a little bit of her day on the new gum, but then most of her day on the regular gum at the usual rate of pay for packing.[56]

The last strike mentioned in the media was the most curious of all, and when it reached the press it coincidentally revealed one of the gum manufacturers' more unusual marketing methods. When the strike took place in New York City in the middle of August 1899 vending machines were then ubiquitous in that city, at least in the offering of a limited range of goods and services. Most of those machines dispensed chewing gum or were weigh machines. Large companies owned all of these machines and, as the labor dispute revealed, they employed people, "decoys" (all men) to do nothing but go from machine to machine and use them, that is, to spend all their working day buying gum or weighing themselves. The idea was that other people in the vicinity would see these decoys so engaged and be struck by the urge to copy their behavior. "The decoy is generally a man of magnetic personality. He marches up to the apparatus in a way calculated to inspire confidence and suggest imitation and he does it in such a way as to attract as much attention as possible." Said a reporter, "In a few minutes the machines are besieged with other customers."

In dealing with the chewing gum machines, the journalist continued, it was the duty of the decoy to insert the wad of gum into his mouth, proceed to chew it "and ejaculate upon its excellent quality." Those decoys were paid $2 a day when they went on strike for higher wages. It was then that the details of the strategy became public. No wage increase was obtained by the strikers but the issue was resolved when the two sides agreed that once a decoy had weighed himself 75 times his day was over and he got his $2. For those decoys working the chewing gum vending machines a day's work was set at the purchase of 100 sticks of gum, from 100 machines. Once the decoy had bought and chewed 100 wads of gum his working day was finished and he had earned his $2.[57]

The strike of the decoys generated an editorial in the *New York Times*. "How many readers of this paper have seen a man extract succulent chewing gum from the alluring penny-in-the-slot machine and instantly felt that the interior of his own mouth would be evermore filled with fur unless he went and did likewise?" wondered the editor. And did the horrid suspicion ever dawn on the reader's mind that the man was a decoy? The editor stated, "The professional gum buyer must also be a gum chewer. It is a part of his business to put the gum in his mouth and then look as if he were a De Quincey in the midst of a most beatific dream."[58]

Competition in the chewing gum business was seriously curtailed at the end of the 1890s when several of the largest concerns in the field joined together in a "trust," as such combinations were called. Combinations were common enough in that era and took place in many, many industries. They were designed, of course, to eliminate competition, to control the industry, and to increase the rate and amount of profit. Trusts became so ubiquitous, and so against the public interest, that much media attention was devoted to the issue. Congress would eventually pass various pieces of anti-trust legislation. A combination of chewing gum makers in America was effected in 1899 with a capital involved in the trust said to be about $15 million. Firms involved in the trust were Adams and Sons, Brooklyn; the Beeman Chemical Company, Cleveland; O.W.J. White and Sons, Cleveland; J. P. Primley, Chicago; St. T. Britten, Toronto; and the Kiss Me Gum Company, Louisville. These firms constituted all the leading chewing gum manufacturers in the country.[59]

1. *The Business of Gum*

Just two years later, in 1901, a reporter noted the formation of the gum trust and said, "Now most of the best brands of gum are manufactured and controlled by one large company—the trust was called the American Chicle Company. It sold an average of 135,000,000 packages of gum a year and its sales were said to be increasing "enormously." At that time about 2,600,000 pounds of chicle were imported into the United States yearly, and that chicle was mixed with many times its weight of sugar, paste, essential oils, and so forth, in the production of gum. American Chicle Company had recently acquired 2.5 million acres of land in Yucatan, Mexico, in order to grow the trees that provided the chicle.[60]

At the end of 1901 a reporter looked back at the formation of American Chicle. According to this piece the trust was incorporated with a capital of $9 million, divided into $6 million common stock and $3 million preferred stock. Since it had been formed its profits had been sufficient to pay regular annual dividends of six percent on the preferred stock and a larger dividend on the common. As of 1901 American Chicle planned to enlarge its capital by issuing $2 million more in common stock and $1 million more in preferred, bringing total capital up to $12 million. Part was slated to be used for development work on the firm's recently acquired huge tract of land in Mexico with the balance of funds earmarked to increase the company's manufacturing capacity.[61]

Journalist James Morrow asked chewing gum manufacturing tycoon William J. White (his firm was one of those that went into the trust) in 1908 who organized the gum trust. White said the preliminary and technical work was done by Charles R. Flint, the man who brought about consolidations in starch, rubber, sewer pipe, scales, woolen goods, and so forth. The gum makers had met a good many times attempting to form a trust but could not agree as to the valuation of the different factories. Nine firms had formed the combination—one of them was in Canada and one was in England. Since American Chicle had organized itself nine years earlier, it had spent $4 million for advertising. It had exclusive rights in several hundred theaters (no firm except American Chicle could sell its gum in those theaters) and whenever there was a large crowd of people, such as at a fair or political meeting, one would find boys selling American Chicle gum. A cross-continent billboard campaign had cost the trust $175,000. When the reporter asked White

This 1906 Chiclets ad was more elaborate, to create the image of a gum that appealed to all ages and to both genders.

if American Chicle had a monopoly, the reply was, "No. Since the early days of White and Beeman hundreds of factories have started and failed. They couldn't stand the pace. It required several hundred thousand dollars to advertise and establish a brand of chewing gum. However, plenty of opposition remains." Then the reporter asked White about his views on "large combinations of capital." White thought it was all to the good for everyone, as it lowered production and unit costs and prices. "I believe, however, that when a corporation

In 1906 trusts (cartels) were everywhere, including in the chewing gum industry. Trusts were then reviled in the media and by the public and this ad for Sanitas touted first and foremost the fact that the company was not a member of the gum trust.

gets control of one of the daily necessities of the people—like oil, for instance—and begins to pinch the public, that the government should interfere. Capitalization, too, ought to be controlled."[62]

When the idea of taxing chicle was under discussion, the *New York Times* editorialized on the topic in 1897. The editor pointed out the chief constituent of chewing gum was chicle and while the substance was then untaxed—that is, it entered the country duty free—the Dingley bill then proposed in the U.S. Congress would impose a duty of 10 cents a pound, "or 50 per cent of the amount which the importers have hitherto been paying for their material. Here alone is enough to ruin the business, those who are in it say." As well, those makers grumbled they were confronted with increased duties on practically everything else they used, including sugar, wintergreen and peppermint oils, tinfoil, and waxed paper. According to the editor, if the bill passed, it would have imposed on the chewing gum manufacturers a tax amounting to $75,000 per year, "and they declare that, as they cannot raise the price of the product, their industry will be killed outright."[63]

At that time the Ways and Means Committee of the U.S. House of Representatives was working hard to complete the tariff bill. It was expected that the free list of the Dingley bill would likely be much smaller than that of the act of 1890. With a war looming, the Congress was desperate to find ways to increase its revenues, and one of the ways to do that was to take from the then duty free list such articles that would stand a small duty without becoming a burden on the consumer. Chicle was then on the free list but it was reported in this story that over 200,000,000 pounds had been imported into the United States in 1896. "A small duty upon this article will raise considerable revenue without in any way increasing the price of chewing gum to the consumer."[64]

That tax of 10 cents a pound was duly imposed on chicle, and in the spring of 1898 the association of chewing gum manufacturers, meeting in convention, resolved not to protest against the government tax on chicle. Said a newspaper editor, "They can afford not to protest for well they know they will not lose anything. Come war, come peace, come weal, come woe, the universal bicycle girl will still have her chewing gum to wag her jaws on."[65]

U.S. legislators debated the issue of whether or not to tax chewing gum once again, late in 1921. At that time there was a war tax on chewing gum but a number of U.S. senators wanted that tax repealed. However, another group of senators, led by Senator Reed of Missouri, maintained that chewing gum was an ideal subject for taxation. Reed declared in the Senate, "If there is anything made and consumed by the human family that is utterly useless, it's chewing gum. A few moments ago you taxed all the telegrams and telephone messages and other means of transmission of messages, $28,000,000, and now you are asking for a reduction on chewing gum. Who made this chewing gum bargain?"

Those comments caused the editor of a Syracuse, New York, newspaper to remark, "But the chewing gum habit must be regarded as mystifying to say the least. Why any person should want to exercise his (or her) maxillary muscles or agitate his (or her) salivary glands, in the way suggested by the chewing gum of commerce, is a query we cannot pretend to answer. It is enough to know that a good many people do." He believed that the admitted absence of reliable statistics notwithstanding, about 20 percent of the population from the age of four upwards chewed gum habitually or occasionally. "The most numerous devotees of the practice, we opine, are sweet unmarried girls of between fifteen and forty-five. Those engaged in gainful industry, in which they have no time to talk, are apparently in the majority," he added.[66]

Still on the question of taxing gum in the U.S. Congress, one month later, Senator McCumber, speaking in the Senate, made the statement that there was but one great trust in the chewing gum manufacturing business: "That trust has driven out of business practically every one of the great companies. There is only one that is still struggling for an existence" (American Chicle was the trust and Wrigley's was the lone outsider). McCumber argued the trust was content to keep the tax up: "With its enormous business it is able to pay it. The smaller concerns all over the country are unable to pay it and continue."[67]

Marketing and advertising of chewing gum was very low-key and barely attracted any media attention during the entire period covered by this book, except for the final few years. It was only in the period of World War I, and onward, that advertising of chewing gum, and everything else, became an incessant and pervasive part of society. Gum produced in the form of "novelty" shapes enjoyed a period of success in the early 1880s. If a manufacturer struck the fancy of children with a particular shape then he had a successful product; if not, he could melt the unsold stock down and reform it into a different shape. One maker told a reporter that "almost every conceivable shape" was easily molded. Gum in the shape of a firecracker was always popular around July 4th, with other popular shapes being a cigar, baby, pig, and a strawberry. For a time one maker formed his product into very thin round pieces that sold well for a time under the name of "needles and pins." Gum shaped like tops or marbles was also popular.

Manufacturers then used several colors for their product—mostly they used white but other colors occasionally used included red, yellow, and chocolate. Manufacturers sold their gum to jobbers who supplied the retail confectionary trade. Those manufacturers were said in this account to receive about 60 cents for a box of 100 pieces—a piece of gum retailed for one cent. Demand for gum was kept up, at least partly at this time, through the prize in the package system with prizes ranging from a ring or a doll up to a clock or a watch. When the prize was too bulky to go in the same package with the gum the retailer retained the numbered prizes separately. Corresponding numbers were put on slips of paper folded up with the gum.[68]

Traveling sales representatives were the principal way for the gum manufacturer to disseminate his wares and to garner publicity and attention for the gum as the agent made his rounds. For example, C. S. Ritz of Mansfield, Ohio, was, in January 1903, going on the road to start his 12th straight year as a traveling salesman for the Beeman chewing gum concern. His sales for 1902 were within a few hundred dollars of $50,000. That was money for direct sales only and did not include any mail or telephone orders from his customers. Ritz worked five states: Ohio, Kentucky, Maryland, West Virginia, and Pennsylvania. He believed there was almost as much gum as candy sold in a year in the United States.[69]

The advertising budget in 1914 for Wrigley's gum was $2 million. A March 1914 *Saturday Evening Post* had an inside double page advertisement done in colors for the gum. According to the Stewart-Davis Advertising Agency of Chicago—which placed the ad—it cost $12,000. It was that agency that released the $2 million figure. Assuming Wrigley made two cents profit on each package of gum, the firm had to sell 100 million of those five-cent packs of gum just to pay its advertising bill for 1914.[70]

Apparently, some ads for chewing gum made it into newspapers disguised as supposed news items. What gave such items away was the slavish devotion and adoration the article lavished upon its subject. A piece that appeared in August 1916 started off by declaring, "Chewing gum is one of the greatest things in the world to drive away laziness. The mere act of chewing awakens a desire to be active." As an example, the article suggested the reader could test that idea at a card party where the game was lagging: "Pass around a package of gum and see how the game will speed up. The mind of every player will immediately be concentrated upon the game." The same effect would occur at a tennis game in which they players were listless. Handing out gum to the players in such a game would cause the play to be "a hundred percent better." Many gymnasium managers had discovered, it was said, that gum was an excellent thing to keep handy to offer their charges when they slowed down in their exercise. "In cases where lively physical exertion is necessary the gum acts in a dual capacity. It puts pep in the one who is exercising and keeps the throat moist and clear." The article said in many lines of work chewing gum helped the workers to concentrate and accomplish more: "This is thoroughly recognized now in hundreds of large factories, and gum chewing among employees is encouraged by employers." In New England and other parts of the United States, factory owners were reported to have gone so far as to install gum vending machines at plant entrances and in lunch rooms because "they find that gum chewing not only checks idle conversation among employees but removes any desire to lag." What gave such articles away as advertising material disguised as news was the lack of a dateline and city of origin; there was nothing to localize the piece to the city wherein the paper was published. Also, no authority was cited for any of the claims made, nor was any specific detail supplied. Even the usually weak and self-serving anecdotal "evidence" was completely absent. Such pieces were generic, national pieces extolling in general the virtues of gum. Those pieces were probably written by the gum manufacturers and submitted, with a fee, to newspapers for publication.[71]

Hype more recognizable as hype began to appear at the time of World War I. Riding high then as a superstar was George M. Cohan of Yankee Doodle renown. He gained fame first as an actor, then as an author with his plays and songs becoming big hits on Broadway and everywhere else in America, then as a producer of plays. In June 1917 it was reported that Cohan had undertaken the management of an "immense" chewing gum factory. He took over the factory and assumed management, but for one week only, and it was only as a public relations stunt for the benefit of the motion picture cameras in connection with his first Artcraft film—*Broadway Jones*.[72]

A large display advertisement for Adams Black Jack Chewing Gum (licorice flavor) that appeared in a Canadian newspaper in February 1918 declared, "The Canadians first introduced chewing gum into the trenches and now there's scarcely a solider on the west front who doesn't consider a good gum like Adams Black Jack a necessity. A stick a day keeps nerves away. Every time you buy it for yourself, buy it for a solider."[73]

Later in 1918 a large display ad for Adams Chewing Gum devoted the top half of the display to a line drawing of Uncle Sam smiling as he prepared to put a stick of chewing gum into his mouth. The caption to his left said, "Why shouldn't he smile?" The text of the ad declared Uncle Sam had become the firm's biggest customer during the war: "We gave him all he asked for. We sent overseas 155,945,000 sticks of Adams gum." And, "The men in the front lines craved it—they couldn't smoke. To the men in the hospitals it was a blessing. The men in the artillery used it to rest their nerves. The men in the Tank Corps fought on it. And to the boys in the air, gum was a great steadier." In conclusion, this ad stated, "Now that peace is here, let Adams Gum become a part of your daily existence. For the soldier boy has proved that chewing gum is an efficiency habit. It makes men fit."[74]

An ad for Adams Pure Chewing Gum that appeared in print in January 1919 was titled, "One stick of gum made the world rosier." At the top was a drawing of a wounded soldier lying in a hospital bed. His head was bandaged and he was unwrapping a stick of gum. Standing at his bedside was a uniformed solider, presumably a friend of the wounded man who had stopped by for a visit. The bedridden solider told his friend (in the ad's text) that he had nothing more than a grin-and-bear-it spirit when they first placed him in that hospital bed, but one of his buddies had brought him a package of gum "and the world honestly looked rosier as soon as I took my first chew. This lad's kindness and the cheer that package of gum gave me impressed me so that after I was able to hobble around I spent five francs, all the money I had, buying gum at the hospital canteen and playing good Samaritan. You can't imagine the good it did for those wounded boys, and the smile of appreciation when they saw that little package." At the bottom of the ad, under the name of the gum, was the single line, "Send a stick in every letter to your soldier boy."[75]

Gum tycoon William Wrigley, Jr., said in an interview in February 1919—he was in the news then as he had just bought Catalina Island off the coast of California—that he spent $3 million a year in advertising his gum and that he had already spent in total over $30 million doing just that. And those funds, he explained, all came from the "lowly" pack of chewing gum containing five sticks of individually wrapped gum and that sold throughout America for five cents a pack. Wrigley claimed he sold chewing gum because he advertised it; the more he advertised the more he sold, and the more he sold the more he advertised, and so on. At the beginning when he started his gum business he had very little money left after expenses but half of what he did have, more or less, he put into advertising. Wrigley said he spent more money advertising his five-cent chewing gum in the *Oxnard Courier* than did 75 percent of the merchants of Oxnard, California. Said the reporter, "The chief value of advertising as proved by Wrigley is in the first place to have something to advertise, something that the people want, then to keep on telling the people about it. If you tell it and repeat it often enough they will believe it."[76]

Ads for Adams gum continued to exploit the supposed link between chewing gum and a more efficient war effort through at least 1919. Ad advertisement for Adams California Fruit Gum that ran that summer was titled "Adams California Fruit Gum shares in the conquest of the air." It spoke of the gum being carried on a dirigible airship, the R-34, and that in that instance, "It did its duty in this triumphant struggle against the uncharted spaces just as it served Valor and Victory in every Allied trench for five grueling years." And it was reportedly put to a specific use on the R-34. The following was supposedly verbatim from the log on the R-34, entered on July 3, 1919, at 2 p.m. "Slight trouble with starboard amidships engine; cracked cylinder water jacket. Shotter, always equal to the occasion, made a quick and safe repair with a piece of copper sheeting, and the entire supply of the ship's chewing gum had to be chewed by himself and two engineers before being applied." The last line of the text of that ad read, "The thinking man's, the fighting man's nerve ration."[77]

Two of the latest type Curtiss airplanes, similar to those used by the U.S. Army, and fully equipped for long-distance flying, were making a tour over eight states in the summer of 1919 visiting 150 cities and towns. The planes carried a consignment of Wrigley's chewing gum for local distributors—reportedly, the first delivery on record of this product by airplane. Those two planes (apparently leased for a short time by the Wrigley firm) were named "Spearmint Number One" and "Spearmint Number Two." William Wrigley had chartered the two planes and had them painted white and decorated with the Wrigley trademarks and packaging artwork. When one of those planes first arrived over each community it was to visit, it dropped 25 small parachutes. Each parachute carried a package of gum and four of them contained a complimentary ticket that would be honored for a free ride in one of those planes. Finders of those tickets rode free while any others in the community who wanted to be taken for an airplane sightseeing ride could do so, at a cost of $15 per ride. Over the four months the campaign was to last the tour was to cover the Midwest and South of the United States.[78]

The Wrigley planes arrived in Sheboygan, Wisconsin, at 1 p.m. on Monday, September 1, and stayed until Wednesday, September 3, at noon. After arrival both planes were used for the rest of the daylight hours to give people quick sightseeing trips. Customers, who paid the $15 each, were taken up one by one for their rides; a total of 40 were taken for a ride that day in the two planes. Sightseeing rides were given all day on Tuesday and on Wednesday, right up until noon.

John N. Hammond, a Wrigley manager from Chicago, was the publicity man for the tour. He dropped into the offices of the *Sheboygan Journal* to explain the novel plan for commercial advertising and deliveries of his company's product. Those two planes had arrived in Sheboygan from Milwaukee, making the flight in 40 minutes. The two pilots on the tour were paid a salary of $500 a month each and the mechanics on the tour each received a salary of $200 a month. Hammond's advance work paid dividends, as the newspaper printed a fawning article about the event, thus achieving what was perhaps a Wrigley goal—to have an advertising campaign treated as news and thus receive fairly extensive, and free, press coverage. According to the article, "Mr. Hammond stated that without exception, Sheboygan is the most progressive city he had ever visited and that he was never accorded such hospitality as he received at the hands of Sheboygan people since his stay in the city." It was also noted that Hammond spoke complimentarily on the "splendid" appearance of the city and the "magnificent" factories in operation.[79]

Wrigley's tour must have proven to be more successful than anticipated, because it was still on the go in the spring of 1920. An ad for the tour that was placed in the *Anniston Star* on March 31, 1920, heralded the arrival in Anniston, Alabama, of Wrigley's gum-delivering planes, under the headline of "Wrigley Flying Circus Coming." Those two planes arrived in Anniston on Thursday April 1, 1920, and departed on Monday, April 5. This ad mentioned the $15 sightseeing rides that were available to all comers, and that tour began with one of the arriving planes dropping those 25 small parachutes, each still carrying the same cargo as before. Much of the ad maintained the idea that the event was more about employing more productive business methods than just being pure advertising hype. One of the lines in the advertisement text read, "Delivery of light package goods by this means demonstrated for benefit of manufacturers and merchants." It was explained that those two planes were carrying a consignment of Wrigley's gum for the firm's distributors (jobbers) in the Anniston area and, in fact, all seven of them were listed in the ad by name. "The local distributors—the first delivery on record of this product by aeroplane" went the text. Further emphasizing that point was the following part of the ad text: "Always a keen enthusiast on the latest developments in any enterprise, and especially in commercial aeronautics, Wm. Wrigley Jr., of Chicago, the largest chewing gum manufacturer in the world, has chartered these planes to exemplify commercial flying."[80]

Late in 1919 an ad for Adams Black Jack Gum, "There's only one Adams Black Jack," targeted young boys. That ad featured a drawing that depicted four boys around 10 years of age who were all outside a house playing with a dog. "There are lots of chewing gums, but to a youngster Adams Black Jack is it. Because of its licorice flavor … boys know that Adams Black Jack eases the throat and takes away huskiness. They know it relaxes the nerves when you're excited. And they know it helps keep teeth sound and white."[81]

Early in February 1905, Thomas Adams, famous as the "inventor" and manufacturer of chewing gum, died at his home in Brooklyn of pneumonia at the age of 87. He had begun experimenting with chewing gum after the end of the Civil War—during which he had served as official photographer for the Army of the Potomac. Initially he had produced gum by hand but soon switched to machinery. For a long time the huge Adams gum plant stood on Sands Street in Brooklyn. However, Adams sold his business to the trust in 1899 and around 1903 the production plant was relocated to Newark, New Jersey. Reportedly, Adams amassed a fortune of several million dollars before he died.[82]

This 1917 ad tried to use banking imagery and equated spending a nickel on a pack of gum as a "wise" use of money.

Reflecting in an Indiana newspaper on Thomas Adams' death, an editor suggested some sort of honor should be paid him, or homage bestowed on him, because, in his opinion,

This 1919 ad for Adams gum claimed the product could steady the nerves and perhaps make one fit to be a pro baseball player.

1. *The Business of Gum*

Adams was an unfairly forgotten inventor. "Modern chewing gum, tender, tensile and tenacious, is an ingenious improvement upon the old acrid exudation of the spruce tree," he said. "In a humble way it typifies the progress of the age. It represents a transition from a childhood delight to a national luxury." The editor wondered how many audiences had relieved dreary waits between acts by chewing "those tenacious strips of floured paste" and how many cooks, mothers, heads of families, and so forth, had chewed gum during periods of tedium. It had solaced boxers in the pain of defeat and refreshed politicians in the stress of oratory, he thought. Concluded the editor, "It is the great vivifier and luxury of the age, accessible to the poor and not beneath the proud. Other men of inventive genius are given their due fame. Why not the inventor of chewing gum?"[83]

William J. White was another of the early gum tycoons. He was born of humble origins in Canada and was brought to Cleveland at a young age. White had a varied past being a Great Lakes sailor, a farm worker, then a shipyard worker. When he had wandered to St. Louis he tried to enlist in the United States Army but they would not take him. Then he tramped his way to Fort Leavenworth and became a cook for the teamsters. He returned to Cleveland with a greasy sheet of note paper in his pocket; it was a recipe he had obtained form an old peddler but soon forgot about. Back in Cleveland he married Ellen Marie Mansfield, a girl from a background as poor as his own. For White it was a constant struggle to make a living for a family that grew to include seven children. Frequently the family moved house. White and his wife divorced in 1906 after 23 years of marriage.

One day during the struggle for existence the Whites found they had a $5 bill to the good and at that point William remembered the old peddler's note. White invested the $5 in chicle and sugar, and his chewing gum business was off to a start. He personally peddled his gum on the street of downtown Cleveland while his wife was making more of it at home over the kitchen stove. Finally, his sales and reputation spread to the point the stores in Cleveland were willing to sell it. White was kept busy delivering his gum to groceries and to drug stores. Then his business grew to the point that he had to hire help, and it kept on growing. He made several fortunes before selling out for $5 million, plus stock, to the chewing gum trust, American Chicle. As of 1906 he was living in

New York City and was president of the chewing gum trust at a salary of $25,000 a year.[84]

When William J. White remarried in October 1906 it was reportedly to a woman who was wealthy in her own right. White was credited with an income of more than $500,000 a year from his position as head of the chewing gum trust. He owned two "palatial" homes in Cleveland and a "splendid" stock farm, which was home to Star Pointer, the first of the two-minute harness horses. As well, he had been elected to Congress as a representative from Ohio (he served from 1893 to 1895; was born in 1850 and died in 1923).[85]

Another journalist, describing White's beginnings in the gum industry, reported that White, a candy maker, knew the popularity of the tough taffies, the so-called "chewing candies," and the idea of making a commercial chewing gum occurred to him. He learned how to make chewing gum from paraffin, or petroleum wax. It was made on his wife's kitchen stove and he peddled it from a street corner. The business prospered in a modest way and then White heard of chicle. He brought some in, made his gum with chicle as a base, and started to advertise.[86]

Dr. Edwin E. Beeman, former chewing gum manufacturer, died in Elyria, Ohio, on November 6, 1906, at the age of 67. Death was caused by a cerebral hemorrhage, after an illness of more than four weeks. He was born in Birmingham, Lorain County, Ohio. His father was a prominent physician in the village, and Edwin, as a boy, decided to have a career in medicine. He went to Cleveland to complete his education and graduated from the College of Medicine in 1861. Returning to Birmingham, he became a physician and in a few years built up an extensive practice. Around 1870 he moved to Wakeman, Ohio, where he continued to practice medicine. It was there that he first began the making of pepsin, which ended up making him a millionaire. At first he prepared pepsin in small quantities for the use of his patients. Soon he found profit in producing it in larger quantities and selling it to druggists and to other physicians.

Seeing the possibilities of production on an even larger scale, Beeman moved from Wakeman to Cleveland in 1883. He opened a small shop on River Avenue and devoted his time exclusively to the manufacture of pepsin; his business prospered. One day by chance he hit upon the idea of producing pepsin chewing gum. Beeman experimented and succeeded in those experiments; the year was 1888. From that time onward the name of Dr. Beeman and pepsin gum were inseparably linked together. Soon he had a large chewing gum factory, which he sold to the gum trust, American Chicle, when it formed. Beeman then retired.[87]

Journalist James Morrow related some of the stories of both White and Beeman in a piece that was published in November 1908. Morrow said the basic facts of the story of gum were related to him by William White when he—White—was a representative in the U.S. Congress. When he moved to Cleveland he eventually learned the trade of candy maker. Entering that business, he peddled candy in a one-horse wagon to small grocers and other merchants. One day White went to a public auction. A little manufacturer of confectionary had gone out of business and his equipment was up for sale. Among other items, a marble slab and a soot-covered pot were offered. White bought them. Candy was boiled in the pot and cooled on the slab. Why not make chewing gum that way, White wondered? He set the pot up in his kitchen at home and tested various gums, including spruce, paraffin, and chicle and different flavors such as clove, wintergreen, peppermint, and cinnamon.

When Morrow asked White if he thought the gum business might fade away, White said, "The gum business will not play out. Americans are so nervous that they must bite on something. Farmers use hay; other men use tobacco." White avoided personal publicity, explaining to Morrow, "There is one thing I will not do, even for the gum. You have never seen my picture in public places. I abhor vulgarity. Besides, I think there is some advantage in mystery.... The absence of my picture from street cars and newspapers arouses curiosity and creates comment; and talk of White naturally involves White's product."[88]

Morrow went on to say that almost contemporary with White was "an odd and leisurely character known as Doc Beeman," who moved on from the practice of medicine to the production of pepsin, which he made from the "inward parts" of pigs and sold to people suffering from indigestion. According to this story, Beeman bought something at a book and stationery store one day and the cashier there suggested to him that he make gum and put pepsin in it. He thought about it, found the idea reasonable, and did some experiments. He allowed that cashier to have a stake in his new business and within a few years she was a wealthy woman. Then Morrow introduced George Heber Worthington, president of the "largest stone company on earth," a firm that owned 50 quarries in the Central West part of the nation. Gum for him was "incidental." In addition, he owned a zinc and lead mine in Missouri, was president of a big national bank that had been established by Marcus A. Hanna; and held an interest in 40 other enterprises. Morrow asked him how he got into the gum business. Worthington said he knew Beeman when he was a physician in a village near one of his stone quarries.

After Beeman had settled in Cleveland and began making gum, Worthington ran into him on a railway train. He told Worthington he was losing money; he had two male partners, each of whom had invested $10,000 with Beeman, but that money was almost all gone. Worthington looked over the books and Beeman's premises and decided that since the gum was good but Beeman's management bad, he would help him. Tell your partners, he said to Beeman, that I will give them $5,000 each for their interests. Beeman did not want to stiff his partners that way and reluctantly declined the offer. So Worthington gave him a check for the full amount of $20,000 and also got Beeman to accept the fact he was a bad manager and to turn over the running of the operation to Worthington—with no interference from Beeman. Although Worthington financed the operation, he claimed he never gave it more than one hour a day of his time. "I sat down with Beeman and talked over a wrapper in which to put our product. Doc was using a label that had a picture of a pig on it. Doc was a genial fellow, but he had hideous taste. 'You are not making sausage,'" I said, 'but a delectable confection,'" explained Worthington. Worthington decided to put a picture of Beeman on the wrapper, "So his philanthropic countenance and fine, old bald head went onto the label, and onto the billboards and into the newspapers all over the land."[89]

When chewing gum magnate William Wrigley, Jr., was profiled in 1919 it was reported that he had moved from being a small soap manufacturer to being the biggest chewing gum maker. He was then also the chief owner of the Chicago National League baseball club. Additionally, he spent more than $1 million a year on the advertising of his chewing gum. After a public school education in Philadelphia, he went to work in his father's soap works in Philadelphia. Young William was an outdoor enthusiast and swimming was his favorite sport. Some years later when he went to Chicago he entered the chewing gum business, coming up with the idea by mixing the juice of the spearmint herb into his gum. Although that idea was derided by others, Wrigley persisted that his spearmint gum was the coming product. Undaunted, he braved his critics' opposition and sneers until, by the time this profile was written, every city and town in America, reportedly, had spearmint as its best selling chewing gum. "The cowboy of the plains, inveterate smoker of cigarettes, will often pull out a stick of spearmint when the high winds prevent smoking owing to the danger of prairie fires. At the restaurant, after a hearty meal, the host offers the pink package of gum to his guest," said the reporter. "At the theater, on the trains, in the streets, everywhere, jaws chew and chew. Even the Kentucky colonel, remembering his mint juleps in these dog days, slowly places a stick of mint gum on his tongue and is happy."[90]

According to the profile, while William Wrigley had caught the fancy of millions of Americans with his spearmint and other gums, "he continues to work with the same zest in extending his field to foreign countries. One of his pet ambitions is to teach the English and the French how to chew. Americans traveling abroad are his best advertisers for Yank abstainers from the gum are few and far between." It was said that every American, in preparing for the worst that might befall him while abroad, carried a supply of gum with him that he had bought and stocked up on in America because chewing gum was not easily attainable abroad: "They haven't been properly educated up to it, as one youthful champion of the gum-chewing habit remarked."

When he was profiled in 1919, William Wrigley, Jr., was 55 years old, in "excellent" shape and worth many millions of dollars. He was described as still an outdoor enthusiast, an expert boxer, a crack swimmer, and held his own on horseback. Also, he had a fleet of automobiles at his disposal, and before World War I his yacht Ada E was called one of the finest afloat. Wrigley owned "one of the most magnificent country estates" in the United States and was a member of a number of posh country clubs.[91]

2

Women and Children

From the earliest mentions of gum-chewing in the media, women were singled out as the major users of the product. In some cases articles said, or implied, that women—and perhaps children—were the only users of the product. Likely that was an exaggeration. Men probably made up a greater portion of the users than the articles would have their readers believe. However, women certainly made up the majority of users, at least in the earliest years. Men were busy chewing something else when gum started to take hold in America as a popular product. They were chewing tobacco, and that was a habit that females never acquired. The spitting involved with chewing tobacco functioned as a line over which no woman would step. By 1890 or so men were clearly involved in the habit, as many articles by then acknowledged, although some stories kept up the idea that it was almost an exclusively female habit for a longer period of time. Articles on the practice up until 1890 or thereabouts for the most part treated chewing gum as though it was only a habit found in women and children.

A gum maker, O. G. Staples of Jefferson County, New York, kept 20 men constantly engaged in 1860 in its manufacture, a sign of the product's popularity. In the six months ending November 15, 1859, he had manufactured and sold over 35,000 boxes—each box contained over 200 sticks or rolls—making a total of 7,000,000 rolls. A reporter with an Indiana newspaper observed, "The chewing of gum has become almost a mania with the ladies in the east, and we are somewhat inoculated with the notion in this Hoosier land." He added, "Pure Spruce Gum, it is said, and it strikes us with reason, will sweeten the breath, make the teeth white, and interferes with scolding. If this be so, we are in for gum, sure."[1]

A few weeks later a New York City correspondent spoke "of the almost universal habit of chewing gum"[2] among women in his metropolis.

In July 1860, a journalist in Milwaukee was worried because he felt little or nothing had been said in the newspapers about gum containing deleterious substances "and so all the children in the schools, all the young ladies in the parlors, all the boys not yet up to tobacco are exercising themselves with this nauseating gum game." In one or two families that he could mention—but did not—where young ladies predominated, "it is an interesting sight to see them in the parlor all chewing, their nether jaws moving with the graceful characteristics of so many cows." And, he concluded, "Not the least objectionable feature in the fashionable habit is the impossibility of young ladies chewing without expectoration. They must spit. Think of the dear creatures spitting like backwoodsmen."[3]

A shocked and appalled editor of the *Council Bluffs* (Iowa) *Times* reported in July 1870 that he had counted within just 15 minutes over 70 females chewing gum on the street in his city. Whether or not he bothered to look at males on the street for evidence of the habit went unreported.[4] In order to excite the ambition of young women in her audience, a female lecturer delivering a talk on woman suffrage in Maine in the early part of 1876 remarked that if women had political influence, chewing gum would be put on the free list (no tariffs) and kept there forever.[5] Women had the vote in Wyoming in 1876 and in an election there in that year it was reported that a man running for town clerk bribed 18 female voters with a pound of chewing gum.[6]

A Milwaukee editor declared in 1878, "Much is said about women chewing gum and all the artillery of ridicule, possessed by man, is directed against this habit of chewing indulged in by the opposite sex." He added that he could not remember so much as one gum chewing female in his circle of acquaintances, but there was a vast array of tobacco chewers, and he then discoursed against that "vile practice." And with all that good material for ridicule at hand, meaning tobacco chewing, "the journalist still will persist in turning his attention upon perhaps one poor little specimen of the gum chewing woman, away down in New Jersey somewhere, and her innocent, cheap, and clean habit is commented upon and ridiculed, and its indulgence sounded from Maine to California, despite the fact she never spit on anybody in her life, or breathed whiskey, onions, tobacco, and other odors into the face of help-less humanity." The editor concluded that if there was less tobacco con-suming and more gum chewing—if something had to be chewed at all—"it would be much better for all humanity, and particularly so for the nearest concerned."[7]

Commenting on the fad of gum chewing, in 1879, a newspaperman from Syracuse, New York, observed, "The habit of chewing gum or wax among children and in many instances young ladies has become one of the silly and injurious practices of the passing hour." He said that if a person happened to meet an assembly of 24 young girls at least two-thirds of them would be compelled "to take a chunk of long, stringy wax from their mouths before they can commence a conversation. The wax is held in their hand, and the moment the conversation ceases it is thrown into the mouth and vigorous work is resumed." And, in case the girl felt the need to leave the room to get a drink of water, "she hands her wax to her nearest neighbor who manages to keep it hot until the return of the owner."[8]

A report early in 1880 had it that actress Mary Anderson, while playing Juliet onstage in Boston, took a wad of chewing gum out of her mouth in the garden scene, stuck it carefully on the railing of the balcony, and picked it up again and put it back in her mouth after her last "good night" to Romeo.[9]

In the state of Maine alone, it was reported in 1881 that 100,000 pounds of spruce gum were sold every year. Of course, Maine was one of the few states where the item was harvested. A reporter commented that this mild "dissipation" was indulged in mostly by schoolgirls and was said to produce paralysis of the tongue and lockjaw. "But we are consoled by the hope that the habit will spread to mothers-in-law, in which case Maine will be unable to supply the demand for case lots for birthday and holiday presents from fond son-in-laws," he quipped.[10]

Another humorous item appeared in 1883 when it was noted that newspapers all over the United States had been ridiculing the Vassar college girls for chewing gum. But, said a journalist, "If Vassar girls do chew gum, it is a guarantee that jaws are not engaged in any worse occu-pation, and gum-chewing should be encouraged accordingly in that seat of learning."[11]

Around 1885 a few articles appeared about a supposedly new craze that was percolating through America—licorice eating. It was, of course, not really happening and articles about the so-called fad disappeared as quickly as they had arisen. Nevertheless, one article speculated whether women would begin to abandon gum chewing in favor of licorice. The consuming of the item involved having a cuspidor handy, that is, spitting was involved. A druggist stepped forward to explain why women would not give up gum for licorice and also explained, indirectly, why women had never taken to tobacco chewing. "It isn't natural for a woman to spit. They only do it under peculiar circumstances. When you find a woman who is frequently expectorating she is doing that which is dia-metrically contrary to the characteristics of her sex," said the druggist. "That is one of the prerogatives of the masculine gender. It is one of the few rights of man with which woman does not meddle."[12]

When a New York City reporter talked to a retailer on Third Avenue in Manhattan in November 1885, the retailer told him that women all did it. The newsman asked him if he meant only young girls did it, to which the retailer replied, "Not a bit of it. Every woman I see in here is addicted to the habit. Young and old, pretty and plain, married and sin-gle, they all chew gum." He said he noticed as many fashionable women engaged in the habit as he did their poorer sisters: "It's as common a sight now to see the richly attired woman with a piece of chewing gum in her mouth as it is to see her with some ugly little brute under her arm or following her at the end of a string."[13]

Near the end of 1891, a Chicago journalist brought up a question he thought had often been raised but never answered satisfactorily— "Why is it that a beautiful woman is rarely found addicted to the gum chewing habit?" If she was, he thought, she certainly never made an exhibition of it in public places. "It may be that she realized the fact that the process of mastication does not enhance the attractiveness of the human face, hence has the good sense to take no chances of disfigure-ment," he speculated. And, he added, anyone who took the trouble to observe "will note that the gum chewer is invariably homely enough to stop a street car without pulling the bell. The same rule holds good in every public place where the gum chewing woman is met." In conclusion, he noted that physicians had condemned the habit as physically hurtful, but that it had "no effect in restraining the jaws of the gum fiend."[14]

Also late in 1891, an article reprinted from the *Indianapolis Star* pointed out the chewing gum habit had penetrated all walks of life. Interviewed was a chemist by the name of Professor Hurty. That scientist told of a ladies' dinner party held recently in Indianapolis at which, after the meal, pepsin chewing gum was passed around to the assembled guests. "The one feature of the affair was the fact that no attempt was made by the women to conceal their weakness," explained Hurty. "Every last one of them chewed gum and seemed proud of it."[15]

A relatively long piece on the subject of women gum chewers was published in March 1892 in the *Salt Lake Tribune* under the byline of Kate Dein. "Almost constantly you meet women or girls gently moving their jaws to and fro as calmly as cows chewing their cuds," said Dein. "Every time you board a street car you will find two or three young women dreamily gazing out of the windows and mechanically working their jaws." There was an individuality about the manner of chewing gum, Dein philosophized. Some women chewed noisily, others quietly; one would chew with her mouth closed, another with her mouth open. A thin, nervous woman chewed quickly and almost nervously. She chewed gum, thought the reporter, just as she did everything else. On the other hand, a calm, self-possessed woman chewed slowly, noiselessly. You could sit beside such a woman for 15 minutes before finding out that she was chewing at all. An indecisive woman chewed slowly one moment and quickly the next with a lateral movement of the jaw. A cautious woman moved her jaws slowly and regularly by straight up and down movements while the vivacious woman chewed and talked and talked and chewed.[16]

Dein observed, "Then, no woman has ever been able to look pretty and chew gum at the same time. Nor is it for want of practice for a gum-chewer chews when she dances, walks, rides, or talks. She never stops, except to eat and sleep." In its favor, the reporter acknowledged, gum chewing was not an expensive habit and an economical girl could stretch out a piece of gum to last all winter. Favorite places to stash used wads of gum for later use were said to be under the edge of tables, on window ledges, on shelves, chair backs, and so forth. When you saw a woman chewing gum in a street car, on the street, in a store or in any other public place, she said, "If you can't tell who she is, you can tell what she isn't. She is not a lady. You can never make a mistake about that." Dein did not say that a lady never chewed gum—she might do it because her physician advised it for dyspepsia or something of that sort. But if she did chew gum she went to her room, bolted and barred the door and chewed in solitude. "No amount of money would induce her to chew gum in public," Dein explained. "There are some things that a lady prizes more than money and self-indulgence. She places value upon herself. The girl who chews gum cheapens herself in the eyes of all who see her."[17]

Commenting on how unappealing were gum-chewing females, a journalist declared in 1893, "If girls only knew how they are so often disillusioned in the eyes of nice young men by chewing gum, they would quit the habit at once." That was because a pretty face, crowned with a yellow bang and featured with a dainty tip-tilted nose, a delicately rounded chin, a smiling and rosy mouth, plump cheeks and a smooth and peachy complexion "can look sadly distorted and homely when the jaws are worked in a passive and lackadaisical way over a little piece of gum. The prettiness goes, and somehow the sight suggests the cow and her cud."[18]

A few months later in 1893 another newsman remarked the gum chewing habit had been in America for some 25 years: "The chewing gum habit is, I know, an old established weakness among the female kind of these United States." As well, he thought the habit was perhaps infectious as people who cared nothing whatever for chewing gum would readily do so when they were with a crowd that encouraged it. "The very fact that they would be ashamed to chew gum all by themselves induces them to do so when two or three other people are doing it." He thought that if a person got on a train car and watched the passengers looking for chewers there was a good chance that at least a dozen people would be chewing gum on the sly. That is, working their jaws very slowly when they thought no one was looking. "Of course most of them are girls and women," explained the journalist. "If you would accuse a man of chewing gum, he would unhesitatingly deny it and swear reluctantly that it was tobacco he had in his mouth. I don't know of any little weakness a man hates to own up to more than chewing gum."[19]

Another long think piece on the topic of "women and chewing gum" appeared in October 1893, originally from the New York *Sun* but reprinted in several other newspapers. The journalist began by stating that a philosopher had earlier explained in the *Sun* the buying of chewing gum by men with the theory that they did not actually buy it for themselves, but they really purchased it for females. While this reporter agreed, as a rule, that was probably so since most of those addicted to gum seemed to be women, he did add, "But undoubtedly it is to some extent a masculine habit also. Several men prominent in public affairs are reported as gum chewers." Then he went on to say that observers in the street cars, on the elevated roads, and even at the theaters revealed that of late they had discovered indications that its use by women was increasing at "an alarming rate" and was also "more frequent than ever." Moreover, those observers reported the habit was not confined to girls, but had also obtained a strong hold on matrons "and many of them women well beyond the period of youth."

For the reporter all of this was remarkable, considering how careful women were of appearances and especially to make the most of their own good looks, since, he argued, nothing detracted more from beauty than the continual movement of the jaws in chewing gum. It took away the charm from the prettiest girl, yet she would continue on with her public gum chewing without the slightest apparent consciousness that she was distorting her features. "At any rate she is careless as to the matter," he wrote. "The practice seems to breed in her a curious indifference to masculine favor. As she chews she seems to be absorbed in the chewing to such an extent that the natural feminine instinct for pleasing is stifled in her." She appeared to have reached the point where, if she had the solace of chewing gum, "she can get along without men's admiration for the time being, and that time is nearly continuous, since she chews almost incessantly, we are told, in her moments of activity and in her intervals of leisure."

Instances had been reported to the journalist, he claimed, where men had actually been seen making love to girls who were chewing gum. "Undoubtedly, too, in order to win favor, they even supply the gum to the girls," he speculated, "though it is for them so distressing a rival and so great an obstacle to the concentration of thought requisite for lovemaking." What, then, wondered the newsman, was the philosophy of this recent American habit, for in its prevalence it was new, and why should it have so "pernicious" a fascination for women especially, even though it marred their beauty "and thus violates the dictates of the universal instinct of women to enhance their charms for the captivation of masculine admiration?" Unfortunately, the readers of this piece were left disappointed. The journalist had no answer for the question he had posed, nor did he even venture to speculate.[20]

When a reporter with the *Salt Lake Tribune* discussed the topic in February 1904, he declared gum chewing was most certainly a habit, and whether or not it was considered a bad one, "it is a fact that too many of Salt Lake's girls spend too much of their time in exercise of the jaws." The practice of the habit, he argued, was not confined to any class or classes, but was indulged in by girls of "every hue and shade, of every age and condition and social standing. They do not confine themselves to chewing at home, but do so in public places and upon the street." As far as this journalist was concerned, it was a habit just as much as was smoking and chewing tobacco. Girls, he continued, were prone to dismiss that idea by saying it may be a habit but it was not a hurtful one. But girls did not realize that a "sick headache" had its origins in chewing gum, or that the undue exercise of the muscles of the face produced a general feeling of languor and lassitude. He added, "They fail to perceive or refuse to take cognizance of the fact that their physical beauty is marred by the overdevelopment of the lower portion of the face. There is nothing so mars the harmony of a symmetrical face as taut cheek muscles and heavy, distended jaws."[21]

A July 1906 article in an Ohio newspaper declared gum chewing was in vogue. It was no longer considered to be a vulgar habit, "for women in the smart set have taken it up this summer and are serving it with bonbons after luncheons and dinners in their country, mountain, and seashore homes," with that information coming from a New York City newspaper. Since pepsin was touted as being an aid to digestion, pepsin chewing gum was the most popular kind. A "prominent" retailer in New York City was queried by a reporter and declared that now when women bought a box of candy or an ice cream soda from his establishment, they also bought a box of gum and furthermore, that with all the standing orders of items that he shipped to the mountains and seashore each week there were also included requests for 10 or 20 boxes of pepsin gum. "I believe that gum is now considered a delicacy and is served with the choicest bonbons after each meal," explained the retailer. "It is not refused at table either, for the orders show that immense quantities of it are daily consumed."

When a society woman told him she wanted to have a standing order for 20 boxes of gum sent each week to her country home, along with the already existing standing order for a 10 pound box of chocolates, she explained to the merchant, "I like gum after a meal, especially the pepsin flavor, and so many persons are afflicted with indigestion and of course don't want to excuse themselves to take medicine that I know I am doing them a kindness by giving them something that contains enough pepsin to have a quieting effect on the stomach." For this society woman, as long as everybody chewed gum it really was not an objectionable habit "and in the drawing room or on the porch for half an hour or longer after meals it is rather a comfort. We women feel as if we were having a dissipation similar to the men's smoking, except that they join us in chewing and really seem to enjoy it."

After meals, though, was not the only time those society women chewed gum. They also indulged during car rides, for example. A different society woman told the journalist, "Gum is the greatest possible comfort on a long auto trip. It keeps one from being thirsty and, I believe, from becoming nervous when sitting quietly for hours. Of course, I do get tired if I chew it all the time, but instead of constantly working the jaws I keep it in my mouth and chew it occasionally."[22]

An unidentified Reno, Nevada, woman told a newsman in 1908, "It's all right to chew gum at home when one is alone but it isn't ladylike to do so in public, though I'm sorry it is considered in that light, for I do like to chew gum." When the reporter told her that a person's health demanded gum, she quickly exclaimed with delight, "Well, that's different, that makes it proper, I'm so glad."[23]

A woman named Frances Aymar Mathews in 1912 criticized the university education of women: "Do the girls who go to college learn there to chew gum and crave excitement and notoriety, and do they live during their years at college like Bohemians in a Latin quarter romance?" Mathews thought they did. Not surprisingly, that set off a storm of disagreement. One who responded was Dean Virginia C. Gildersleeve of Barnard, in a lengthy article in the *New York Times*. With respect to manners, Gildersleeve stated, "Miss Mathews says a great deal about manners. In the first place, Barnard girls do not chew gum, and I don't think any college girls do. They do, I suppose, drink soda water—why shouldn't they?"[24]

If adult females who chewed gum came in for verbal condemnation—and they did—the treatment handed out to schoolchildren of either sex who indulged in the habit was often much harsher. A 15-year-old female student at a Kenosha, Wisconsin, school was flogged with a piece of rawhide by her teacher for the offense of chewing gum in 1860. The girl was identified only as the daughter of E. F. Morris while the teaching master was a man called Mr. Pope. Details were not given but Pope ended up being arrested for his actions and tried in court. Evidence at the trial indicated Morris was flogged across her back and bare neck with Pope administering five or six stokes, drawing blood. The charge against Pope was not specified in the news accounts but whatever it was the jury could not reach any agreement on a verdict. Pope was released on the basis of what sounded like a hung jury.[25]

A November 1870 account stated that the community of Janesville, Wisconsin, was much exercised by the wholesale floggings that were said to prevail in its public schools. The instrument of torture used was, generally, a strap 16 inches long and 1¼ inches wide, made of thick cowhide and limbered with oil. One boy was reported to have received 99 blows on the hand for chewing gum in class while another pupil was flogged for 10 minutes for "smiling." The tone of the article was very much against corporal punishment in the schools.[26]

One week later Janesville was still grumbling, but this time it was about the large number of newspapers around the country who picked up on the stories of floggings in the Janesville schools—most of them concentrated on the story of the boy who received 99 strokes for chewing gum—complete with large exaggerations. Said a Boston editor, "The semi-savage residents of that backwoods village have recently adopted as a rule in their schools that the punishment for the offense of chewing gum (which is readily obtained from the tamarack trees abounding in the region) shall be 999 blows with the Russian knout, large numbers of those instruments of torture having been imported for that purpose. This punishment has actually been inflicted on a little boy but three years of age." And the following account appeared in a Memphis paper, "The inhuman residents of that city have recently adopted in a mass convention called for that purpose, the bastinado as punishment in their public schools. One little boy of seven years was recently flogged for three hours on the soles of his bare feet, and then compelled to stand for five days on those same feet, for the mild offense of chewing gum."[27]

It was declared in 1885 that gum chewing had become so universal with LaGrange County, Indiana, schoolgirls that the county school superintendent had introduced the command "Attention! Remove your gum!" into the school drill commands.[28]

On an April 1888 day a little girl in the Lincoln Avenue School in Freeport, Illinois, was chewing gum. It annoyed the teacher to the extent the pupil was ordered to throw the gum in the garbage. That caused the child to begin to cry as she tearfully explained she did not want to throw out the gum as it belonged to her mother. The teacher then relented and let the child keep her gun and take it home to her mother.[29]

A young boy, pupil at the North Jefferson Street School in New Castle, Pennsylvania, was reported to have been "severely whipped" in that school in 1894 by a young teacher—the offense for the flogging was the chewing of gum. A day or two earlier the child had been warned that if he chewed gum he would be whipped. On the day in question he started to chew gum in school again and was kept after class. When school was dismissed for the day the whipping began. Punishment was inflicted by the female teacher who kept whipping the boy until he finally broke down and cried. He resisted crying for as long as he could but finally broke down after what he said was a half hour of flogging. His teacher was determined to keep whipping the boy until he did cry—it was a battle of wills. His mother noticed his damaged back when he finally arrived home, and brought the matter to the attention of the press.[30]

Around the same time, in the winter of 1894–1895, a West Side grammar school in Chicago suffered what was described as an "epidemic" of gum chewing. Teachers at the school at first thought they had stamped it out by the time-honored method of singling out the miscreants and compelling those children to throw their gum out of the window. But then the epidemic returned, this time "in violent form." Some of the teachers tried "despotism" to stamp out the returned habit but, as they had nothing with which to back it up, that method was not successful. Other teachers used ridicule and sarcasm; still others tried arbitration. With the latter method, the compromise consisted in giving students permission to leave their gum in the cloakroom. So each girl put her hat on her own particular hook in the cloakroom and stuck her gum on the wall above it, "and her rights were respected." However, a boy came along one day and stole all the wads. After that, the gum chewers put their wads on their inkwells at their desks. However, the wads were so close to the owners and in such plain sight that the temptation was so great that method had to be abandoned.

In another room in the school a teacher ignored the situation for a time and the gum chewing went on without interruption. Then one morning when the children arrived the teacher was sitting at the front as usual "but with the absent minded, vacuous expression characteristic of the confirmed gum chewer on her face." All day long this teacher chewed gum going through all the usual facial expressions and contortions. It was said that it slowly dawned on the children that she was giving them an object lesson. Did they look like that? During the noon recess the children discussed the matter among themselves and the next morning, reportedly, there was no gum in that classroom.[31]

With the consent of Miss Howard, the principal of the Washington School in Victor, Colorado, a teacher there named George Reeder had been trying to "cure" children of the chewing gum habit by making them chew quinine, a very bitter substance. A female pupil named Urquhart was punished in that fashion on the morning of May 21, 1903. That caused her brother Clarence Urquhart to complain to Howard, and even threaten the principal. Reeder was called in and he threw Clarence out of the room "with great violence." As a result his body struck the door casing and his shoulder was severely bruised. Later that same day some male pupils banded together and mobbed the teachers as they left the school for the day, pelting them with rotten eggs and rocks.[32]

On March 7, 1907, discipline was applied at the McMynn School in Racine, Wisconsin, to a dozen pupils of the higher grades who were "continuous offenders" of the rule against gum chewing during school hours. They were supplied with a stock of their favorite flavor of gum and made to stand before the rest of the school and chew gum during the entire school day. It was said the offense was one that had been particularly pervasive in the school and Principal Martin had been induced to threaten drastic measures. When the offenses continued Mr. Martin appeared at the school on the morning of March 7 with a number of packages of gum, selected out all of the worst offenders as they arrived for school and hauled them before the entire student body for punishment. Several of the pupils so singled out refused to chew, which prompted Martin to declare they would "be punished in another manner." The others chewed on for hours; one was a girl and the others were boys from the 8th grade. At noon, instead of agreeing they were being punished, the offenders declared themselves delighted with the treatment and resolved to chew all afternoon. Martin then decided to take even more drastic measures to impress on the pupils the fact they were indeed being punished. They were given more gum for the afternoon session but to their shock found the gum had been treated with a liberal application of quinine. Before the afternoon was over, the offenders yielded and all of them promised to adhere to the school's chewing gum ban in the future.[33]

Five weeks later a follow-up to the above story indicated that Principal E. S. Martin had become "famous throughout the United States" because of the gum chewing incident. Since the quinine incident McMynn School had been, reportedly, free of gum chewing during school hours. Many newspapers picked up and published the original account. Martin received several hundred newspaper clippings from various cities around America commenting on the affair and many letters requesting him to write feature stories about his method of dealing with the habit. Out of the many newspaper articles that flowed from the incident, it was said, only one criticized Martin's action "and that was mild indeed."[34]

Pupils at the public school in Winchester, Virginia, were no longer allowed to chew gum during school hours, as of October 1907, under penalty of dismissal. School principal N. D. Cool had reported to the school board that a large number of pupils were "addicted" to the chewing gum habit and that it "had a tendency to demoralize and interfere with study." Because of that report the school board promptly banned gum from the school and instructed the principal to summarily dismiss all pupils caught with gum in their mouths.[35]

In a public school in the west side of Philadelphia in 1910 a teacher was having difficulties enforcing the injunction barring the use of chewing gum during school hours. As a result, the teacher decided to make an example of the two most willful boys. She stationed the pair in one part of the classroom where they would be conspicuous. Then she gave

"GUM RACKS FOR PUPILS! WHY NOT?" ASKS NORMAL SCHOOL PRESIDENT

Children chewing gum in school were seen as a terrible problem in this period, and this 1916 sketch spoofed the idea that gum racks should be available in schools. The idea was that the gum chewer would leave his wad of gum on a rack, beside his name or number, and retrieve it from this storage space after school, and then reuse it.

each boy a roll of clean white paper and told him to chew it. The boys, with their cheeks bulging out with the paper pulp, were compelled to chew steadily for 15 minutes.[36]

Principal Karl E. Whinnery of Sandusky High School in Ohio, in a talk before the 800 pupils of that school in 1921, told them he would not permit any boy students to meet their "best girls" in the corridors of the building, nor would he permit couples to loiter about the grounds. Additionally, he declared that gum chewing by students would not be tolerated and that the excuse of having an appointment with the dentist, to explain an absence, would henceforth be considered "passé."[37]

3

Popularity and
Pervasiveness

The Atlantic *Telegraph* estimated in June 1886 that fully one-third of the young people of Atlantic, Iowa, made gum chewing an important part of their existence, from the girl who chewed spruce gum to keep her jaws in practice to the small boy who chewed Black Jack to make people think he was tough.[1]

Later in 1886 it was reported that at least 30 kinds of commercially-made gum were on the market in Chicago, and that was not all. The southern balsam gums did not find their way into Chicago, as they were made especially for the home market. Said a Chicago confectioner, "The gum counter is now a recognized part of our business. Lately favor has been setting toward the spruce, but there's a call for the sweet varieties."[2]

Another report from Chicago a year later, in July 1887, declared that if chewing gum was popular a year earlier "it is a perfect rage now." A druggist said that his sales of chewing gum were getting to be "enormous." When a man went to investigate its prevalence at Geneva Lake (cottage country for Chicago), he complained that he found wads of gum discarded everywhere. At the hotel where he stayed he found wads on the columns of the hotel veranda, under the arms of the rustic chairs there, and even on the edges of the chairs in the hotel dining room. He found it even on the logs people sat on at the edge of the lake. "People seem to be getting over the old prejudice against chewing, and it has come to be a regular thing among all classes of people," he wrote. "Many men use it to avoid using tobacco. Women say it is a solace."[3]

Orders for spruce gum were reported to be up at the start of 1888: "Gum chewing has become so fashionable that there is an unusual demand for it and it is one that promises to last." It was said that the chewing of gum aided digestion and whitened the teeth. Elderly men took to the product due to the first reason while the second reason made the practice popular with women. One firm was said to have made a fortune by producing a candied chewing gum that was sold by druggists, tobacconists, confectionists, and at elevated railroads. "The chewing gum habit has got away beyond the school girl, and there's no telling where it will stop at its present rate of progress," concluded the article.[4]

A reprinted story that first appeared in the *Baltimore American* early in 1888 exclaimed that the habit of chewing gum by men, women, babies, young and old in the West was gradually working its way east. "It is a matter of common practice at many health resorts, and strikingly so at the Hot Springs in Arkansas, and nearly all the physicians in these sanitariums commend the exercise as materially aiding digestion, cleaning the stomach, and as a help in breaking off chewers from the use of tobacco." Just a few years earlier, and even then, continued the journalist, in staid eastern cities, "a young lady who chewed gum would be shunned by other fair ones and held up as an example as one on the direct route to perdition." However, in Chicago, Kansas City, St. Paul, Minneapolis "and all the rest of the progressive west and northwest cities and towns if one can't chew a nickel's worth of gum per day one is not up to the standard."[5]

In the period 1888 to 1890, the product really captured the public's attention and media articles became more numerous. A brief piece in April 1888, for example, observed the gum chewing craze was "raging" in Freeport, Illinois, with men, women, and children all using it.[6]

A report later in 1888 remarked that in days gone by the "gentler sex" had a complete monopoly on the gum chewing habit, but in the last little while a change had taken place. It was now not unusual to meet half a dozen men, young and old, in a one block journey and find they were all working their jaws over tutti frutti, spruce, or some other favorite brand of gum. "It is a period of moral revolution. The young man desires to refrain or abstain from the use of tobacco, and what is more natural than that he should seek solace in gum." Among the male members of the chewing gum fraternity, the reporter commented, the legal profession was taking a high rank. Among lawyers the old-fashioned spruce gum was said to be the type generally preferred—that is, "the purest and healthiest" chewing gum. As a rule the boys did not take so kindly to the brands preferred by the girls. When females declared the brand Yucatan to be the best, the men opted for Barley Malt, Tutti Frutti, Sapota, and others. Many members of police forces had also adopted "this harmless habit, which they look upon as much more clean than tobacco chewing and it affords a great comfort, so those addicted to it say, in passing away the weary hours upon the beat, where there is often no one to talk to for several hours at a time." Another advantage of the habit pointed out by this journalist, and many others over time, was that it was a very economical habit, much cheaper than tobacco."[7]

So popular was gum chewing becoming that a recipe for homemade gum was published in newspapers in 1888, despite the economical nature of the commercially-prepared product. Take of prepared balsam of tolu two ounces, white sugar one ounce, and oatmeal three ounces, soften the gum in a water bath and mix in the ingredients. Then roll in finely powdered sugar or flour to form sticks to suit.[8]

Still in 1888, an article reprinted from the *Chicago Tribune* remarked, "In spite of the manifold warnings of physicians, and in spite of all the contemptuous and sarcastic remarks which are constantly appearing in the papers, gum chewing in this country is rapidly on the increase." The author of this piece believed that two-thirds of girls were gum users. He was also of the opinion that gum chewing was not exclusively confined to the female sex as was smoking to the male, for many men used gum to help kill the craving for tobacco, "thus jumping from the frying pan into the fire, perhaps." When he asked himself why it was that women chewed gum he offered the thought that no one knew the answer, including the users themselves. One girl said she chewed because she could; one said she chewed because her mother told her not to; another said she indulged because she liked the taste and besides, everybody else chewed. Concluded the reporter, "They really did not know why they chewed and had never thought to ask themselves the question."[9]

An item that was originally from the St. Paul *Pioneer Press* and reprinted in the *Washington Post* (among other papers) in July 1889 stated that the gum chewing habit was certainly on the increase throughout the nation. "An epidemic has fastened itself upon the best and fairest of America's daughters from Maine to California and from five years of age up to those uncertain days that lie beyond the hope of matrimony," was how it was described. "And from the daughters and wives and sweethearts this form of maxillary calisthenics has been communicated to fathers, husbands, sons and lovers, until America has become a nation of gum chewers." Reportedly, the sales of chewing gum in Minneapolis had nearly doubled in the past year.[10]

A few weeks later the *Trenton Times* (New Jersey) repeated much of the material cited above. However, the piece did add some, presumably, original material. Pointing out the mania for gum had spread faster in the previous year than ever before, it added that years ago most of the gum sold was the "genuine" spruce variety (mostly from Maine). But in 1889 the gum sold "is nothing more or less than rubber with various kinds of flavoring to suit the taste and fancy of the women folk." When the New Jersey reporter asked a druggist in Trenton if he sold much spruce gum, the man's reply was that he did not, that 90 percent of the gum sold was "made of rubber or some other substance that is far from healthy." Added the druggist, "I have seen more women chewing gum on the streets within the past year than I ever did before" and not one out of 100 of them used spruce gum.

The reporter found several Trenton confectionary stores selling gum, all of which told him the sales of chewing gum had gone up markedly in the past year. One of them commented, "I am doing a bigger gum business today than every before. Everybody chews gum lately. It is not spruce gum I can assure you." And: "Most of the gum I sell is made of rubber. All of the women are chewing gum nowadays. It's made of candy. You see, this gum I sell is sweetened and it tastes more like candy than anything else. I think that this is the reason why so many women chew gum lately."[11]

That same year, 1889, a report in the *Indianapolis Star* remarked, "It is as natural nowadays for a Hoosier, at least in the Hoosier capital, to ask for or offer a piece of gum, as it was for an old-time Hoosier to request or companionably offer a 'chaw of terbaccer.'" In Indianapolis it was said that everybody chews, including "doctors, lawyers, merchants, that picturesque aggregation, the city council, and the entire baseball nine." When the habit of chewing gum was confined to giggling schoolgirls, he said, it was an object of ridicule: "When the girls' fathers began chewing they formulated ingenious excuses for it. Now everybody chews and nothing is said. Any one bringing up the old-time objection is either ignored, laughed at or looked upon with interest as a relic of antiquity."

At that time there was a chewing gum factory located in the southeastern part of Indianapolis where it produced its gum out of chicle, sugar, and flavorings. Five flavors of the gum were manufactured there—licorice, mint, pineapple, wintergreen, and sarsaparilla.[12]

When a Greenville, Pennsylvania, reporter asked, at the start of 1890, when could one find gum chewers, his answer was "at all hours of the day." Gum chewers could be found, he said, "in the church and in the den of vice; in the gorgeous parlor and in the hovel; in school room, opera house, and on corners of the streets, and it may be asked where they may not be seen." The users, or "victims" as he described them, were: "the society belle and street walker, the fashionable gentleman and the debauchee, and all intermediate grades. This habit does not respect classes. It finds willing devotees everywhere."[13]

Out on the West Coast in March 1890, a journalist with the Oakland *Tribune* asked the druggist at Kirkland and Trowbridge's drug store in that city about the demand for gum. "Yes, it's just a fad. There's a gum craze on, and you'd be surprised at the amount of the stuff chewed in this city. I suppose gum chewing has increased two or three hundred percent in the past year," he said. Everybody was at it, he continued, old and young, men and women, boys and girls. "We never kept the stuff until about four months ago. Then we found that people were coming in all the time for it, and greatly disappointed when they found we hadn't a stock on hand." As a result he began to stock gum, and he then kept eight or ten varieties on his shelves, but he grumbled the wholesalers had some 15 brands and he had to keep increasing the number of brands he stocked. "I think these baseball fellows are largely responsible. Did you ever notice them during a game—every one of them chewing away like a sausage cutter. The tutti-frutti people use the ballplayers as an advertisement, furnishing them their cuds just for the notoriety they give the brand." Another reason he thought might be a factor was that the manufacturers "are putting the stuff up in such an attractive shape that it catches the eye. I suppose there is a sort of calm satisfaction about chewing the stuff, though I'd never marry a chewer, especially one of these street masticators."[14]

Late in 1890 a reporter declared that the cynics pointed out that no fancy of the American people had become such a craze as the public indulgence in the gum-chewing habit and that no craze had flourished so in the face of public odium. The habit had reportedly reached the stage then that made it impossible for a New Yorker to go to the theater or church, or enter the street cars or a railway train or walk on a fashionable promenade, without meeting men and women whose jaws were "working with the activity of the gum chewing victim." And, he continued, that spectacle was maintained "in the face of frequent reminders that gum chewing, especially in public, is an essentially vulgar indulgence that not only shows bad breeding, but spoils a pretty countenance and detracts from the dignity of those who practice the habit. Cynics who observe it have sighed for the return of the sturdy discipline of their youth, when the schoolmaster used to spank everybody caught chewing gum in public." For this reporter one of the few "rays of hope" was that many observers in the know felt, or hoped, the present prevalence and swift rise of the habit would mean an equal swift fall to obscurity, and soon.[15]

A retailer of gum in 1896 in Massillon, Ohio, stated: "The demand for chewing gum among Massillonians is getting to be something enormous. It is now a daily occurrence for men who are old enough to chew tobacco to buy 25 or 30 cents worth of gum at a time. Everybody chews gum and we're glad of it for the sale is really lucrative, there being more than 50 percent profit in it."[16]

A reporter who believed that 70 percent of bicyclists chewed gum while they were on their bikes wrote a brief piece in 1897. Although he wondered about the link between bicycling and gum chewing, he presented no answers to the question, nor did he venture to speculate.[17]

In the waiting rooms of all the rail depots in Fort Wayne, Indiana, in 1902, one could find the "chewing gum machines" (vending machines),

CELEBRATING   CHEWING   GUM'S   FIFTIETH   BIRTHDAY

This 1916 sketch celebrated the 50th anniversary of chewing gum (by its calculations) by featuring illustrations of chewers.

The Humble Birthplace of Chewing Gum.

A sketch of the birthplace of chewing gum, published on the product's 50th anniversary.

a reporter told his readers. You put a penny in a slot and you pulled out a stick of chewing gum. In the busy south depot were two gum machines, and they took in on average some $6 to $7 each. The weighing machine—one cent per weight—took in $7 to $8 a week. Those machines were placed there not by the railroads but by large commercial firms that owned and controlled the machines. Owners of the sites hosting the machines got a percentage of the revenue for allowing their premises to be used. Railroad employees emptied the machines on a specific schedule and sent the money on to the commercial firm, who settled later with the railroads. "There is big money in the business, for this is an age of gum chewing girls and women—and men too—as evidence of which witness the jaw motion of about three-fourths of the audience attending the theaters and other places of public entertainment," concluded the article.[18]

Above and following page: **This pair of sketches show the contrasting ways that chicle was gathered in 1916, on the streets of New York City and in the jungles of Central America.**

In the summer of 1905 a *New York Times* story asserted: "Chewing of gum has become almost a national habit. To its credit may be set down the fact that among men it has to a great extent driven out the chewing of tobacco. Chewing itself seems to have some obscure necessity

behind it as if, like the exercise of the teeth in squirrels, rats, mice, and other rodents, it were an instinctive act for the purpose of keeping the teeth sharp and in good condition." This report made a brief mention of non-commercial gum, remarking that in the country it had always been a habit with children to collect the gum from cherry and peach trees for the purpose of chewing that exudation.[19]

One of the leading chewing gum dealers in Reno, Nevada, remarked in 1908: "There is a peculiar thing about gum in Reno. It is one of the commodities which has no ups and downs in its sale ... chewing gum goes right along steadily, month in and month out." Reno was said to be a heavy user of gum.[20]

A Charleston, South Carolina, journalist commented in 1911 that time was, "and that not very long ago, when ladies did not chew gum; or if they did it was in the privacy of their homes. But they chew it now, not in Charleston, but elsewhere. It is stated on good authority that almost twice as much chewing gum is sold in the country today as was sold a few years ago. We are becoming a nation of chewers, chewing everywhere, in private and in public."[21]

Mabel Chadband was the writer of a September 1914 article on the popularity of chewing gum in Cedar Rapids, Iowa. One retailer told her his sales amounted to 3,200 packages a month. At that rate his store sold 38,400 packs annually or about five sticks to every resident of Cedar Rapids, estimating the population at 38,000—and that was just one retail outlet. In Cedar Rapids gum was sold chiefly in the confectionary, drug, novelty, and department stores. And in all the places Chadband visited she was told that gum consumption was on the increase and sales were far in excess of those of former years. That increase was particularly noticeable over the previous year. Explained one dealer, "We have sold more gum, I believe, because we have pushed it. We have given a large space in our store to the display of all makes of gum, and back of us has been the manufacturer who has spent much money in advertising. One brand of gum has cost the manufacturer more money in advertising than all the other makes combined." Another reason this dealer mentioned was that gum was being sold cheaper than heretofore. Some of it was being sold at the rate of three packs for 10 cents, other brands were going for two packs for five cents, but by the far the greatest number were still being sold at the standard price of five cents a package (containing five sticks). Chadband observed that not all gum chewing was done by women. "Far from it," and many men were said to be buying it after they had quit smoking. She related: "In the east a few years ago the chewing of gum was looked upon with disfavor but even this attitude toward the gum chewer in that section of the country has changed recently. An easterner told me that here in the middle west he found

more people chewing it than in his part of the country." An eastern manufacturer of gum said American consumption of gum had gone up since
World War I began. He said; "Everybody has taken on a case of nerves
over the big scrap. Men become so excited over war bulletins they keep
puffing or chewing all the time. Women have to take theirs out on something else and it has fallen to the lot of chewing gum to take the edge
off their nerves." Spokesmen for the chewing gum factories were
reported to say their plants had been working 24 hours a day to supply
"the greatest demand in their history."[22]

A reporter for a Brownsville, Texas, newspaper asked himself in
1918 if there was much chewing gum used by the residents of the lower
Rio Grande Valley. His answer: there certainly was. For proof, he referred
his readers to A. S. Livingston and L. L. Graves, who were traveling representatives for the "famous" Adams Black Jack gum, "a commodity that
has become famous through its unusual flavor." Those two men were
then in Brownsville, and they told the inquiring reporter that the
Brownsville area was a good chewing gum section, citing as evidence
the large number of orders they had received from area wholesalers, the
largest for one ton from Cattarelli Brothers.

Graves stated World War I had wrought many changes with one of
the most interesting and important ones being the departure of the former attitude toward chewing gum. "A short time ago, the chewing of
gum was believed to be, in certain circles, a vulgar and obnoxious habit,"
he explained. But the fact that it had been found to be a "necessity" in
the U.S. Army and Navy, coupled with the fact that gum had been sanctioned and purchased in large quantities by both the American Red
Cross and the U.S. federal government, had to a great extent caused people to give the product more serious thought and a stronger desire to
know more about it. Enthusiastically, Graves then outlined briefly to the
reporter how gum was manufactured, calling it "the pure, wholesome
Habit of the Alert." Hospitals were using chewing gum in large quantities, claimed Graves, declaring it to be very beneficial when a patient
came out from under ether. He said his firm, the American Chicle Company (the trust that contained Adams, among other makers), had
recently received the following letter from one of New York City's biggest
hospitals regarding their Black Jack gum. "Your licorice flavored gum,
Black Jack, seemed to be far more efficient than any other. The pleasant

flavor, plus the medicinal virtue possessed by the licorice, leads one to recommend for your consideration that this particular type of gum be recommended as of value in post-operative thirst," went the letter. "Our experience would thoroughly justify you in the claim that this gum has virtue which should be brought to the attention of hospital authorities." Additionally, Graves remarked that advertising had played an important part in bringing chewing gum to the forefront. While many manufacturers were curtailing their ad expenditures for 1918 due to the war, American Chicle planned to continue "to conduct their huge advertising propaganda."[23]

So pervasive had the habit become by 1920 that expenditure on the product was held up as an example of wasteful spending, compared to more deserving aspects of society. In this case gum prevalence was compared to the "deplorable" state of affairs that existed in respect to donations to the Presbyterian Church in the United States. "That many church members spend more for chewing gum in a day than they give to the church in a year" was one of the statements made in a survey of the Presbyterian Church. That survey and conclusion came from the New Era Movement of the Presbyterian Church, which grumbled that many church members had heretofore given as little as 14 cents a year.[24]

In a piece published in the summer of 1920, the president of American Chicle Company was cited as saying the people of the United States were spending $100 million a year for chewing gum. Supposedly the demand for the product had tripled since 1917, and the chewing gum manufacturers were said to thank the arrival of Prohibition for that situation. However, the journalist who wrote the story thought the makers could just as well thank advertising for that increase in demand, as they all had bought extensive space in the newspapers and magazines. This reporter also posed the question why it was that people chewed gum. "Nervousness? Yes and no, say the scientists," he wrote. "They have a theory that the chewing gum habit results from modern man's eating soft foods, and that gum serves as a safety valve to give vent to the surplus energy of the jaws that in the olden days was directed at tough meats, forest roots and coarsely cooked foods."[25]

Another news item, later in 1920, declared, "Gum chewing has not only been increased by the absence of booze but is enjoying added vogue because of the high price of sugar." This article also argued that more candy was eaten by men who could not get booze. Chicle had dropped in price from 75 cents a pound to 55 cents, and with annual sales of chewing gum at $100 million, around nine million pounds of chicle were consumed in its manufacture. One pound of chicle costing 55 cents was said here to make $11 worth of gum.[26]

Molly Lee had her own newspaper column (probably syndicated) in 1921, titled "Molly Lee Says Today." In her May 2, 1921, column she asked her readers in the subhead, "Have you the gum chewing habit? Or has the gum-chewing habit got you?" She started off by writing, "There was a time—though it is so long ago that few remember it, or care to consider it—when it was considered very bad taste to chew gum in public. Ladies did not chew gum at all—others may have chewed gum, but not in public places." Lee added, "But now the casual observer would decide that EVERY man, woman and child in the country chews gum." If anyone doubted that, Lee advised such a person to look around at people attending events such as concerts, plays, movies, church services, or in the streets, and "at first glance there is nothing to indicate that there is hidden away a wad of succulent sweetness. But after a while there will come an exciting episode in the picture and the cud will be shifted to the other side of the jaw and an expression of peace will steal over the features of the chewer." Lee added that others would be there in those groups, others "who chew with a champing regularity and utter disregard for the book of etiquette in which may be found a simple rule suggesting that the mouth be kept closed—when full."

She noted that in the early days of the history of the United States gum chewing was in its infancy. The Pilgrims may have occasionally chewed some of "the fragrant, spicy spruce gum with its aromatic taste bordering on the bitter" simply by scraping it off the tree, but the modern young person would scorn such primitive methods of obtaining gum. For the modern young person, all that was involved was a trip to the store with a nickel. Concluded Molly Lee, "Men have taken to the gum-chewing habit to a striking degree and the constancy they show toward the little sticks of sweetness indicates that they are an incentive to great activity, and also to deep and creative thinking."[27]

Taking a contrary stance was a June 1921 article in a California newspaper that insisted there was then a drastic fall off in the sale of chewing gum. However, no details were provided, nor were any numbers or other evidence introduced to reinforce that claim. There were not even anecdotal reports presented—such as an anonymous store owner stating sales had fallen off by some percentage. Nonetheless, the reporter pressed on, saying that some manufacturers blamed the lack of a war for the supposed drop. As well, Prohibition was saddled with some of the blame. In the old days, it was said, husbands used to buy gum at cocktail bars each afternoon to chew on the way home to kill the smell of alcohol. But all that ended with the arrival of Prohibition.[28]

4

Usage, Geography and Consumers

A reporter from the *New York Sun* went in July 1882 to a building near Bleecker Street west of Broadway that bore the sign "Chewing Gum Factory," wherein the proprietor informed the journalist that demand for chewing gum came and went. There was less demand when school was out, and in the fall when children returned to school demand for the product went up, "for chewing gum is a quiet comfort during school hours." If a pupil brought in taffy or candy then sticky fingers and smeared books were the result. As well, the rustling of a candy paper wrapper might catch a teacher's attention. As a result, gum was easier for a child to bring to school and, of course, it was economical. A pupil might stick a wad of gum in his desk when called upon by the teacher to recite, and when it dried it became fresh and crackly again, as good as when it was first bought.[1]

A different reporter, with a different New York City newspaper, wrote in 1883: "In the upper circle of society chewing gum is frowned upon as being vulgar." But in East 10th Street in New York there was said to be a club of ladies called the Spruce Club. They met twice a week in winter, ostensibly to chew spruce gum. But that was just an excuse, noted the reporter, because during the two hours the women chewed gum they worked on making baby clothes for poor people. Each member of the club contributed 50 cents a week, which bought the linen and the gum.[2]

When still another reporter for still another New York City newspaper spoke to a gum manufacturer at his New York factory in 1884, he asked the man if chewing gum had any merits. The owner replied that plenty of people used it to relieve their dyspepsia and cure their indigestion. When he was asked by the reporter who were the users, the owner said it was mostly children. "Women and young girls do their share. Men chew to considerable extent, and I have known many a case where slaves to tobacco have been cured by chewing gum. If men did not chew tobacco they would be as fond of gum as women are." He added, "Negroes are fond of gum, and you never meet a colored girl that has not got her mouth full of it. The great gum-chewing states are Kentucky, Illinois, and Ohio, in the order named." Then the reporter asked the proprietor if gum chewing was an economical habit. In reply, the man said he had a piece he had been chewing for three months and it was just as good and as big as when he first put it in his mouth—he could not wear it out.[3]

A St. Paul, Minnesota, druggist said that he had read abut a supposed craze for licorice chewing among women that had taken hold in the East. He said, though, that fad had not struck St. Paul and there was no demand in his city for licorice. School children, he explained, chewed licorice and slippery elm because those things were sweet and they varied the "monotony" of their mastication with chewing gum. "It is rarely you will see a woman chewing" anything, he thought. In his opinion there had been a general decline in all chewable things and he thought it was related to the increased availability of candies. "I've known people to masticate tolu gum. Now that's hard stuff to chew, because it clings to the jaws, and once in the mouth is difficult to get out again," he said. It gave a person a sort of a "lock-jaw. We tell people about that when they call for the gum; but some of them, if they happen to be a little pig-headed, won't believe us, and insist on having the gum." But, he explained, tolu gum was then made up into a kind of taffy by mixing it with other things "and in that form can be chewed, and is pleasant to the taste." A man from Louisville told this druggist that in the Kentucky city "every other person one meets on the street is chewing the gum." The druggist concluded there was no craze for licorice there but there seemed to be a craze for tolu gum.[4]

When a traveling sales representative for an unnamed chewing gum manufacturer was passing through Elyria, Ohio, in 1885, he said he sold 3,000 boxes there each month, which totaled 36,000 boxes a year, or 3.6 million sticks of gum. A reporter commented, "Thus the men, for men do chew it, women and children pay out over $30,000 per year for a foolish useless, idle, worthless habit."[5]

A reporter and a companion were standing in front of a New York City hotel on an August day in 1886 when an "obviously wealthy" man drew up to the hotel in a posh carriage. The companion told his reporter friend that the man in the carriage was a chewing gum manufacturer. "Look around us and you will see that about three out of four of the women, young or old, are chewing gum. The awful gum habit has taken hold of the jaws of the fashionable women throughout the country this season," he added. "Just as you observe it here so it is at every resort. The fascination of gum-chewing equals that of opium, I do believe, and its slaves are slaves indeed." According to the companion, the man in the carriage invented it five years ago when he kept a little candy store in a back street of New York City. His customers at first were the pupils of a public school nearby and the gum pleased them. Demand soon spread and the manufacturer marketed his gum systematically over a wider area. Children throughout the land became "victims" to it and then, continued the companion, "Lately the demand was extended by a truly fashionable craze."[6]

A journalist with a Detroit newspaper declared in October 1886 that there was no basis upon which to estimate the percentage of American women who chewed gum, "but the number has been put at from one-half to two-thirds of the feminine population. The practice is confined to no particular class. The lady in her parlor and the maid in the kitchen exercise their jaws over the tasteless substance with the same industry. It is far more common among women than chewing tobacco is with men." When a Detroit retailer was asked who were the biggest users, the response was: "Probably the girls employed in the large factories are the most confirmed gum-chewers." A prominent Detroit candy dealer said, when asked the same question, "Yes, two-thirds of my lady customers when they visit me lay in a supply of chewing gum, although the principal demand for it comes from school and shop girls. A few men buy it regularly, but they are generally persons who have been addicted to chewing tobacco and are endeavoring to conquer the habit. The dudes use it quite extensively and usually want a highly-flavored brand. It is all harmless."[7]

A San Francisco correspondent for a New York City newspaper declared in 1886, "There is a ludicrous habit in this country, which shows how childish some of the people are. It is that of chewing gum.... It is,

I think, a habit imported from Missouri, or else it was acquired among the foothills when tobacco was scarce." A "noted" Massachusetts professor who had recently moved to San Francisco was supposedly surprised because the reporter did not chew gum. That was meant to indicate, perhaps, that the habit was more prevalent on the East Coast than on the West Coast.[8]

According to a November 1887 news story, St. Louis, Missouri, annually handled $250,000 worth of chewing gum. This report stated that represented 25 percent of all the gum consumed in America, a claim that was, of course, not true. It was pervasive enough in St. Louis that it was then stocked by every druggist in the city. "However, this habit— for it has reached that stage—is confined to the Western states, most of this immense sum of chewing gum being consumed west of the Alleghenies. The Westerner has become a gum chewer."[9]

When a New York City reporter spoke to the unnamed chewing gum manufacturer at his Brooklyn plant, he asked him what class of people were the greatest gum chewers. "Formerly children used to be the chief consumers, but in the last three years, since the roller skating rink craze began, adults have used it more," he said. That caused the reporter to ask what roller skating had to do with the subject. The explanation was that in the rink the dust made by the skaters caused the throat to become very dry and it was found the gum relieved that dryness. "Of course there are a great many young women who chew the gum simply because they like it, but I have noticed of late that men are taking to it," he added. He said he met a great many men every day who chewed gum to help break themselves of the tobacco chewing habit. And, he claimed, there were a great many people who worked better when chewing gum, and he knew plenty of men who could not figure with any degree of satisfaction unless they were chewing tobacco or gum. Bicycle riders and baseball players often chewed gum, he pointed out. "It's an odd fact but you can't go among any professional baseball club without finding half of the members using this article. Then again, there are persons who chew it merely for the sugar and the flavor," continued the manufacturer. "I have seen men at a game of ball or the races buy 50 cents' worth of gum and chew it up in an afternoon. Of late it has become quite the thing as a preventive of seasickness."[10]

An article that appeared in the *Waterbury American* in June 1889 discussed "prominent" gum chewers. Giving some idea of popular images of the time was the article's subhead, which appeared all in capital letters: "Secretary Blaine [United States Secretary of State James G. Blaine] enjoys the schoolgirl's habit." If the reporter was to be believed, Washington, D.C., was a city of gum chewers; more so perhaps than any other city on the middle or southern Atlantic coast. "Gum chewing here is not a craze. It did not spring suddenly into popularity. It resembles Topsy's idea of her own evolution; it 'jes' growed,'" he said. "The daintily flavored saliva increaser is not only popular with schoolboys and schoolgirls; it permeates society form top to bottom, and a census of the men who delight to roll the waxy morsels under their tongues would be a surprise to the country." Then the journalist wrote about the man who (next to the president) controlled and directed the foreign policy of the current administration, noting he "uses a great deal of gum, but he takes it straight. It is the pure product of the spruce trees which are so numerous in his native State. He says that gum chewing is not, with him, an unreasoning habit." Blaine himself commented, "It aids my digestion. I chew simply because of the good effect it has upon my stomach." Reportedly, Blaine's wife also chewed gum but "not in public, though, for there is no greater stickler for submissive yielding to the 'proprieties' than Mrs. Blaine." As well, said the reporter, "there is gum at the White House. Mrs. McKee is an expert chewer, and when Russell Harrison married ex–Senator Saunders daughter it didn't take the Western bride very long to pick up the habit from her sister-in-law." For this observer the use of chewing gum was widespread throughout the nation's capital: "Go where you will, in the store, or on the street, at the office, around the public buildings, and the gum-chewer, like the poor, ye have always with you." Many of the society women in Washington were also said to be users. "Two of the judges on the supreme bench of the District of Columbia are incessant chewers, and so is Justice Gray, of the Supreme Court of the United States."[11]

When a local journalist dropped into Nasby's Bazaar (apparently a sort of social club for men) in Reno, Nevada, in June 1889, he found the club members discussing gum chewing. Since he wanted to learn all he could about the habit, he immediately became interested. One of the reasons for his curiosity was that in a "virtuous" attempt to quit the use of tobacco, he had substituted gum one day, a week earlier. He chewed the wad, which was about the size of a walnut, industriously and energetically, until 5 o'clock in the afternoon, when he was completely exhausted and quit. His jaws ached and his stomach felt like it had an air pump in it. So hard did he work with the cud that he did not recover until the next day, when he arrived at the conclusion "the remedy was worse than the disease." At the club he discovered the subject and discussion, however, was confined to the subtopic of young ladies chewing gum on the street, and if they could have overheard all that was said on the subject he had no doubt they would never take another chew.[12]

One of those who spoke at Nasby's was W. L. Bechtel, who said concerning women chewing gum: "The look of it was enough to disgust any sensible man without the habit, to say nothing about its demoralizing effect on the health." Dr. Lewis, in attendance at the club, was then appealed to with respect to the health effects of the habit. He said, "It may not seriously affect the health, but I must acknowledge that it affects the personal appearance very materially and I should call it a pernicious habit." Another who spoke on the topic was the Rev. Mr. Lucas, who said "it was undignified and unladylike to be constantly chewing gum." As well, he argued the effect was to cause wrinkles to come about the eyes and make one prematurely old. Lucas denounced the habit forcefully and said that if a young lady addicted to the habit could but see herself as others saw her she would quit the habit at once. At that point Nasby himself came to the defense of the gum-chewing girl. While he acknowledged the practice was not very dignified, he said: "But what vice can a young girl have that won't be criticized; they can't chew tobacco, smoke or drink whisky, and I say if they can derive any pleasure from chewing gum let them enjoy it."[13]

A brief newspaper editorial from Ohio in 1894 spoke briefly to the growing awareness that men also indulged. "Chewing gum is becoming noticeably common among men, and if indulging in this clean and harmless habit they may break themselves of more obnoxious ones, I say—chew on—and on," the editor wrote.[14]

Later that year an editorial reprinted from the New York *Herald* addressed the same topic, arguing that gum chewing was no longer a feminine habit only. "I think not now, though the time is not so far gone when the practice was limited to children and young misses. It is different now," stated the newspaper man. Partly, his conclusion was based on what he saw on a train leaving New York's Grand Central Station. As was the custom on trains then, a train boy went around offering gum and other items for sale to all the passengers. In the train car in question 16 of the 29 men in it bought gum and chewed it in public. On inquiry, the train boy told the journalist that the percentage of male buyers was much higher in the "purely masculine retreat, the smoking car." Said the train boy, "It's the best selling article we carry and the men use more of it than the women."[15]

By the time 1900 arrived, articles concerned with the usage of gum tended to become a bit more sophisticated, focusing more on geographic factors and, occasionally, on the psychology behind the product. One such article appeared late in 1900 in the New Orleans *Times-Democrat* and featured an interview with J. J. Amend, a traveling representative for one of the largest chewing gum manufacturers (unnamed) in the United States. Amend said, with respect to New Orleans, "this is a very poor market locally for chewing gum…. The worst in the Untied States." When the reporter asked him why, Amend admitted he did not know, but "I know lots of towns in other parts of the country that use ten times as much chewing gum—yes, 50 times as much—as New Orleans, and they are not nearly as big as this city, either." He explained that he had been around to the drug stores since he had arrived in New Orleans and he found their sales to be very light. "The first-class stores tell me that sometimes they don't have a call for chewing gum more than once in two or three days. They only keep one or two kinds on hand, whereas in such stores in the North and East a dozen different kinds will be kept constantly for sale, and the demand is steady at all times."

Asked where the best gum market was in the U.S., the salesman replied, "All West and North of St. Louis. Lots of gum is sold throughout Kansas, Nebraska, the Dakotas and Minnesota. Kansas City is a great town for it." Then the reporter asked Amend about the situation in Chicago. "Oh, Chicago is one of the greatest chewing gum cities in the country. Chicago has gone ahead of New York, in this respect." New York he thought, used to be a great town for it, and one could not go anywhere in the city without seeing girls working their jaws as if their lives depended on it. "But the caricaturist and the paragraphists made such fun of the habit that a great many of the girls stopped chewing and the sales fell off very heavily. Boston was a pretty good gum town at one time, but never so good as our Western cities," he said. In the opinion of Amend, the newer the city, the better was the chewing gum trade therein. He found that in an old city like New Orleans the people did not seem to take to the habit at all. As well, he thought the French element in New Orleans hurt the trade, "for the French are not gum chewers. The Germans don't chew gum, either. In some of the places where there are many Germans, as in some cities of the Northwest, we sell but little chewing gum," he added. "The young people like it but the old people won't let them use it. I have seen many a boy spanked by his German mother for using chewing gum."[16]

Less than a year later, in 1901, J. A. Morris declared, "America is par excellence the land of the gum chewer.... Soldiers and bicyclists are the chewing gum manufacturers' best customers, and Chicago is probably the best chewing gum town on the American continent." For Morris, New York City was the second best town with St. Louis standing in third spot.[17]

Another report, late in 1901, also declared American soldiers were, perhaps, the chewing gum makers' best customers. During the war with Cuba the sales of gum were described as "enormous." After soldiers, bicyclists were the next best customers, "the habitual visitors to race tracks are said to be the most confirmed gum chewers in the world."[18]

A 1902 report in the Kansas City *Star* remarked that the market for gum extended over the whole nation, although the South and the West provided the heaviest users. Also, there was said to be a heavier consumption of gum in the summer than in the winter, and that was because gum relieved thirst. Natives of the tropics chewed rubber or gum for that very reason. As a final thought, he added that bicyclists and "people under a nervous strain" were addicted to gum.[19]

Every month in 1902 there was sold in Sioux City, Iowa, $3,500 worth of chewing gum, said John C. More, general manager of the Iowa Candy Company. In Chicago for 1901 the figure was over $150,000. "It is a fact that within the past two years the sale of chewing gum has almost doubled. These days people seem to have stronger jaws than ever before due, no doubt, to constant practice, and I presume this is why more gum is chewed every month," said More. "Then, too, people have come to recognize in some brands of gum certain medical properties, and they chew it to aid digestion as well as to exercise their maxillary machinery." More thought that men chewed gum as much as did females. Peak selling time was just before Christmas and More thought that was because people liked to eat sweet things at holiday times.[20]

An employee of a vending machine firm, refilling a chewing gum machine at an elevated rail line in New York City, was asked in 1904 if more gum was sold at certain times of the year than at others. He thought there was not much seasonal variation but perhaps a bit more was sold in the spring months of March and April: "Then, perhaps, the people buy more chewing gum; but as a general proposition people chew gum the year round."[21]

The *New York Times* of October 16, 1904, featured a report that declared, "Men buy chewing gum as freely as women and girls." At the Polo Grounds and at the American baseball league park several boxes of the product were sold each game to men in the grandstands and in the bleachers. "Some of them do it to assuage a craving for tobacco, and many of them because they get nervous if their jaws are not continuously working," said the piece. The players chewed gum as well as the fans. Players could chew gum on the field if they wanted to, and it was reported that most of them did. Jake Stahl of the Boston Americans was said to use a large wad of gum. When he came in from the field to the players' bench he stuck the wad on top of his cap, where it looked like a large button. Then, when he went out into the field again he took it from his cap and put it back into his mouth. All the way along the streets that led from the elevated railroad to the baseball grounds boys sold chewing gum to fans going to the game. "It is the same at the race tracks. Boxes and boxes of it are sold in this way every day," said the reporter. "This has nothing to do with the medicinal gum that men chew for indigestion and other stomach complaints. It is just the gum-chewing habit, which is one of the standard jokes that men like to bring charges on against women and girls."[22]

Automobiles were, at first glance, an unlikely catalyst for increased gum usage, yet that is just what a 1905 article claimed to be the case. One female explained to another why she started to chew gum: "The chewing gum habit is the inevitable outcome of the motoring habit.... By some psychological principle a high rate of speed maintenance for any great length of time produces an uncontrollable desire to keep the jaws going.... Everybody chews it, from dare-devil drivers down to the most timid passengers." According to this article, druggists and confectioners told the reporter that the sale of gum had increased 50 percent with the craze for automobiling. "It used to be just that way when cycling was the fashion. Scorchers all chewed gum, and bought it in large quantities. With the waning of the wheel's popularity the demand for gum fell off. Automobiles have revived it," he explained.[23]

A Denver, Colorado, druggist explained to a reporter in 1906 that he sold a lot of chewing gum "and, queer as it may seem, a great many of those who buy it are men. Why do they get it? Well, I'll tell you. They buy it to use in breaking themselves of habits. A man will think he's smoking too much and will want to quit. He'll drop tobacco and take up chewing gum." He added, "Another man will quit drinking. He wants something to do with his mouth.... Therefore he takes to chewing gum. I have even known dope fiends to use gum in order to quit using the drugs. Gum is a great thing as a habit breaker." In his opinion, women chewed lots of gum but men used almost as much.[24]

An article that appeared in 1907 repeated the conclusions that had been appearing off and on in the media for many years, that, contrary

Real Chewing Gum

COLGAN'S *VIOLET* CHIPS — THE GUM THAT'S ROUND

COLGAN'S MINT CHIPS — THE GUM THAT'S ROUND

It's New!   It's Great!

"Mint Chips" and "Violet Chips" are the latest Colgan Gum Co. creations. Differently delicious in flavor and form—for the chips are round and sold in a round metal box.

"Mint Chips" have the wonderful flavor of old fashioned mint stick candy. "Violet Chips" are flavored like the aroma of sweet violets. Supreme as a breath perfume.

Sold everywhere.   5c the box.   Avoid imitations.   Insist upon Colgan's.

COLGAN GUM CO., Inc.,   **Louisville, Ky.**

A 1910 ad for Colgan's. An attempt to appeal to the public with a strange shape, and to produce a gum that seemed to be more candy than chewing gum.

to popular belief, it was not American women but soldiers and bicyclists who made up the chewing gum manufacturers' best customers. And that Chicago was the best gum chewing town in North America, followed by New York City, with St. Louis in third spot. Added to this account was the story that a man from Milwaukee had been a gum chewer for five years and during that entire period he had no desire for tobacco. Reportedly, an old solider from California considered gum to be conducive to longevity.[25]

Perhaps showing that chewing gum had really, and finally, arrived in America was a lengthy piece that first appeared in the New York *Herald* in December 1910 and dealt with not just usage of the product but with "the psy-

A New Delight

A palate tickler of such delicious flavor and real worth that you'll fall in love with it, whether you've ever used chewing gum or not.

And it's good for you, too! It will keep your teeth clean and sweet, your gums healthy, and aid your digestion.

Ball Player's Picture in Every Box

In Round Metal Boxes

Unusual chewing gum — in flavor, shape, freshness and purity. Ten round dainty chips in each box.

Mint Chips

Flavored like good old-fashioned peppermint stick candy.

Violet Chips

Like the perfume wafted from sweet violet meadows.

By all means enjoy these delightful morsels to-day! They're sold everywhere. If not sold near you, send 10 cents in stamps for a full box of each.

COLGAN GUM CO., Inc.,
LOUISVILLE, KY.

5c

Another 1910 ad for Colgan's.

chology of gum chewing"—as the title of the piece asserted. The journalist began, "This seems a gum chewing age. Once a pastime of childhood, the practice has increased so that persons of all ages may be seen wearying their head hinges with the motion, while their cheeks bulge and their foreheads even contract with the vigorous exercise." He wondered what the psychology of gum chewing was and what the hold it had on the American people was. "The custom may be considered as a symptom of American unrest—as a nerve strain and shock absorber, as a muscular divertissement something like the double shuffle or buck and wing dancing or, indeed, it may be frankly regarded as a relic of barbarism, for such it is considered to be by Dr. Carleton Simon, a well known physician," speculated the reporter.

He thought the first explanation that could be offered concerning gum chewing was so superficial that it could be forgotten without giving it a second thought: "Nice persons do not chew gum." Admitting that gum chewing was not sanctioned by the highest social circles in any way, he argued that posters existed that represented young women in evening gowns sitting in fashionable restaurants receiving large consignments of sugar coated gum from deferential waiters (presumably he was referring to ads). And he had heard that not so long ago a "brilliant gum party" had been held in Cincinnati and, in any case, countless people all over the country were chewing gum. "Let it not be said, either, that Americans chew gum because they like the flavor of it, for after a minute or so of work the substance becomes a neutral base without savor," he said. Next, he pointed out that people chewed gum everywhere, in the streets, on public transit, in public places, and so forth, and it was also used by athletes, including baseball and football players. Some $10 million worth of chewing gum was then sold yearly in the United States, about one billion sticks of gum, with the standard ration of chewing gum (stick) being a thinly rolled slab, about 2½ inches long and 1 inch wide. Major manufacturing centers for the product were in New York City, Philadelphia, and Cleveland, with those makers buying around six million pounds of chicle yearly in order to produce the product.[26]

Returning again to the mysteries of the psychology of the habit, the reporter declared, "The true inwardness of the habit is not to be found in the yearnings for digestion nor in the desire for aromatic flavorings, but it is in the very act of chewing itself." (This was a strange thing to postulate since most journalists, including this one, admitted virtually no gum chewing existed in the world outside of North America.) Dr. Carleton Simon asserted there seemed to be a peculiar desire on the part of humans to chew or gnaw: "It is not caused by the habit created in childhood and must be sought in racial ascent. It is a relic of barbarism, and it has its origins in the yearning for food. It is a love of the exercise of the gustatory secretions." Simon argued chewing gum was nothing more or less "than a latent instinct brought down through a long period of time from forefathers who chewed the hide when they could not chew the meat."

Agreeing that was one theory, the reporter said there were those who found, however, that the habit "partakes largely of the nature of a sedative for American unrest.... It lacks the narcotic effect of tobacco or the betel nut, yet its milder influence upon the nervous system is held by those who use it to be highly desirable." In conclusion, he said the average American was not happy unless he was doing something. "If he cannot smoke he may chew gum. If he cannot read he may resort to chicle and paraffin. There are some women who may have no taste for newspaper reading, nor yet for the latest novel, who while away a shopping journey by invoking the elastic gum."[27]

A report in 1911 told of a man who did a count of gum chewers in a cinema in New Castle, Pennsylvania. In the audience he found that 65 percent to 70 percent of the females were chewing gum, as were "many" of the males.[28]

An *Indianapolis Star* article that looked at the subject in depth in March 1914 said that many exaggerated claims had been made concerning the virtues of chewing gum "and, by all odds, the most original is that it is a powerful aid to love making. A Chicago young woman, who handles the question with a certain technical authority, declares that gum chewing is soothing to the nerves, and leads one into delightful reveries." She continued, "From reveries to love is merely the distance between two pairs of lips! A wad of gum in the mouth is not favorable to beautiful oral expression of sentiment; but the fair proponent meets this very point by industry that the most eloquent love making may be wordless." The journalist went on to state that close observation of the phenomenon had shown that nearly all gum chewers believed they were receiving some specific benefit from it, "From the comedy of love making to the big drama of American national growth, chewing gum is a considerable factor." Dr. T. H. McClintock, of the New York Hospital, was cited as saying, "It is an American habit and an American industry, and kept alive by hundreds of immigrants landing here every day, who adopt

LET'S BORROW YOU GUM TILL RECESS AND SEE WHAT WE CAN DO WITH IT

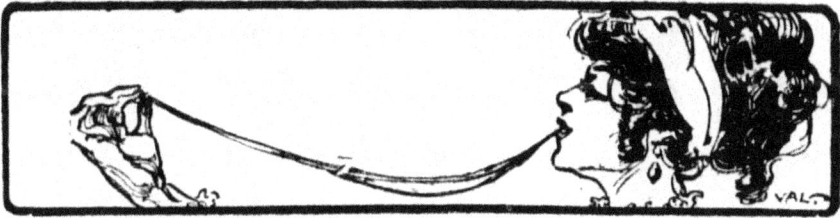

This 1910 sketch mocks two habits then prominent among chewers. One was to create a string by pulling some of the gum out of the mouth. The other had to do with the sharing of gum, a not unusual happening at the time. A person would chew gum for a time and then pass the wad to a friend or classmate who would then chew the same wad.

This 1910 sketch tried to capture the chewing motion of various types of chewers but was not very successful.

THE CHEWERS—By Berton Braley and J. Campbell Cory.

"What a wad of chewing gum each cheerful chewer chaws!"

Another sketch showing the contortions gum chewers went through, often unknown to themselves. This is from 1913.

it in their process of evolution, and thus become the largest asset of the gum manufacturer." During 1913, he added, some eight million pounds of chicle were imported into the United States, which was used to make chewing gum with a market value of more than $34 million.[29]

Usage of chewing gum increased greatly in the years of World War I, as the media also played up its impact. For example, a July 30, 1917, article started out by declaring: "That American chewing gum is playing no small part in helping to win the war is evidenced by the many stories from the front where chewing gum, once regarded as a luxury, is now listed as a necessity by the Red Cross Society." It was said to be advocated by "numberless prominent men" including ex-president Taft, who was chairman of the American National Red Cross, and Lord Northcliffe, the "famous" London, England, editor who was then in the United States on behalf of the British government. Hundreds of thousands of large packages of chewing gum were said to be delivered daily to the various army commissariat departments for distribution among the troops, and "millions of men of every nationality who never chewed gum before have come to regard it as a solace in times of loneliness, stress and suffering."

Because of the immense relief chewing gum afforded U.S. soldiers, subjected to all the nerve-racking strain of modern warfare, the keenest interest had been developed in the item by the Army medical authorities, he explained. The beneficial results obtained from the constant use of chewing gum by the soldiers, and especially the wounded, "who are often enabled to bear terrible wounds stoically if only they may chew gum," meant "the Red Cross Society now lists chewing gum as a war necessity." Lord Northcliffe urged that chewing gum be sent to the fighting soldiers of all the allied nations in generous quantities. Speaking from what he had actually seen when he visited the various war fronts a little while previously, Northcliffe "emphasized the importance of chewing gum in field hospital work and spoke in glowing terms of the relief it had brought countless pain-racked men, while costing their benefactors practically nothing."[30]

Canadian solider Sergeant Major G. H. Macleod was interviewed in the summer of 1917 on his experiences at the Western Front. He had been overseas to fight on two occasions, being wounded each time and sent back home for treatment each time. Macleod was also notable because he had been used as the model on a well-known recruiting poster that invited all eligible men to rally to the colors. When interviewed, he was attached to the British military recruiting mission headquartered on Broadway in Manhattan, New York. He made a strong plea to an American reporter for soldier "comforts" to be sent to the camps and to the trenches. Macleod laid particular emphasis on the soldiers' "great demand" for American chewing gum that, he declared, had saved many a poor fellow from the terrible tortures of thirst as well as helping on the line of march. Recalling a continuous march of more than 28 miles near the French frontier with the going hard and many of the men beginning to lag behind after some eight to 10 hours of steady marching, he declared, "I, myself, did not feel equal to another mile, when one of my chums gave me a stick of American chewing gum. In a few minutes the fagged-out feeling had completely left me, and I felt equal to another ten miles at least." He explained that he knew of dozens of other cases in the front line trenches of men who had been so completely worn out by the incessant shell fire that they were unable to go to sleep, and in 15 minutes a piece of chewing gum "had so quieted their nerves that they dropped into a peaceful rest."[31]

Macleod said he felt confident that the American public would realize the urgent need of sending large quantities of chewing gum to the soldiers, especially since the first contingent of U.S. troops had arrived in France. Macleod thought the public would agree that chewing gum was of great value to the troops when they knew that it was handed out to the wounded at all field hospitals. Furthermore, he declared, "It wouldn't be going too far to say that chewing gum had acted as more than merely a thirst quencher, valuable as that is, for I know cases myself where many wounded men managed to keep themselves going on chewing gum after rations, consisting of a can of corned beef, two Oxo [beef stock] cubes and army biscuits, had been exhausted and until assistance arrived." Macleod hoped a wide appeal would be made all over America for soldiers' comforts, and especially for chewing gum. At the close of the story the reporter added that a number of public spirited Americans had rallied to the cause and were giving of their time and services free in order to start a fund and collect money to send chewing gum, and other comfort items, to U.S. fighting men.[32]

Commenting at the same time on the subject of troops and gum, an Iowa journalist observed, "Washington has just discovered something new in munitions—a sinew of battle that you can buy from a street peddler. It is small, harmless and inexpensive—yet it is a part of the fighting equipment of our troops in France." He argued that thanks to the war chewing gum had assumed a new and drastic importance since "it ministers to one of the subtlest and strongest needs in modern fighting. It satisfies a basic psychological craving of the man in the trench." And, "It makes him fight better and die harder. England—slow, stolid England, which made fun of gum-chewing America—is now ensnared in the meshes of the elastic chicle. Her Tommies chew gum in action and her munitions factories are manned by gum chewers." Concluding his article, the reporter said the trench fighter is under a terrific strain, whether he knew it or not: "In such stress, relief is to be found in gripping something with the teeth. People in all climes and in all periods soon learned this elemental fact. The sailor who chewed a bullet when he was being flogged knew it."[33]

An article that appeared in U.S. newspapers around Christmas 1917 was an appeal for funds to be sent to W. W. Pilkington at 26 Broadway, Manhattan, New York City. People were urged to send in money so that chewing gum could be bought and sent overseas to the troops. Those people who opposed sending tobacco to the soldiers at the front—to prevent the troops from being encouraged in a habit that was "looked on with disfavor," said the piece—could now do something for the men without encouraging the tobacco habit. Men found that in many cases gum worked to steady their nerves and thus, a fund was being raised to provide the item to the troops. Continuing on, the plea said there was no great need to go into detail on the benefits to the troops of chewing gum. Suffice it to say, "The one big outstanding fact is that they positively crave it and they can't get enough of it. It stimulates the brain, quickens the digestion, and calms the nerves. A very famous English general has chewing gum served every night at mess. 'Where men must be alert you will find chewing gum,' has become a proverb."[34]

The same article about the plea was published in another newspaper with this comment included, "For instance, one of the most amazing and often amusing spectacles of the war is to find a man from any of the great universities insisting upon getting his share of chewing gum— a commodity, let it be whispered, that the same gentleman considered plebian before the war."[35]

Louis Ludlow reported in September 1918 on the topic of gum and war by writing, "Chewing gum, usually spoken of derisively as a cud for giggling girls, is performing a more dignified and important function during the present war than it ever performed before. Chewing gum has come into its own." An announcement from the U.S. War Department emphasized the part chewing gum was playing in winning the war: "Orders have just been placed by the quartermaster corps for 2,300,000 packages of chewing gum for the army. It has been found that on long marches and where troops are unable to get sufficient water, chewing gum is very effective in relieving thirst." When the commanding officer of a regiment of field artillery was embarking for overseas service, he was reported to have stated that 250 pounds of chewing gum would save hundreds of gallons of water when most needed, pointing out that gum was cheap and there were times when water was very expensive and at times unobtainable.[36]

A few weeks later a story started off by observing it was a sad day for the American soldier overseas when the United States Post Office declared it could not accept package mail intended for members of the

American Expeditionary Force. It meant no candy, no cigarettes, no chewing gum, and so on. However, someone came up with a plan to get around that prohibition, at least for chewing gum, and that plan was presented in the newspaper. Readers of the piece were advised to write G. I. Joe his regular weekly letter on the usual sheet of linen notepaper—but to leave the lower half of the first page blank. Next step was to buy a package of the soldier's favorite chewing gum, remove the outer wrapper of each stick, dab a bit of library paste on the folded ends of the inner wrapping of wax paper that was around each stick, and paste them to the notepaper—the five sticks straight across, sided by side. Then the letter was to be folded as usual and put into the envelope. The advice was to send no more than one package of gum in each letter, any more and it became too heavy. If a reader wanted to send more gum at the same time he was advised to send two letters in two separate envelopes. A final piece of advice was to not send gum alone in an envelope, as it had to be pasted to the paper that kept it spread out flat and firmly in place.[37]

When the war was over, an editor of a New England newspaper observed that a YMCA secretary who recently returned from France was of the opinion the American soldier would probably be remembered by many French people for two things associated with him—cigarettes and chewing gum. Noting the general folly of making snap judgments, this editor went on to do just that: "The jaunty cigarette, the nervous habit of gum chewing is but a surface indication of the highly strung and active American manhood."[38]

5

Editorials, Commentaries, Reformers and Religion

While a small fraction of the editorial writers, notable commentators, and the like had the odd good word to say about the uniquely American habit of chewing gum, the overwhelming majority were opposed to the practice, often vehemently so. Reformers, crusaders and religious figures waxed long and loud against the practice as well.

One of the earliest attacking editorials appeared in August 1870 in a newspaper published in Massillon, Ohio. In that editorial the newspaperman declared: "One of the most filthy, disagreeable habits in existence, and one which ranks side by side with tobacco chewing among men, is the practice of chewing gum, which is so much in vogue among many who consider themselves young ladies." Using a style of writing then in vogue that attempted to scare the reader with horror stories, the editor added, "The most nauseous liquid foam is put in to whiten the gum."[1]

An editor with the *Greenville Argus* [Pennsylvania] presented a list of things "we like to see." Of course, the list was presented in sarcastic, ironic fashion. One of the items was, "We like to see young ladies keep their jaws in constant motion, endeavoring to masticate a huge ball of chewing gum; it looks so lady-like!"[2]

Two weeks later, still in 1873, an editor with Reno's *Nevada State Journal* noted that many of the city's young ladies were in the habit of chewing gum and went on to remark, "We can't for the life of us see why they want to smack their lips over such miserable trash, when the mouth of every young man they meet is watering for them."[3]

Writing in the Port Jervis, New York, *Evening Gazette* in 1879, the editor observed that the habit of chewing gum, which so many people had, "girls particularly ... is not only silly but dangerous." As examples he cited a young lady in Louisville, Kentucky, who "chews so incessantly that she cannot now control the use of her jaws" and of another young lady who attended Albany High School in New York and who was "so afflicted by this unfortunate practice as to excite the commiseration of all who have seen her. At times her sufferings are painful to witness." He continued, "Eminent physicians have exhausted their means to alleviate her condition, notwithstanding which her jaws continue to open and shut with a violence that threatens dislocation."[4]

One of the first editorials that, while it did not have anything positive to say about the habit, did not say anything negative, appeared in late 1881 in the pages of the New York *Herald*. For this editor, "The mastication of gum is a more cleanly and less debilitating habit than snuff dipping or tobacco chewing." And, "Let the gum chewers go on; their occupation may not be deserving of high honor, but it is harmless compared with many others in which the human mouth is chief operator."[5]

When the editor of the *Daily Huronite* (Huron, South Dakota) dealt with the chewing gum habit, in November 1887, he stated, "Victims of the chewing gum habit—a most detestable one, by the way—sometimes apologize for the practice by asserting that it is wholesome, and is an actual aid to digestion. Any well informed physiologist will deny this at once." Chewing gum produced a flow of saliva into the stomach at a time it was not needed by that organ, he explained. That saliva burdened the stomach and forced it to abnormal action to get rid of it, and at the same time the salivary glands were robbed of the secretion and obliged to do double work to produce the saliva necessary for digestion. Concluded the editor, "So far as the stomach is concerned, chewing gum is as injurious as chewing tobacco."[6]

With respect to the habit of "ladies" chewing gum, the *Indiana Progress* (Pennsylvania) commented at the end of 1889, "This most disgusting habit is being indulged in to an alarming extent. If you see some of our young ladies on the street, their jaws are working like a cow chewing cud. At church you observe the same performance." The editor added, "If these ladies could see themselves as others see them they would discontinue this disgusting practice at once. It is a practice beneath a lady, and those who continue it will inevitably lose the dignity and respect which is due to every sensible lady."[7]

Equally vehement on the topic almost one year later was a piece published in newspapers that was reprinted from the *Jenness Miller Magazine.* "The gum chewing girl is an eyesore to all refined people, and it is astonishing that even well dressed and well conducted women indulge in this altogether reprehensible habit without appearing to realize that it is unladylike and insufferably vulgar," fumed an editor. Continuing on he declared, "If chewing gum is such a delicious pleasure, the women who are slaves to the habit should practice it in the seclusion of their own chambers and indulge in its delights behind closed doors, just as they would smoke the surreptitious cigarette which is tabooed in public."[8]

At the start of 1891 an editorial in a magazine called *Youth's Companion* (reprinted in newspapers) asked whether gum chewing could be regarded as harmful to any degree. In reply to its own query the piece said, "The habit is unnatural. It meets no normal need, as does the chewing of the cud by the cow and some other animals. Whatever is abnormal is presumptively injurious, even though we may not be able to trace its effects. It took a long time to find out that tobacco chewing caused one of the most fatal diseases of the heart." According to the article, every secretion of the body had its natural limitation, and artificial stimulation beyond that point had to be hurtful. That was termed a "general law." Gum chewing stimulated the salivary glands vastly beyond their normal limit, and the result had to be injurious. A constant swallowing of saliva in a sort of churned state carried into the stomach a large amount of air, which became a source of discomfort and often of positive injury. It was observed that air swallowed that way became greatly expanded by internal heat. Also noted was the idea that muscles were enlarged by use—cited was the blacksmith's arm compared to that of the scholar. While the normal use of the jaw muscles tended to keep them in proper working condition, their overuse in gum chewing "must tend to their undue enlargement and thus to the disfiguration of the face."[9]

Later in 1891 a newspaper editor addressed the subject of whether a woman who spent the evening chewing gum should occupy a private box at the opera. Said the editor, "The public generally will take the ground that the more private the box the better." And, he added, if a woman knew how "hideous and disgusting" she looked chewing her gum she would leave it behind her altogether when she attended the opera: "Or if the gum business has become a habit, and the gum and woman have become inseparable, she had better remain at home and inhabit her closet and chew, chew, chew."[10]

In the spring of 1891 a report noted the net profits for the previous five years of the principal firm engaged in the manufacture of chewing gum were $655,735. The New York *Tribune* commented, "Think of the number of human jaws that the stuff which produced this large sum has set in profitless motion, oftimes, too, to the annoyance of the unwilling witnesses of the operation." He went on to say, "The chewing gum habit is far from being a survival of the fittest. Some physicians, it is true, claim a therapeutic value for chewing gum, but like the application of a blister, use of this curative agent ought to be entirely private."[11]

The *Sandusky Daily Register* (Ohio) raised the question in May 1891 of whether gum chewing was injurious, citing mixed reviews from medical men, and said the answer was maybe yes, maybe no. "To say the least it is a beauty-destroying habit. The ugly wrinkles about the corners of some women's mouths come from continued gum chewing."[12]

Virtually all the editorial comments about gum to this point treated the topic as though it was only females who indulged in the practice. One that appeared in the *Union Star* (Iowa) at the beginning of 1894 dealt mostly with female chewers but also acknowledged that men were also users. Wrote the editor, "The habit of gum chewing is again taking front ranks among the gentler sex and how unladylike and distasteful it is to civilization. It is not solely with the female portion of humanity, but many young men harbor it and especially at public gatherings." He ventured, "You sometimes meet a woman on the street swinging her mouth wide open and shut fast, squeezing the life out of a stick or two of California Fruit, Tutti Frutti or Blood Orange. If a fly was to happen that way it would be in jeopardy, and many times meet with sudden death."[13]

A more positive editorial came in September 1894 from the pages of the *Middletown Daily Argus* in New York. Herein the newspaperman declared, "While it must be admitted that some girls can chew gum without detracting much from their charms, it is a fact that most of them do not appear to good advantage while continuously wagging their jaws." However, he thought there was a benefit to chewing gum. The act of chewing increased the flow of saliva and thus aided digestion: "Good digestion makes a good complexion and good complexions make pretty girls. Hence it is just possible that pretty girls chew gum to make themselves pretty."[14]

A Newark, Ohio, newspaper commented on the "dreadful" habit of chewing gum in 1897: "There is nothing true which can be said in favor of such a habit. It is unclean, unhealthy, and disgusting. It ruins the teeth, the throat and the digestion, no matter who tells you otherwise." Then he went on to cite an editorial from the *Boston Herald* that remarked, "Gum chewing is a most unpleasant spectacle for the disinterested observer. That wagging of jaws looked at persistently has been known to drive one insane, and the desire to seize the chewer and make him or her disgorge is only controlled by getting out of the way as quickly as possible." For the Boston editorial writer the eternal chop, chop of the jaws brought into a play a set of muscles that eventually disfigured the face, "while causing an expression of bovine idiocy to settle upon it. Where is the human being's natural vanity while that piece of gum is being masticated? If the victim of this gum chewing habit will kindly look at herself or himself in the mirror during an hour or so of the operation, it may have the effect of curing her or him of it."[15]

A reader known as "The Grumbler" wrote to the *Iowa State Reporter* (Waterloo) at the end of 1897 wondering why the local mothers' group did not take up the issue of gum chewing on the streets of Waterloo and in public places. Recently, wrote The Grumbler, he counted 27 girls and young women while walking just three blocks, with each of them "chewing the cud." In reply, the editor of the newspaper said, "If chewing gum is an actual necessity to the comfort or pleasure of a girl, the masticating should be done within the home. The street is no place for such exercise, and it is an exhibition of vulgarity that should be avoided."[16]

An editor with a Colorado Springs newspaper wondered why, in the summer of 1903, so many of the girls, young and old, women, middle-aged or old, chewed gum so persistently in public places. He brought up the subject of men chewing tobacco in public, and while he thought that was bad enough, he also felt people were used to it, as it had been going on for so long and therefore was no longer objectionable. "But it does not create the painful surprise nor utter disgust that comes over one upon seeing an apparently refined bit of femininity chewing away like mad, for all the world as though she were a cow." When he journeyed by train, this newspaper man calculated the numbers and stated that half the women in his car bought packs of gum from the train boy on his first trip through the car. "Gum chewing goes on everywhere on the street and in the cars that run up and down there. If only once the women could hear the masculine comments they would be so ashamed that a complete revolution would take place," he concluded. "If the reprehensible practice was abandoned by the woman, the millionaire owners of chewing gum factories would be forced out of business."[17]

According to the editor of the *Titusville Herald* (Pennsylvania), in the summer of 1904 a new nickname had been coined for the gum-chewing girl of Chester, Pennsylvania, "The Gum Dolly." Reportedly, preachers had recently spoken from the pulpit about the girls who persisted in chewing gum on the streets and in public places. So pervasive was the habit then said to be in Chester that a well known society woman recently passed around chewing gum to her guests after refreshments. "Upon every highway in the city girls from good homes, who liked to be classed with the smart set, middle aged women and girls from the slums, can be seen chewing," he reported. "The girls chew gum on the trolley cars, in church, at the playhouses, at the baseball games—everywhere it is one incessant grind. When out walking in the evening with their escorts many young women prefer chewing gum to ice cream."[18]

An editor with an Iowa newspaper started off his 1905 rant by writing, "My dear young woman, don't get the habit. The evils of the chewing upon the economy of your physical system are vividly explained by Dr. Joseph S. Diamond of Bellevue College, New York, who ought to know." Diamond declared the chewing of gum delayed digestion and put the user at the risk of microbes. Besides, said Diamond, "gum chewing is a neurotic manifestation—that is to say, there is something jangled about your nerves. They are not what they ought to be. You have developed a sort of jaw unrest that is no trivial thing." All of that caused the editor to conclude: "Gum chewing habitually followed up, will destroy some of the beauty of your mouth and chin and sooner or later put ugly lines in your lower face. It is the honest truth." And, "Nothing is here said concerning the ugly spectacle made by this perpetual motion of jaw machinery."[19]

The *Nevada State Journal* returned with a comment in 1906 when the editor declared, "Nobody needs to chew gum.... Chewing gum certainly is deleterious for it continually deludes the digestive system into the idea that it is getting something to eat, and makes the stomach waste its gastric resources on nothing at all." The editor went on to compare its use to the economy of a miller who kept his mill going and wearing out the machinery when he had no grist to grind. "The habit of chewing gum is, moreover, a repellent and afflictive thing."[20]

In the *New York Times* in August 1906 an editor argued, "The present recrudescence of gum chewing, however, dates from the bicycle craze, which it outlasts. It came to be believed by the bicyclist that chewing gum allayed the pangs of thirst." To some observers it seemed that the gum-chewing habit was far more prevalent than ever before, and it seemed to have "attacked" the female sex with especial fury, he said. If one looked around in any of the elevated cars or in the subway cars and if by chance there was a row of young women of the "saleslady class" opposite the observer, the chances were "they will be seen masticating in a sad sincerity, like so many cows in a row in a stable. They seem to imbibe a solemn satisfaction from the process. In many cases they would rather chew than chatter, and that is saying a great deal." He admitted that the male of the species was sometimes seen doing the same thing, but that it was the females "who mainly munch and munch and munch, like the sailor's wife in Macbeth. A foreigner going about New York would be quite justified in concluding that the American young woman was a ruminant animal."[21]

But after some 35 years of overwhelmingly negative editorial comment on the topic, the editorial attacks suddenly faded away. Apparently, the topic was just about exhausted. A couple more pieces appeared in that first decade of the 20th century, but they were favorable items, more or less. One, in an Iowa newspaper in 1908 started off by citing a New York psychiatrist as saying that gum chewing relieved the ear drums of the roar and rattle of the city. An observer would find half the passengers in the subway trains chewing gum, he said, and it was because of the noise: "People take the only method their subconscious thinking arrangement suggests to relieve the condition."

Then the editor inserted himself to say that any excuse for chewing gum was welcome and that the manufacture of gum had become one of the great national industries. A great deal of capital was invested in it, and millions of people were involved in that industry, mostly as chewers.

"Considering the great fortunes made in it, let none regard the chewing of gum as a useless, frivolous, senseless practice," he wrote. "This great national industry is the subject of constant satire and ridicule. This is because it is not understood, and it may be because it is mainly a female accomplishment." He pointed out that some observers believed the practice arose from nervousness—the idle desire to be busy without doing anything—and because it filled up the vacuity in conversation. As well, he said some observers regarded it as in obedience to the feminine instinct for the cultivation of patience and self-denial—patience in a fruitless activity and self-denial in the eternal act of mastication without swallowing. However, he argued the habit was no more related to those virtues than it was to the habit of the reflective cow in chewing her cud. At that point the editor moved into ridicule, declaring the true explanation for the practice was a more philosophical one, and related to a great modern social movement. And that was to strengthen and develop and make more masculine the feminine underjaw. "If women are to take men's place in world affairs, they must being by shifting from the men to the women the heavy determined lower jaw, which, as everybody knows, is the most distinctive mask for prowess and power."[22]

A 1909 editorial in the *Baltimore Sun* (reprinted in other newspapers) began with a worry about the consequences of a possible decline in the world availability of chicle: "It is, indeed, one of the most important of all agents for combating that universal wreck of nerves which threatens to engulf every one of us." Next he declared that human existence in this "hysterical" 20th century was not static, but dynamic—not a being but an eternal and painful becoming. People lived at breakneck speed and crowded a million complex and fatiguing acts into every hour; we were said to be a non-stop people, on a psychic joy ride. As a result, people sustained a frightful battering of the nerves, an enormous using of the emotions, an unbearable running amuck of the faculties. Something was needed to deal with all of that—some brake, as it were, or governor—to keep the human machine from rattling itself to pieces.

For the editor that something was "technically known as an anodyne, or dope" and of all forms of dope, chewing gum was at once the most effective and the least harmful. It furnished a safe escape from excessive nervous energy; it gave the bones and sinews, from the waist upward, constant and agreeable exercise, and it deadened the intellect "without engendering actual imbecility. Nothing else produces so certainly and pleasantly that vacuity of mind necessary in many professions." To the chorus girl, the floor walker, the congressman, the motorman, the theatergoer, the diplomat, and the lonely shepherd it was a "pearl beyond price. Without the malleable and inexhaustive gum to occupy them, all of these persons would think indignantly, and thinking would soon drive them to the sanatoria that dot our rural hillsides— broken in body and smashed in mind." Chewing gum, the editor declared, was no longer a toy and no longer a luxury: "The world needs it and the world must have it, and if the chicle trees dry up, then more chicle trees must be planted." Because, he concluded, "Not the poppy, nor mandragora, nor all the drowsy syrups of the east can take the place of chewing gum in civilization."[23]

Running parallel to the anti-gum pieces from newspaper editors were equally negative articles form various other authority figures such as educators, scientists, actors, and columnists. One such piece came in the form of an address from the Honorable A. P. Edgerton (he was president of the U.S. Civil Service Commission) delivered to the school board and graduating class of the Central Grammar School, Allen County, Indiana, in June 1885. Most of his speech was about the need for universal education, the benefits from it, taxation to support it, and so forth. A year earlier in Allen County there were 25,078 people age six to 21, but only 10,349 (41 percent) of them were enrolled in the public schools. Later Edgerton went on to say there were some things outside the public schools deserving of educators' attention for the purpose of correction by those educators. Bad habits, he thought, were brought from the homes or the streets into the schools. So, to stimulate reform outside of the schools, Edgerton felt he had to converse with the public. He observed that an unsolved mystery was why the natural attractiveness of the human face should unnecessarily be marred by gum chewing. Remarking that the human mouth could never excel a cow in the chewing business, he declared, "The panorama presented by the skating gum chewers at the Princess rink, is a study in its facial contortions, for an artist. Unless other means fail to prevent gum chewing in the public school, the trustees propose to select a class for exhibition as facial contortionists." Edgerton concluded: "A fine woman, like other fine things in nature, has her proper point of view from which she may be seen to the most advantage; but, when she makes herself a public gum chewer she is not a fine thing in nature and is not seen to the best advantage."[24]

According to a scientific exchange's 1888 report, the habit of gum chewing in the United States was producing a race of hollow-cheeked young women. That was because the constant exercise of the masseter muscle hardened it and removed the fatty covering that led to roundness. Thus, "not only is the fullness of the cheek destroyed but there is a tendency to wrinkle the skin, a natural result of the falling away of the parts beneath it."[25]

At an 1890 meeting in Pennsylvania of an unidentified club, a member rose to complain to the group about the habit of gum chewing. He declared the habit was as disgusting as that of tobacco chewing and cigarette smoking: "Some there are who are bitterly opposed to the use of tobacco, and in the very midst of their vituperations against it, chew gum made of old, dirty cast off rubber shoes, with such avidity and motion of their creaking jaws as to render themselves disgusting and offensive."[26]

A 1903 letter to the editor of the *Portsmouth Herald* in New Hampshire urged the paper's readers, "For heaven's sake, sharpen up your pencil and stab the young girls, the girls not so young, the middle-aged women, and the old ladies who chew gum on the streets. Just tell them how the practice appears in masculine eyes. This morning I met six, chewing away like mad. It was positively disgusting." He fumed that he could not understand why they went out in public to make exhibitions of themselves and remarked he had even seen "very nice girls" do it, "girls one would imagine too refined to indulge in so vulgar a pastime as chewing gum on the street." Still in a fury, he concluded, "Haven't modern girls interest enough to occupy their minds without stealing the only recreation of the cow?"[27]

Enid Lid was a columnist who lived in Fort Wayne, Indiana, in 1903 and wrote for the hometown newspaper, the *Fort Wayne News*. In her column of October 2, 1903, she said she had been at the theater a few nights earlier she was sitting where she had a pretty good face view of a large part of the audience, and she observed that about 75 percent of the women in that audience were chewing gum. "Their jaws were going like so many meat chopping machines and I almost imagined that I could hear the grinding thereof," she wrote. Lid explained that gum-chewing habit of the women was not confined to the theater. She had observed the same general habit among them at other public gatherings. "I see it on the streets, in the electric car, in the store, in the office and the factory. In fact, about everywhere one goes nowadays he finds the gum-chewing woman with her jaws in everlasting motion." She added that it was a mystery to her why a woman would spend an hour or two at home in preparing her toilet to go to some public gathering and then mar the whole effect of her attempt to make herself beautiful "with the distorted features that the gum-chewing habit always brings."[28]

Lid pointed out that a tobacco-chewing man looked bad enough, but a woman, "with her naturally refined ways and charming equipage, presents a horrible appearance, to my way of thinking, when she is rolling a big stick of chewing gum around in her mouth." Enid decried the easy availability of chewing gum with retail venders everywhere, street hawkers all over the place and in front of stores and at every transit depot, drug store, restaurant, and candy store chewing gum could be found for sale. When she compared men chewing tobacco and women chewing gum, she argued that with each of them the habit was strong. And that it was just as difficult for a woman to give up her chewing gum as it was for a man to give up his tobacco: "Both are slaves, bound by the chains of a habit that is as senseless in one case as in the other." However, she felt women had worse habits than the gum-chewing practice, "which perhaps has no stronger objection to it than it looks bad in public." Among the worse habits women had, argued the journalist, were the use of slang, the smoking of cigarettes and, worst of all, their alcohol consumption.[29]

Another female columnist—Mrs. Mikkel Vip—was on a tear against gum in an August 1906 column wherein she declared that, sanitarily viewed, the habit of gum chewing was condemnable. American dentists of late were said to have become conscious of the fact that the altogether too many poor teeth in America were due to the excessive use of gum. The fact that women who chewed gum were permitted to appear in society circles in America had always been a riddle to her. "I do not understand it. Anywhere else in the world, the doors would be closed on her just as rigidly as they over here are closed to ordinary ladies who indulge in the smoking habit."

When she considered the argument that was it not equally bad to see men chew tobacco, she said, "Of course it is, ladies! But admit that you find nowhere in what you could call decent circles any men who chew tobacco." And, she continued, a man chewing tobacco would be admitted nowhere in America to the homes or circles of intelligent and cultured people, at least not if he had the audacity to chew his tobacco in the presence of ladies or gentlemen. Thus, for Vip, socially seen, the habit of chewing gum or tobacco was equally bad: "As the tobacco chewing man is excluded from decent society, the gum chewing girl should be likewise."

Vip stated that in any case, merchants of all kinds should make it a point to prohibit their employees from chewing gum in the presence of customers. Any store where the employees and clerks were permitted to chew gum or tobacco should be placed under a boycott. "It is the most foolish thing in the world—this, to chew gum and tobacco." Financially, the habit was not so bad, Vip admitted, "But it is bad enough. It is entirely useless. It is a sign of incomplete culture, barbarism, and lack of respect for others." She thought that foreigners visiting America held, as a dominant impression, that it was a gum chewing nation. Concluded Vip, "America is worthy of a better fate. But America cannot expect more respect from foreigners until she abandons some of her uncivilized habits. And gum-chewing first."[30]

Ben R. Rogers was a retailer who operated the Utopia in Little Rock, Arkansas. In 1907 he remarked that the habit of chewing gum was one of the worst that a person could possibly contract. "You take a man who chews gum day in and day out and you'll find an extremely nervous individual and one who suffers more or less from indigestion," he explained. "A little gum is all right occasionally. It aids digestion and gives exercise to the stomach and heart muscles." Rogers said he had been selling gum for 10 years but did not chew himself. "It sounds strange for a fellow to be knocking his own game, but I know what I say will not have any effect upon gum chewers and just as much of the stuff will be sold in the future as in the past."[31]

On a Saturday evening in March 1908 the Forum and Athenaeum societies held a literary program in Stevens Point, Wisconsin, the leading feature of which was a debate—"Resolved, that to be a slave to fashion was a greater evil than to chew gum." Mr. Bacon and Miss Gilfillan supported fashion while Mr. Spindler and Miss Savage upheld the cause of gum chewing. At the end of the debate the jury decided in favor of gum. Highlight of the debate was reported to be Spindler's rebuttal in which, by a few well chosen remarks, he swept aside the arguments of his opponents.[32]

Blanche Bruce was a syndicated columnist who apparently operated out of Nashville, Tennessee. In one of her October 1911 columns she told her readers she could tell many girls why they had missed their chance of marrying. "While they may be good looking and may dress well, if they have that awful habit of gum chewing there is not one gentleman out of five hundred who will take one of them for a wife unless he is a habitual gum chewer himself," she declared. Bruce wondered why women persisted in chewing in public "when it is, as we all know, a vulgar habit? If one must chew gum for indigestion one should do so in the privacy of one's room at home." She stated she had talked to dozens of men, both in business and in professional life, "and they tell me that the gum chewing habit is so repulsive that it makes them often lose a valuable acquaintance or a business deal." Blanche asserted she had a young male cousin attending Yale University and that he would not make the acquaintance of a young woman who chewed gum. "He and his companions formed a club, and there are now 150 in this club of young millionaires and lawyers and doctors, who have signed pledges never to marry a young woman, no matter how attractive she is, who chews gum in public."[33]

Superstar actress Lillian Russell weighed in with her opinion of the practice in a newspaper opinion piece, which appeared under her byline, in February 1912. She argued that a certain class of people considered the practice to be bad form and would not be guilty of its use, outside of the privacy of their own rooms. In her view, the innovation of putting the digestive pepsin in the gum was probably responsible to some extent for its popularity. For the addition of pepsin had made an "obnoxious habit" a beneficial one and given chewing gum a medicinal quality. Russell argued that gum should not be used, however, not even just enough to bring about the desired effect—aid to digestion—because the action of chewing gum for any length of time would cause little wrinkles to form at the corners of the mouth, in front of the ears, and under the chin. "I would advise girls to avoid chewing gum in public, as it is a habit that is injurious to facial beauty," she explained. "It distorts the features unnecessarily. If you do chew it, chew it in your own room and make it a remedy for something, and do it correctly." Russell believed that in the audience at a play the effect of a woman chewing gum was ludicrous. If she could observe another woman unconsciously chewing gum while watching and being interested in the play, she would never be guilty of doing it herself. "It is positively the most unbecoming action a person's face can take," the actress concluded. "See for yourself sometime when you are at the theater. Pick out one who is chewing gum and watch her face when she is off her guard and you will understand what I mean."[34]

Later that month an editorial comment on Lillian Russell's opinion piece was published. That editor said the chewing gum habit had received many hard knocks from physicians, preachers, teachers, and editors, "but it probably never received so hard a jolt as one which has just been aimed at it by Lillian Russell ... who in recent years has become a regular contributor to the newspapers in the department of health and beauty hints and advice." The editor went on to sarcastically observe that "Airy Fairy" Lillian Russell has just confided "to the public her expert opinion, gained through long and careful observance of conditions affecting female beauty that chewing gum constitutes a subtle and insidious enemy to good looks," noting her argument that persistent chewing produced facial wrinkles, the terror of all women. "And as most of the gum chewing is done by womankind, it naturally follows that the reminder of Miss Russell will have the effect of weaning and curing many girls and women from the desire to indulge in this practice, knowing the penalty they will later have to pay," he added. The idea that some female gum chewers might give up the habit was one he could embrace.

He continued on to explain the gum business, as everyone knew, was in the hands of a trust, a trust that had made millions by persistent efforts to initiate as many as possible into the order of gum chewers. For that purpose a systematic advertising campaign was waged and statistics indicated more gum was being consumed than ever before. Becoming sarcastic again, the editor concluded, "If we are not mistaken, however, Miss Russell's shot will have a telling effect on the gum chewing business and may even put a crimp in the trust."[35]

Elizabeth Thompson was another syndicated columnist; hers was the Agony Aunt style of answering readers' questions in print. Two young females, both in high school in grade 10 (15 years old, or so) wrote to Thompson in October 1917 to ask, "When out with a fellow and he offers you gum, should you take it even if you don't like to chew gum? Our mothers do not like us to chew gum. Do you think it is vulgar?" To Billy and Winifred, Thompson replied: "No, just say 'I don't care for it, thank you.' Yes. I think it is vulgar. Next time you are on the street look at the girls who are chewing gum and notice how repulsive the habit seems to others. Your mothers are wise to teach you not to acquire the habit."[36]

Still another syndicated columnist was a woman named Molly Lee. In the subhead of a May 1921 column she wondered if a person had the gum chewing habit or did the habit have the person. Molly never addressed that question in her column. However, she did conclude it was a habit that often fixed itself upon the person who indulged through a desire to work off nervous energy and the high level of tension that the "rushing strenuous life of the latter days has brought. It is most unbecoming and if we were only granted that priceless boon for which Bobbie Burns wished, that we might 'see oursel's as ithers see us,' there would be many who would refuse to be tempted by gum."[37]

Annie Laurie was another syndicated advice columnist. A letter that appeared in one of her columns in August 1921 came from a young woman who explained she was deeply in love with a "splendid" young man. She was afraid, though, his affections were for another, as he never spoke of his love for the letter writer, but she felt he seemed to care at times. She wanted to know what she could do to win his love, explaining to Laurie that she was in the habit of chewing gum occasionally, which he objected to very much. Since he indulged in tobacco, the letter writer added, she could not see why he should ask her to give up her "little pleasure." She asked Laurie if perhaps it was the issue of gum chewing that kept the man from telling of his love for the letter writer. Annie Laurie replied: "Do not ever chew gum; if you must though, do it when no one is around, it is a vulgar habit for one to get into especially in public places, there is nothing more unattractive than to see a girl continually chewing gum. It is only natural for a man to use tobacco." Laurie stressed one could do nothing to win another's love except to be natural. "Just be natural and be sweet, but take my advice and stop chewing gum; you never can tell that may help, then too, if you really cared for him it should be no sacrifice to stop chewing gum," she added. "I should imagine you would do it just because he asked you to."[38]

From time to time those labeled by the media as reformers or crusaders arose to do battle against the plague of chewing gum. Sometimes they were alone, sometimes at the head of a small or not so small group. And sometimes very little detail was provided. For example, a very brief item in 1883 related that a New Hampshire reformer had commenced a crusade against chewing gum, claiming it tended to lead the user to take up tobacco, and finally it led on to "ruinous" alcohol.[39]

One year later one of the biggest names in the anti-everything brigade turned his attention briefly and somewhat indirectly to the issue of chewing gum. In March of that year notorious puritan Anthony Comstock announced he had unearthed a lottery scheme for children and soon thereafter four chewing gum and confectionary firms were made painfully aware of his activity. At the end of February a New York citizen tipped off Comstock to what he saw as a scheme for making gamblers, conducted by Adolph Sachs at 35 W. 30th Street, Manhattan. Sachs ran a small retail store at that location dealing in items such as candy, chewing gum, and so forth. One brand of chewing gum sold by Sachs was known as the "Silver Hook Crystal Panorama Easter Egg Package." For each piece of gum, about the size and shape of a pen, customers paid one cent. The gum was displayed in a handsome box that contained, besides some ordinary candy, three large pieces of confectionary in the shape of eggs. With each piece of gum the customer received a number that entitled him to some sort of prize. It might be a piece of ordinary candy or it might be one of the eggs. Comstock arrested Sachs for running a lottery. Sachs decided that if he had to take the blame, others would go with him. As a result he informed and gave the names of four different firms that manufactured the gum and put up the prizes. He also told Comstock that the gum drawing the capital prizes was not mixed in with the rest but was put up in a separate package. That package could be put to one side by the retailer. Then customers could buy the gum until doomsday with no chance of getting the capital prizes. Thus, those capital prizes could be used as decoys for months, or could be sold off by the retailer for a profit.[40]

After he unearthed all the details of the scheme Comstock went before Justice Power and swore out four arrest warrants. Two were for retail outlets wherein Comstock, accompanied by police officers, arrested several employees at each outlet. The other two warrants were against manufacturers of gum, one of which was Charles Grimm and Company. All of those arrested were charged with conducting and aiding a lottery. That fourth warrant was for the well-known chewing gum maker Adams and Sons, 77 Murray Street, New York City. It was one of the oldest firms engaged in the manufacture of gum in America and the two owners were arrested. At their six-story building on Murray Street, they employed 50 to 75 employees and did a huge business in gum. For the previous five to six years the firm had been using prizes as an advertising gimmick to move their product and claimed they were driven to it by the competition. They did not consider their advertising ploy to be a lottery. In those raids, nine and one-half cases of prize gum were seized with each case holding 100 packages of 150 pieces of gum, a total of almost 150,000 sticks of gum. No outcome of the case was reported.[41]

An 1886 account reported that college boys in Iowa were "waging war" against chewing gum and had decided "to kill the next dude who treats the girls to gum." The reason for this crusade was that the girls, after chewing, put their gum on the boys' chairs, causing their pants to stick to the chairs, and so forth.[42]

Mrs. C. Jump organized the Albany, New York, Women's Christian Temperance Union early in 1887. When the group held its first annual session in June 1888 it re-elected Jump president. Then she secured the adoption of resolutions deploring the increasing use of chewing gum among young ladies, and resolutions boycotting grocers who sold whiskey.[43]

With respect to gum, the Albany group believed "it was about time action on this evil was taken." According to the group, when a young girl began the habit she said to herself that she could chew or let it alone but "before she is aware of her danger she is on the downward path to a gum chewer's grave." And when a young man called at a house where there were three or four inveterate young female gum-chewers, and took a seat on a chair, "he feels, when he attempts to rise, as if he had an abnormal attachment for the particular piece of furniture, which sticketh closer than a brother." After noting the passage of the anti-gum resolution, a reporter said, sarcastically, "Let there be anti-chewing-gum clubs organized in every county and State in the Union before it is everlastingly too late to save our girls from a fate worse than matrimony."[44]

An editor with a Galveston, Texas, newspaper noted that Mary Hetherington declared in the *Texas White Ribbon*, the official organ of the Texas Women's Christian Temperance Union, that one of the first causes of snuff dipping was gum chewing. That caused the editor to remark there were many reasons why the mastication of gum was proper: "We have often noticed that those hopelessly addicted to gum chewing are also strangely lacking in intellect. This being the case, the use of gum is a blessing, for by keeping their mouths full, it prevents them from inflicting nonsense on those who are unfortunately thrown in their company."[45]

Elkhart, Indiana, had a new club for men in 1894. Its membership of 55 had pledged its word and honor to "wage relentless warfare upon the chewing-gum habit." One of the strategies to be employed by the group was to boycott every girl that chewed gum "and force all such to the choice of pining away in hopeless despair as old maids or give up the offensive habit." One of their arguments was that a girl chewing gum on the street looked as bad as a young man smoking a cigarette. Another one of the rules of the club was for the members to turn their backs upon all girls who used "complexion powder."[46]

At the Rush Temple of Music on a Sunday in November 1902 Dr. George F. Hall delivered an attack on gum-chewing women. He declared he had as little patience with a female who habitually chewed gum as he had with a male who everlastingly chewed tobacco—both were "nasty and expensive" habits. When he saw a woman chewing gum in public he claimed he felt like shouting, "If those women must chew let them take to the basement." Grumbling, he said that on street cars, in theaters, at ball games and races, in the parlor and everywhere, it was a common sight to see girls and women of mature years chewing gum. "It is a habit which has scarcely a redeeming feature and I for one wish to use all the influence I have in discouraging the same," Hall fumed. "It distorts the face, induces excessive saliva and gives the breath a sickening, drugstore-like perform." Concluded Hall, "I can most assuredly say that in public at least gum-chewing is indecent. A bevy of wax twisters always suggests to me insipidity in conversation and rudeness of manners."[47]

A 1903 news account from Racine said there was some talk of an anti-gum chewing society being organized in Racine. Reportedly, many ladies there claimed that women chewing gum was as bad a habit as men chewing tobacco. On the streets of Racine girls and women could be seen "with their jaws working like the piston rods of an engine." Those women, thinking of forming an association, believed the habit was "becoming a vulgar fad, especially among young girls at matinees at the opera house, at entertainments and social functions. They believe that it is at all times a transgression on good taste and that in time the person seen chewing gum in public places will be stamped as a vulgarian by people of refinement."[48]

Two years later in Racine a number of women congregated on a September evening. Apparently they were a club, formally or informally. They grumbled about females chewing gum in public, causing the reporter to speculate there might be a movement forming to ban the practice in public places. One of the women present said that at a certain entertainment in Racine a few evenings earlier no less than seven young women were chewing away. A second woman at the gathering related she had been at the opera house one evening and counted 14 women chewing gum. At the meeting a vote was taken, wrote the journalist, "and it was unanimously agreed that gum chewing in public places was obnoxious and beneath the dignity of all well bred women and that some movement ought to be made to stop it." An opinion expressed at the meeting was that gum chewing by women was just as bad as tobacco chewing by men, the only difference being that the "filthy spitting was eliminated."[49]

A few years later, in 1907, in Richfield, Sevier County, Utah, it was reported that 16 Richfield girls had taken the pledge not to chew gum, evidently believing themselves to be intemperate in the use of chewing gum. They were not in accord as to the reasons behind the move, although a majority of those pledging agreed with the idea "chewing gum in public don't look nice." Those taking the pledge bound themselves not to chew gum in public places such as theaters and skating rinks between February 10, 1907, and July 1, 1907, although the time limitation was not explained. Also, it seemed the pledge to not chew gum did not apply to private quarters such as a person's home.[50]

Captain J. T. Hollinberger of the First Police Precinct in Washington, D.C., announced in November 1910 that the police would immediately commence a crusade to prevent children from selling chewing gum on the streets at night. For several months underage children—as proscribed by the child labor law—had functioned as chewing gum vendors on the streets of the nation's capital at night.[51]

Religious figures were another group that often spoke out against the habit. A violent discussion broke out in one of the city churches in Placerville, California, in 1879 over the question "Is it wrong for a Christian and a church member to chew gum?" The majority of the church members appeared to be disposed to admit gum chewers to the church but felt determined to draw the line rigidly somewhere, such as, for example, allowing only the "moderate" use of gum.[52]

A certain Miss Ryder of Chicago, described by an Illinois journalist as an authority on the management of Sunday schools, was asked in 1882 what she would do with a child who persisted in chewing gum in Sunday school. Ryder replied that she would take the child aside and explain to her "infant mind" that although gum in many respects might be an excellent thing, it was never given by God to be chewed in a Sunday school.[53]

A very brief item in February 1890 noted only that the Congregational minister of a church in Sedalia, Ohio, had preached a sermon the previous Sunday against gum chewing.[54]

In September 1890 the people of Grace Methodist Church in Jersey City, New Jersey, discussed a letter sent to Mrs. Joseph Autenreith by the church official board. That letter complained that Autenreith's two daughters disturbed the public church service by their conduct and begged the mother to exercise her parental authority over them. It was said the two young women chewed gum during the service and the smacking of their lips was a sound that disturbed those about them. Complaints were made to the official board and the letter to Autenreith was sent under its direction. Friends of Autenreith declared, however, it was all part of an old feud on the part of Pastor Dutcher to crowd out the old members of the congregation. The Autenreith family had gone to that church for some 20 years. At a recent church meeting those old members, including the Autenreith family, asked that the Rev. Mr. Tinger (who had been temporarily in charge) be retained permanently. But others prevailed and Dutcher was brought in from the Far West, and many veteran members of the church were annoyed by that result. Dutcher was said to have then gone on to make things uncomfortable for the older members of the congregation who had opposed his call to their pulpit.[55]

Also in 1890, a report from New York City stated that a congregation at an unnamed church was agitated over the gum chewing question. That is, several girls had been censured for chewing gum during church services. "This is something new in ecclesiastical offenses, for although chewing gum is prejudicial to health and also to good looks, it has never previously been made a matter of church discipline," said the journalist. He thought that preachers who detected gum chewers among the congregation would have the best chance of "curing" them of that bad habit by telling them it not only tended to lead to disease but it also impaired that personal appearance, "which at present is so important a feature in the church-going crowd. If this be not effectual the case must be of a very hopeless character."[56]

Mrs. Ballington Booth talked before a large audience in the Salvation Army headquarters building in New York City on the night of September 1, 1895. Her topic was the "New Woman" and in her address Booth went on to differentiate between the "new woman" and the "advanced woman." While she denounced in scathing terms the new woman, she just as forcefully praised the advanced woman. With respect to the new woman Booth declared she had an "insane" idea that she was emancipating her sisters. "She is taking the reins in her own hands; tries to beat down man, belittle him, makes out that he is no good, and then turns to us and tells us that she is going to emancipate us," said Booth. "We, the true new women say, however, that we do not want her to emancipate us. For we are trying to raise man to a higher sphere and to be a helpmate to him, while she is trying to tread him under foot." When she asked herself what she would do with the new woman, Booth stated, "Her disgusting books of realism, which brings the blush to any pure girl's face, I would burn, together with the gum and cigarettes."[57]

A case in the police court at Cumberland, Maryland, featured two young girls as prisoners appearing before the bar of justice. Rev. Mr. Gillum, pastor of a church at Cresaptown, swore out a warrant against the girls charging them with disturbing public worship. They were committed to jail and held overnight until about noon the next day, when they were taken before the judge for trial. On the stand Gillum said he had been conducting a service and the girls had a habit of taking a front seat in the church and chewing gum in such a noisy manner as to disturb his congregation. He added that he told a brother of one of the girls about it and while he was conversing with the brother his sister came up the aisle and made a face at Gillum. As the minister remonstrated with the girl, the other girl came up and interfered with the situation, whereupon the minister placed his hand on the second girl's shoulder and told her to leave the church and never come back. Both girls then left the church and dared Gillum to come outside. He did so and a "regular scene" took place in which one of the girls shook her fist in his face and called him a liar. Several other witnesses were called to the stand and all of them swore the girls had disturbed public worship by chewing gum and laughing and talking. The magistrate imposed fines and costs on the girls amounting to a total of $27, a sum that was immediately paid. According to the reporter, "The girls are extremely pretty, and have always been considered ladylike heretofore."[58]

When a reporter wrote about an attack on gum by Bishop John S. Vincent of the Methodist church in 1888, he was naive enough to start his piece by declaring, "The gum chewing habit has fixed itself so firmly on the people that but few are found to condemn it." The reporter described Vincent as being bold enough to condemn it. In an address before the Kansas Temperance Union, Vincent appealed to his listeners to attack the gum chewing habit and "to persevere until it is crusaded out of the state." He argued the habit did no good whatever and encouraged other "dangerous habits" (unnamed) among the people. Vincent went on to declare the foundation of temperance reform should be laid at the chewing gum age of childhood, as the habit was a sort of self-indulgence that should be restrained. "If the child's will was educated to resist this habit, it could be easier trained to resist other habits," he explained. In particular, the bishop was critical of the gum-chewing girl "and urged that she should be made to understand that the indulgence of the habit was to her discredit."[59]

Many newspapers around the country picked up the article cited above that featured Vincent's attack. One paper published in Iowa, the *Bedford Free Press*, ran the piece with the editor adding a comment of his own at the end, after the Bishop's criticism of female gum-chewers. "Kansas is not the only state that should take this matter up. If gum chewing is a bad habit in Kansas, it certainly should be considered so in Iowa and elsewhere," wrote the Bedford editor.[60]

Nickell Magazine ran an editorial on Vincent's attack (itself reprinted in several newspapers) in which the publication stated the Bishop's objections to gum were not the usual ones of acquiring a "gum-face" or the loosening of dental fillings, "but he seems to see a great moral danger lurking within this popular habit." As far as this editor was concerned it was not necessary to deny children innocent pleasures in order that they might be fortified against pleasures that were not so innocent. For this editor the only objection to chewing gum was on the ground that it was not a becoming habit to many people, but he saw no great danger in the small boy's indulgence in the "delights of talc and resin." He concluded that Bishop Vincent took life too seriously "and perhaps a little masticatory in the shape of pepsin gum might aid his digestion."[61]

Gum Chewing Indefensible

By RT. REV. F. D. HUNTINGTON,
Bishop of Syracuse.

Chewing gum is an indefensible habit on every ground and evidences bad manners. I consider it one of the forms of deterioration of society. There is no justification for it, and it descredits good breeding. Its unnatural action distorts the jaws, and in time cannot but affect the looks of the perpetual indulger. I should think that that alone would be enough to deter anyone from indulging in the habit. They say that it whitens the teeth, but I do not believe it, and I never heard from a medical standpoint that it was good for anyone. The indefensible and low-bred habit of gum chewing seems to me to be on the increase.

The kind of rant shown here, from 1904, was typical of the reactions religious figures had to the gum chewing habit.

At a Methodist summer camp near Wesley Lake, Ocean Grove, New Jersey, Aaron E. Ballard was acting head of the Camp Meeting Association in 1907. In that capacity he issued an order banning the sale of gum from the booth located on the Wesley Lake campgrounds. He declared that the chewing of gum too much resembled the "obnoxious practice" of chewing tobacco. Ballard also observed that when it came to gum chewing, the ladies of the resort were "the principal offenders."[62]

On November 11, 1907, three members of the Baptist Church choir at Hazelton, Indiana, were arrested on the basis of an affidavit filed by Rev. Samuel Bettis. Overton Decker, Salvan Pearson, and Bais Cunningham were charged with disturbing religious services by chewing gum while seated in the choir. In the middle of his sermon Pastor Betts stopped to talk to the choir of 10 members, scolding the three boys and four girls in it who, he said, had disturbed him by chewing gum. Returning to his sermon, Bettis did not get very much further when the gum chewing was resumed as energetically as before. Again he stopped to state how he felt about gum chewers among the singers. At that point the seven gum-chewing members of the choir picked up their songbooks and departed from the church as one. Bettis went to the nearby community of Princeton and filed affidavits against the three males who had disturbed him. According to a reporter, "It is said that he was advised by local citizens not to proceed against the young women of the choir." No outcome was reported.[63]

Late in 1920 gum chewing was added to smoking and other habits on the taboo list of the religious community in Zion City, Illinois. Voliva, overseer of the church, announced that if he found anyone chewing gum "like an old cow chewing her cud," he would hand them over to the police. Notices had been posted in the community forbidding gum chewing. Also placed on the banned list at that time were low-necked dresses. A method of dealing with that issue was to have female inspectors equipped with spare shawls, among the congregation in church, and whenever they saw a woman with a low-necked dress they would throw the shawl over the miscreant's shoulders.[64]

6

Physical and
Mental Effects

And then there were all the purported effects that chewing gum had on the body and, more rarely, on the mind. Many of them came from respectable physicians and other scientists and many came from other sources such as the media, wherein stories on the effects of gum were sometimes presented without being sourced. Overwhelmingly, those supposed effects of chewing gum were negative, but on occasion a positive article appeared. Most common claim for gum in the positive camp was the idea that it cured dyspepsia (indigestion) or upset stomach.

One of the earliest articles to mention the bad effects of chewing gum on the body appeared at the end of 1859. In order to have sound teeth in middle life and old age proper precautions had to be taken in childhood, said the reporter. "The habit of chewing gum is like applying small air pumps to the teeth. When the gum is separated from the tooth the consequence is a violent strain on the dental nerves." Bad results might not appear immediately but the boy or girl who indulged in the habit "may calculate on having rotten teeth when in the prime of life. Nor is this all." Like tobacco chewing, warned the piece, the gum chewing habit induced an unnatural flow of the "humors" toward the mouth, where it had to be ejected as saliva. "This is bad enough when it can be ejected; but when, from sickness or other causes, the habit must be discontinued, the result may be, and has been, fatal. Let young persons and their parents take heed."[1]

Another theme that emerged from time to time with respect to gum chewing was the idea that the habit was addictive. A reporter on a Reno, Nevada, newspaper said in 1871 that the habit of chewing gum grew on a person who indulged in it as much as did that of drinking liquor, and the sudden breaking of the habit was injurious. A young girl who had chewed gum regularly for years suddenly swore off the item and since then, he wrote, she has had "regular jim-jams" and has had to be sat up with every night.[2]

One of the earliest items that paired dyspepsia with chewing gum appeared at the end of 1872. And this story, unlike the majority of such stories that claimed gum cured dyspepsia, argued the product did, in fact, cause dyspepsia. According to the story, many young people and even quite small children were troubled with dyspepsia "and we know that many of those cases are caused by the pernicious habit of chewing gum." The glands of the mouth pour out saliva when anything was chewed and when they are working the stomach was also at work, he explained, pouring out its proper fluid, and as the stomach was empty part of the time, that fluid acted on the coats of the stomach, causing indigestion and dyspepsia.[3]

A female employee at Crane's paper mill in Westfield, Massachusetts, suffered a severe attack of lockjaw one day in May 1876, in which the jaws were set, or locked, for more than one hour. The attending physician gave it as his opinion that the "disease" was the result of a long and daily practice of chewing gum and that if the young woman persisted in chewing gum "a fatal return of the disease could be expected."[4]

A few good points, or at least non-negative points, were raised in the product's favor by a reporter in 1879. He explained that chewing gum did not, like tobacco, require that the saliva be expectorated; it did not, like smoking, excite the nerves, nor like an abundance of food and drinks, hurtfully overload the stomach.[5]

Late in 1879 another article about gum that was designed to alarm the reader appeared in a Syracuse, New York, newspaper. The piece told the story of Ida Smith in Louisville, Kentucky, who had been a chewer of gum for about one year. One Saturday night she took the gum out of her mouth to get a glass of water but to her horror, and that of her parents, her jaws kept moving rapidly. Her parents sent for a doctor but he was unable to stop the movement in the 11-year-old girl's jaws. He put a tight bandage over her face but it only helped a little—it spread to a facial twitching. Finally, the next morning, Ida Smith reverted to a normal state. When she was restored, said the account, "nothing in the world could induce her to again chew wax."[6]

A very brief mention in the press in 1883 told of gum and dyspepsia from a different angle. Herein the use of chewing gum after meals as a cure for dyspepsia was "all the rage."[7]

Also in 1883, a dentist who practiced on 34th Street in New York City and was said by a reporter to be "of great reputation" declared, "Of course any kind of chewing gum is injurious to the teeth, and spruce gum just as much as any other. It is not the gum itself, but the process of mastication which is bad." He explained that the suction affected both the enamel of the tooth and the nerve "and is often the cause of pulling out the filling of a tooth, no matter how strongly it may be put in. I will have nothing to do with a patient who uses chewing gum, for it is labor lost."[8]

Another mention of gum chewing being a cure for dyspepsia appeared in a Milwaukee newspaper

Chew

Beeman's

Pepsin Gum

IF YOU WANT A GOOD CHEWING GUM.

The practice of chewing gum is old. Our great grandfathers used to be gum chewers. They gathered the gum themselves in the woods. But perhaps you've tried chewing "spruce gum." That was the olden time gum. There wasn't any better gum then. Life is too short to chew any other sort but BEEMAN'S. It's up-to-date. It's ready and chewable from the start.

Mr. Beeman says there is a small amount of pepsin in each tablet. You know that pepsin aids digestion. We have customers who affirm that their digestion has improved since they have chewed BEEMAN'S GUM.

Have you ever tried it? It's a five-cent experiment.

Give the children BEEMAN'S GUM. It's better for them than candy; it's cheaper; it won't upset their stomachs.

Beeman's Pepsin Gum,

THE PERFECTION OF CHEWING GUM.

A Delicious Remedy

For all Forms of

INDIGESTION.

CAUTION—See that the name **Beeman** is on each wrapper.

Each tablet contains one grain pure pepsin. If the gum cannot be obtained from dealers, send 5 cents in stamps for sample package to

BEEMAN CHEMICAL CO.,
76 Bank St., Cleveland, O.

These ads for Beeman's Pepsin gum appeared in 1894 and 1895 and promoted the gum as a particularly effective remedy for indigestion.

DON'T SPITOCUTE YOURSELF.

DƆ YOU USE TOBACCO ?

MR. ASHE USED TO.

SEE ! MESSRS. WELLMAN & MINSEL—Gentlemen: Regarding the ANTI-BACCO CHEWING GUM I bought last August, will say that after using one box of your gum I found the desire for tobacco had left me and I feel free to say I am entirely cured of the habit I contracted in the army 35 years ago of smoking and chewing tobacco. Very truly yours,
J. S. ASHE (head miller Maumee Valley Milling Co.),
Nov. 4th, 1896.   DEFIANCE, OHIO.

TRY ANTI-BACCO CHEWING GUM
(TRADE-MARK REGISTERED.)

And NOTICE how soon that awful tobacco grip will begin to loosen, and you feel like a new man. ONLY 10 CENTS A PACKAGE—10 CHEWS SOLD BY DRUGGISTS—or sent postpaid on receipt of price.

MFD. BY WELLMAN & MINSEL, DEFIANCE, OHIO.

This 1897 ad was a pitch for an anti-tobacco gum. Just by chewing this particular gum a smoker could free himself from the grip of tobacco, or so it was said.

later in 1883. In this case the evidence consisted solely of a reporter who interviewed one man (unnamed) who claimed it had cured him. No other evidence was given. Reasoning behind the idea that gum helped relieve dyspepsia was that chewing gum between meals enabled the dyspeptic to reinforce his stomach with saliva and thereby to digest what he had eaten. When asked how long he chewed gum each time he indulged, the man replied, "Oh, till my jaws get tired—that is, long enough to flood my stomach with saliva." Despite the paucity of evidence, this piece was titled "The gum cure for dyspepsia."[9]

When a chewing gum manufacturer was interviewed at his New York City factory in 1884, he told a reporter that people had told him gum was good for dyspepsia and that he knew personally several confirmed dyspeptics who had been cured by using his chewing gum.[10]

Under the heading of "gum and mathematics," an 1885 piece that originally appeared in a Macon, Georgia, newspaper spoke to the issue of the effect of gum on the mind. The question of whether or not chewing gum affected the student and his studies had been around since the product had become popular, said the reporter. It was left to a Macon school teacher to put the question to the test. One afternoon as a certain school was being dismissed for the day, she told the children the arithmetic class, consisting of 12 pupils of both sexes, would be divided into two groups on the following Monday. Six of the pupils were to be provided with all the chewing gum they could use while the other six would be allowed no gum. The teacher would then administer a test to all of them that contained 29 arithmetic problems. When the experiment was concluded it was found that the gum chewers had correctly answered 21 problems while the pupils denied gum correctly answered only eight of the problems.[11]

Doctors began to weigh in on the subject beginning around the middle of the 1880s. By that time, presumably, gum chewing was a much more pervasive habit involving many more people. At the beginning of 1886, Dr. W. G. Priest remarked, "A popular craze that is daily growing is that of chewing gum. Men chew it openly and above board as much as girls, and the practice has gone so rapidly beyond its old confines that the fame of Vassar college as a shrine where taffy tolu received its greatest share of worship has long ago dried out." In the opinion of Priest, the popularity of the gum-chewing habit was due to the fallacy that some health journal (unnamed) had promulgated a while back declaring that as gum-chewing preserved the teeth and developed the gums, it should be encouraged. He argued that gum chewing stimulated the salivary glands to a degree that was draining and exhaustive and when those secretions were increased they had an injurious effect upon the stomach by increasing the digestion, without the food. At the same time it excited the glands of the stomach, the liver, the pancreas, and the entire glandular system connected with alimentation; it wasted the products of those glands, or diverted them from their proper use, and by so doing injured the system. "So you see, gum-chewing is not only a ridiculous and a vulgar habit, but it hurtful to health and should be stopped."[12]

Many more medical comments on the topic appeared in print in 1886, most of them negative. A piece reprinted from the *New York Medical Record* offered the thought, "Physicians in general will quite agree, we think, that the practice should be indulged in only with the greatest moderation." And that was because "the practice of stimulating one's secretions for the sole purpose of experiencing sensation connected with their flow is not a safe one. There may be inebriety in chewing rubber-gum, and real sensuality in persistent indulgence in aimless mastication."[13]

In Rhode Island it was reported that an epidemic of lockjaw was making the rounds and, said a journalist, "Although it is not stated that the habit of chewing gum is directly the cause of this epidemic, it does not take a very great stretch of imagination to believe that such is the case." He also observed that a young woman in Des Moines had recently ruined $15 worth of teeth fillings by an over indulgence in Black Jack licorice gum. She exercised her jaws, it was said, until she had loosened every filling in her head.[14]

Another piece in 1886 attacked what it called "black chewing gum." According to this article, "It is generally made out of refuse gum arabic—stuff that can not be used in the apothecary shops, and is flavored variously with the cheapest of cheap extracts, licorice, wintergreen, peppermint, or more usually, one of those poisonous flavors that are compounded from acids." Young men and young women chewed it, argued the journalist, because the manufacturers who made it advertised that it perfumed the breath, that it aided digestion, cleared the voice, and was a harmless and "beautiful" substitute for tobacco. But, said the piece, it was not. According to the reporter, the physicians of Amsterdam, New York, had just declared that the practice of chewing this black gum is most harmful and pernicious. They had traced directly to it innumerable cases of sore mouth and sore throat that they have treated of late. Their brethren in the medical profession in New York were reported to have agreed with them, and not only condemned black chewing gum, but all chewing gum of whatever color. The physician in charge of one of the throat dispensaries in one of the largest hospitals in New York said, "Day after day patients, nearly all girls between 8 and 18 years of age, come in here and complain that it hurts them when they swallow, or else that their mouths sting when they drink anything warm. On examining their throats I find the delicate mucous membrane marked here and there with little inflamed patches. In nine cases out of ten it is caused by chewing gum." When he was asked why the gum was hurtful, he explained that the flavoring was usually poisonous and by its constant presence, in however small a quantity, it set up an inflammation. But, he added, the habit was also pernicious in other ways. The untiring motion of a gum chewer's jaws provoked a superfluous flow of saliva and wore out the saliva glands. Gum-chewing worked to retard digestion. If a woman filled her stomach with water or saliva she drowned the gastric juices; "also the interminable attrition wears out the teeth, and foreign flavor by degrees renders the breath more and more disagreeable. The practice is bad in every way."[15]

Dr. Hannaford remarked, in 1886, "The use of chewing gum is useless and worse, since it excites the flow and loss of saliva, when it will be needed for the next meal." Of the saliva, and gastric juices, Hannaford explained, there was only enough secreted for daily use, "the supply indicating the real needs of the system; just enough to repair the waste. The food will need all of those that it may be properly digested." A journalist added his opinion when he said, with reference to Hannaford, "If the increasing and disgusting habit of gum chewing could be controlled by the above scientific statement, backed as it is by common sense, it would be a blessing to the community."[16]

A Detroit journalist presented both positive and negative medical opinions on the topic in 1886. A Detroit physician stated that girls working in large factories where there was a great deal of dust were positively benefited from the use of gum. It caused them to swallow or to spit out the dust they inhaled, which otherwise would lodge in their lungs. Not only was one Detroit dentist unconvinced gum could injure the teeth, he believed it actually improved them, as the constant friction kept them free from tartar and other deleterious substances. However, he warned that the continued use of gum for years would in time wear down the side of the jaw not used in the mastication of the product. Lately, though, wrote the reporter, there had crept into Detroit a substance known as "black chewing gum," made out of tar, which was said by medical men to be extremely harmful and pernicious. It was becoming a great favorite with chewers but physicians asserted its use was conducive to sore mouths and innumerable throat diseases. Put up in fancy paper, sold at a penny a block, flavored with some unknown ingredient, and christened with a sweetly-sounding name such as tutti-frutti, for instance, declared the journalist, "the black chewing gum is forcing its entrée into all grades of society, and driving its rivals to the wall. But it is nothing but tar—cheap tar at that—mixed with gelatine and flavored with—heaven and the manufacturer only know what."[17]

One of the leading physicians of Burlington, Iowa, advised a newspaper reporter in that city in 1886 to "tell the people to stop their children chewing gum. The habit is bad, has nothing to recommend it and occasions diseases in many cases." And he added, "Tell them particularly that the common custom among the little people, of trading gum which they are chewing, is a potent means of infection. Throat and lung diseases, skin diseases, all sorts of infectious diseases in fact, are thus conveyed."[18]

Still in 1886, several of the leading physicians of Chicago came forward to endorse the chewing of gum, provided the practice was limited to 15 minutes or so after eating. They especially recommended it to those suffering from indigestion or heartburn, giving a preference to unflavored spruce and balsam gums. According to this account, many dentists declared that gum chewing was a benefit to the teeth. One Chicago druggist on the north side of the city said that whereas five years ago he bought one dollar's worth of gum to retail, now it ran up into the hundreds of dollars: "It seems as if the demand for gum increased each week."[19]

Some six months later another Chicago physician was asked by a journalist if it was harmful to a person if he chewed gum. "A good deal has been said on both sides of the question but you can put me down as saying that people who have ordinarily good stomachs need take no alarm. A moderate amount of gum chewing won't hurt them."[20]

A lengthy article on the dangers of gum was published by a newspaper in Freeport, Illinois, in September 1888 and which carried the blunt headline, "Stop chewing gum." A subhead for the article, all in capital letters, stated; "A word of warning to the Freeport young ladies— chewing gum spoils their features and ruins their eyes." It was a necessary article, thought the reporter, as the gum chewing craze had taken a firm hold on the people of Freeport. "Men, women and children are afflicted with the habit and it is hard to tell when it will end," he lamented. A well known physician told the reporter, "If the girls only knew that their eyes are being ruined by chewing gum, they would shrink from it as they would from a viper. We all know to what extent this gum chewing is carried on, and what a nasty habit it is. If they have a big wad in their mouth while reading this interview let them throw it out and swear off, as the drinkers say, for in one respect these dainty girls are like drunkards." He argued that if they were chronic gum-chewers they were heir to all the infirmities that afflicted the chronic whiskey drinkers. However, he held out some hope, noting he had three girls who were addicted to that habit but he was able to break them of it "after a great deal of persuasion and some trifling punishment. The oldest girl has evidence of the habit, though, and will take them to her grave."[21]

This piece was one of the earliest ones to link gum chewing to eye damage. The reporter asked the doctor how the eyes were affected. The muscles of the jaw connected with the spine and from the spine there were little fibrous tissues running in all directions, he explained. A number of those extended to the eyes, and were called the optic nerves. If you watched a person eating you would notice a palpitation of the temples when the lower jaw moved up and down in the process of mastication. That was caused by the working of the optic nerves. Those nerves were tender and sensitive and when they were overworked they became shrunken and enfeebled, and then the process of deterioration in the eyesight began. The shrinking of the nerve drew back into the socket and, as it was connected to the pupil of the eye, that also became affected. "The consequence is that the eye becomes weak and loses its color; it becomes an unnatural looking gray, and the vision is so much impaired by it that eye glasses must be resorted to," said the physician. One of his female patients, he continued, wore glasses just because she chewed so much gum. "Her eyesight is practically ruined, and she has crows' feet wrinkles about the outer corners that were caused by the flesh of the cheek being forced upward by the action of the jaw. She is also troubled with indigestion from the same cause. These are all the symptoms exhibited by a person who drinks whiskey plentifully, and hence the comparison." For his concluding advice this physician—who talked as if only young females chewed gum—urged parents to take the matter in hand and see if they could rid their girls of the habit, because "it is a filthy one outside of the terrible effect it has upon the human system. If the parents will keep from their girls some of their little perquisites until they stop chewing gum they would soon give up the habit."[22]

One of the physicians in Chicago told a journalist in that city in October 1888 that chewing gum was "a practice in which grown people should not indulge, and which parents should not tolerate in children." Was it a worse practice, asked the reporter, than chewing food? To which the doctor replied that it was a thousand times worse. A girl would do enough chewing on one cent's worth of gum in a day to masticate her food for a whole week. "The hinges of the jaw are made for the ordinary work of an ordinary life, and they won't stand anymore." This medical man also compared chewing gum to drinking because one nip called for another and one crunch began another. "The continued chewing excites the nerves which lie about the jaws to a kind of perpetual motion, which doesn't cease until their strength is exhausted. It also tends to affect the nerves of the eyes."[23]

When a New York *Sun* reporter spoke to doctors in New York City in 1888 about the statement in print that gum chewing was harmful to the eyes, they all told him the idea was nonsense. A New York ophthalmologist pointed out the optic nerves were completely removed from those governing mastication and could not possibly have any effect. Another physician agreed, but added, "The bad effects of chewing gum are felt by the digestion only." If there was excessive gum chewing so much saliva was secreted and carried to the stomach as to perhaps impair digestion. Also, much chewing could weaken salivary glands so that insufficient saliva would be produced for digestion. However, he added that gum chewing was not so dreadful a habit as it was painted: "Its evils are grossly exaggerated by those who consider the habit to be ill bred and vulgar." This physician went so far as to say, "There are cases where moderate gum chewing is positively healthful. In fact, physicians sometimes prescribe it." For example, he continued, people often bolted their food down and did not have enough time for proper salivation. Thus, it would be "an excellent thing to chew a bit of harmless gum after the meal, and in that way induce the secretion of more saliva."[24]

In an article at the end of 1888 a journalist stated that physicians differed considerably in their views on the subject of gum. An "eminent [but unnamed] doctor from Ohio said that gum chewing seriously affected the eyesight and that he never failed to detect that a patient used gum, by an examination of the eye. Another physician said that the muscles of the jaw and face near the temple were enlarged and hardened from the habit and the curve of the lips was destroyed. On the other hand, doctors "without number" advised its use to cleanse the teeth and aid digestion.[25]

The *Washington Post* presented a piece in August 1889 that said those pretty young girls who chewed gum constantly "had better take warning in time, if they prize their beauty. It appears that a young society belle of this city has so exercised her masticator muscles that they stick out like the biceps which helped John L. Sullivan win the prize of [boxing] champion." Reportedly, the young woman no longer went out in pubic "as her unusual facial development is anything but attractive, and the only prescription that it is possible to give her, is the advice, 'don't move your jaw,' which she is endeavoring to fulfill in the seclusion of her home." Dr. Magruder, president of the medical department at Georgetown University, was visited by a *Post* reporter and asked what effect the use of chewing gum had on the chewer. "The chief effect would be an enlargement of the masticator muscles. This enlargement would follow as naturally as it would from the exercise of any other muscle or set of muscles," he explained. "It would not add anything to the appearance of a young lady to have her jaws stick out prominently from this cause." Magruder declared, also, that chewing gum had no effect on digestion but was "a little beneficial in cleaning the teeth."[26]

Another clash of gum and the mind came to light when the New York *Sun* remarked in November 1890 that the constant chewing of gum had produced "weak minds" in 14 cases of young girls then under medical care. It seemed the constant movement of the mouth caused too great a strain on the head, but no other details were provided. Admitting such cases were the "extreme results" of the gum chewing habit, the newsman went on to assert that cynical critics argued such cases indicated what the county was coming to unless the pernicious habit was curbed.[27]

Nor would the idea that chewing gum damaged the eyes easily go away. In 1891 a Pittsburg journalist had a talk with a city optician by the name of J. Diamond about "the effects of the gum chewing craze that has spread from one end of the land to the other; and it is doubtful if as many of the belles and followers of the habit will continue their chewing after they learn of one of its most injurious effects." Said Diamond, "Does gum-chewing hurt the eyes? Most certainly it does, and that is one reason why I am so antagonistic to it and denounce it. Not only myself, but every scientific optician will tell you the same thing. And it is this, with its attendant injurious effects, that makes the habit so repulsive." Diamond said that just a few days earlier a woman came to him with her eyes in very bad shape and he thought there must be some other cause for it—the patient was not old or otherwise ill. He queried her and discovered she had chewed gum from the time she was old enough to know what it was. "Here was the cause without any further looking. Why, she had to take the highest power of glass I had, and her sight was as bad as though she were eighty."

According to the optician, the constant chewing of gum affected the nerves that led from the spine to the optic nerves, and strained the latter until they weakened and gave out. It was the same, to a degree, he said, with tobacco-users, but gum chewing was worse because its "victims" chewed more constantly, and thus kept up more irritation. He claimed he frequently had cases that were caused by that same habit: "Many young ladies who continue the habit feel its effects, and I have a good many cases lately of very young girls with poor sight, and weak eyes that, as I find from the use of my instruments, and from inquiry into the habits of the sufferers, arise from no other habit than that of gum chewing." If one would notice, concluded Diamond, one would observe that gum-chewers did not have the brilliancy in their eyes, or the vivacious and full-of-life look; their physiognomy looks pale and unhealthy. "If this habit is kept up as a craze the effect upon the eyes will be more evident," warned Diamond, as there would be many more cases.[28]

Curiously, a connection between ocean travel and gum was presented in a brief report in February 1894 wherein it was explained that when an English woman wrote to an English friend she said, "I wonder how it is we know nothing of the wonderful American chewing gum as a remedy against seasickness." Reportedly, when crossing the English Channel a U.S. woman had given the letter writer a piece of gum to chew, and it had worked for the letter writer.[29]

Adding to the idea of muscular jaws was one Dr. Edson, speaking at the end of 1895. Previously, he had recommended gum for dyspepsia and was then expressing the idea that the chances were much in favor of the American people moving to become a square-jawed race if they kept up the gum-chewing habit, and if the habit continued to spread pervasively as it had been doing over the previous few years. "Necessarily the muscles which constitute the hinges of the jaw will enlarge if they are overworked. The future human face may have to be drawn with a square rather than the line of beauty," Edson said.[30]

A destruction of beauty was another effect mentioned fairly regularly in the media. "The chewing gum face is the latest scientific discovery, and it is argued by the discoverer that no one who chews gum can possibly be beautiful," stated a reporter in 1896. He thought that the fact should prove a deterrent to gum chewing to all who thought they had good looks but not, of course, to the "homely." Perhaps, he concluded, "the ceaseless chewing habit of the dromedary, who chews as fastidiously and industriously upon a peanut as upon a squash, is the real cause of that useful quadruped's haggard, gaunt and infinite homeliness."[31]

"Gum makes wrinkles" ran the headline of a December 1896 news story. "Girls, if you want your face wrinkled before you reach a hale old age, keep on chewing gum. That is what doctors say," said the reporter. He had talked to a Wabash (Indiana) doctor outside his office on the street. Pointing out a woman passing by who was not chewing gum, the Wabash physician declared, nonetheless, "There goes a woman who is chewing gum incessantly. She would not chew it in public, of course, but the habit leaves its marks on the cheeks, about the eyes and the corners of the mouth most unmistakably. It is impossible that such a grotesque and unnatural exercise of the facial muscles as is required by this champing of the jaw for hours at a time should not only throw the mouth out of shape and must, sooner or later, bring on wrinkles." Explaining further, he said the first to appear were little fine lines just below the temples. Then a deep, ugly line began to take up a permanent residence at the corner of the mouth, and next in the mouth. The plumpest cheeks that ever bore a rose hue would soon wrinkle under the force of that "ugly gum chewing habit." He stressed that he wanted to draw attention to the fact that the chewing gum habit brought on premature wrinkles, "And she that doubts the assertion may consult her mirror or the faces of some of her tutti frutti friends."[32]

A New England dentist described as "noted" was the authority for the "remarkable statement" delivered in 1897 that the people who had the soundest, best preserved teeth were the ones who were "inveterate chewers of gum." Another "eminent" dentist declared that the texture of the teeth was improved and strengthened by constant chewing, just as the muscles of the arms were hardened and developed by constant exercise. Said the disbelieving reporter, "There are theories and theories."[33]

Without reference to any specific articles, a piece published in November 1897 stated, "The English medical journals have opened a crusade against the gum chewing habit, which is increasing in England at a rapid rate." And, "It has been common to claim for gum chewing that it tended to alleviate the pangs of dyspepsia and stimulate the digestive organs, but the medical journals are now asserting that the habit has an effect directly opposite to this." Supposedly those medical journals were also calling attention to the enormous growth in the output of gum, and sounding a warning against the "filthy makes" that were the "legitimate result" of competition. Much of the chewing gum then on the market was said to be made from ingredients that were far from being "pure and healthy." All of this caused the American editor whose newspaper had printed this piece to say, "The American people are rapidly becoming a nation of gum chewers and the wagging jaws seem to be moved by a perpetual machine that never stops. But the medical journals may warn from now until the crack of doom, and gum chewing will go right ahead. Present pleasure has more attraction for mankind than future health."[34]

BORG'S CHOC-TO Chewing Gum

A Delicious and Healthful Confection!

THE PUREST AND BEST GUM

EVER OFFERED TO THE PUBLIC!

ITS MEDICINAL PROPERTIES ARE INVALUABLE!

IT CURES

SORE THROAT, COUGHS AND COLDS,

AND IS HIGHLY BENEFICIAL TO DYSPEPTICS.

It whitens the teeth and sweetens the breath, imparts a pleasant taste to the mouth, and an agreeable feeling to the stomach.

Borg's Choc-To Gum is the best, try it once, and you will use no other afterwards. If any dealer you ask for it, has not got it, take no other, but go somewhere else. You will find all progressive dealers have it, that is the class of dealers to patronize always for anything you want.

CHEW BORG'S CHOC-TO GUM,

MANUFACTURED AT

59 & 61 S. CANAL ST., - CHICAGO, ILL.

HARTZ & BAHNSEN,

Wholesale Agents for Rock Island.

Medicinal claims were regularly made for chewing gum, as can be seen in this 1892 ad for Borg's Choc-To gum.

The idea that gum prevented seasickness surfaced again in August

Nix-E-Won't Tell!

Tablets or Chewing Gum

Destroys Odor of Liquor, Onions and Tobacco.

For Sale Everywhere.
Nix-E Co.,   -   Chicago

Boston Candy Co., Minneapolis.
Distributors.

Boston Bitter Sweets, Chocolates.

This chewing gum, as outlined in 1904, covered up the odor of onions, tobacco and liquor.

The Only Beneficial Chewing Gum

Gum-Lax is the one chewing gum that really does you good. Chew it just like ordinary chewing gum. It's a tonic laxative in a new form. It doesn't act violently, spasmodically, harshly— but gently, easily, thoroughly. There's no special time for

Gum-Lax

The Laxative Chewing Gum—Cures Constipation

Can be chewed morning, noon or night. Before or after meals. Looks and tastes like the ordinary chewing gum, but really benefits you.

For Sale by Caswell-Massey & Company, Hegeman & Company, Wm. B. Riker, Son & Company, J. Milhau's Son, Killsh Pharmacy, Walter S. Rockey and two thousand other druggists in New York City. If your druggist does not sell GUM-LAX, send us ten cents and we will mail you a box.

GUM-LAX MFG. CO., 29 Broadway, New York City

The laxative chewing gum was on the market at least by 1907, when this ad appeared.

135

1900. At that time there was an old man who sold gum in New York where the Long Branch and Rockaway boats used to depart. As part of his sales pitch he proclaimed, "When you're seasick don't blame the old gum man," to the crowds as they hurried to the boats. Said a cynical journalist, "Its potency is due to the frequent publication of statements that chewing gum will prevent seasickness."[35]

In October 1903 a reporter began his article by stating, "For years the habit of chewing gum has been regarded as one of the most useless and nonsensical of the practices to which mankind is addicted. Aside from the manufacturers of chewing gum and the victims of the habit, there has been nobody found who had a good word for the habit." He then implied the makers and sellers of the product had professed to find medicinal value—such as helping dyspeptics—in the item. But now an "eminent" neurologist from Minnesota had come forward of his own volition to declare that the chewing of gum would sometimes cure and always relieve the mental condition of insane people. In the insane asylum of Minnesota chewing gum in large quantities was included in the list of supplies that were furnished to that institution. Reportedly, it had been found that gum chewing had a very beneficial effect upon patients, soothing them when they suffered violent attacks and enabling them to concentrate their minds upon various forms of work. This information caused the writer of the article to conclude, "If the chewing of gum can be confined to insane asylums, the public would experience great relief. There has long been an opinion that the insane asylum would be a good place for the chewers of gum, and this Minnesota discovery tends to establish the fact that the asylum is the place for the indulgence of this habit."[36]

A Philadelphia dentist remarked in 1904 that gum chewing was generally regarded by the parents of children "addicted to it as a pernicious habit." And yet, he added, in certain cases he had no hesitation in saying that it was a most excellent item. In fact, on more than once occasion had he advised the parents of children whose faces were narrow and whose jaws were not sufficiently developed to make them chew gum. The constant exercise derived from the habit had a tendency to widen an otherwise narrow jaw and thus make room for teeth that showed evidence of crowding each other out of shape. He felt the constant chewing of gum for two hours every day was sufficient exercise to bring about "a most desirable result in the dwarfed formation of a child's jaw." Even when no such treatment was necessary this dentist saw no reason why children should be forbidden to chew gum: "It can do no harm and may possibly do good in keeping the teeth white and clean."[37]

A French scientist by the name of Dr. Leon Meunier wrote in a French publication on the habit of chewing gum. It was reprinted in various American publications in 1906. Meunier related that during a trip he made to the United States in 1904 he was struck "by an empirical treatment which has been employed by Americans for many years to facilitate stomach digestion." In all cities of the United States and Canada he saw large numbers of people chewing a substance to take the place of the "vulgar" wad of tobacco; "that substance is sold everywhere under the name of 'chewing gum' or 'pepsin gum.' He analyzed that gum and found there was not a trace of pepsin in it. In all cases he found the gum was an insoluble aromatized resin. Despite that finding, Meunier ran some experiments of his own and concluded chewing gum was good for the digestion and "gum juice judiciously chewed empirically exercises real therapeutic action on the stomach digestion."[38]

Someone described as a "beauty specialist expert" told a New York City reporter at the end of 1910, "The worst enemy we beauty specialists have to combat is the gum chewing habit. You may not believe that chewing gum destroys a woman's good looks, yet I can assure you that it does." He explained that he had a young client who "fell off" in her looks in spite of all the beauty experts could do. One day he studied her face to discover the reason and he saw that her jaw was becoming square; there was a heavy look that was destroying the oval of her face. When the expert asked the young woman if she chewed gum, his client admitted she did. "Well, stop it," said the expert. "It is making your jaw square, and as your face gets heavy-jawed your eyes grow smaller. The eyes must be set in an oval face to be effective." According to the report from this expert, the client took his advice and stopped chewing gum. As a result, the beauty expert declared, her jaw "seemed to subside. Perhaps it did not really grow less, but her cheeks got plumper and the squareness was not so apparent."[39]

A warning against the excessive use of chewing gum was issued in January 1913 to the 2,500 athletes of the YMCA by Dr. S. H. Greene, Jr., dean of the association's physical examination staff. "The immoderate use of chewing gum may lead to stomach disorders and occasionally may also be a conducive cause of weak eyes," said Greene. He emphasized that he did not mean to say that a large number of the YMCA athletes carried the practice of chewing gum to the point where it became a vice, but some had. "Gum chewing in moderation has very little or no ill effect and at times it may even help digestion, but the gum should be thrown away when the sweetness has left it, for by that time the pepsin, which is the beneficial part of the preparation, has been entirely extracted."[40]

Dr. H. W. Wiley was a scientist who was described in news accounts as a "famous" former head of the U.S. government's chemistry department. He set in motion a storm of controversy when he proclaimed in 1914, "Gum chewing is bad as it weakens the salivary glands and should not be indulged in." A reporter on the *Fort Wayne News* in Indiana set out to interview local medical men and present their opinions on the topic. Said Dr. H. Bruggeman, "Strengthening the jaws of the chewers would seem to me about the most direct result of indulging the gum chewing habit. I can't see that it would have any very serious effect on the stomach." Dr. John Gilpin offered the opinion that chewing gum would hurt no one: "It, in the worst view, is only a habit lacking in delicacy. The salivary glands perform only an unimportant function in the process of digestion, and I hardly believe that the little overwork to which they might be subjected as a result of the undue excitement created by gum chewing would seriously impair them. "Dr. Eric Cruff believed that chewing gum was a habit that was vicious only in the sense that some people might falsely believe that by chewing gum they were going to cure a lot of stomach diseases. Cruff expressed serious doubt that gum would do any particular harm to a person's stomach and wondered whether Wiley could have been misquoted in the original piece. According to Dr. Edward Krause, chewing gum increased the flow of saliva and therefore aided digestion. But, he said, continued use of gum caused the saliva glands to deteriorate and after a time the proper flow of saliva could be produced only by the constant use of gum. That was where the danger came in. "Chewing gum itself is not dangerous, but by continually causing an excess flow of saliva the glands are weakened to such an extent that they refuse to perform their proper functions."[41]

One of those Fort Wayne doctors who was very emphatic in

describing the injurious effects of gum chewing was Dr. L. L. Gardner, who said, "There is nothing to this idea of gum aiding digestion, for instead of being an aid to digestion and a remedy to dyspepsia it is really a cause of dyspepsia." The habit of chewing gum stimulated the salivary glands to such an extent, he argued, that they became weakened after a time and were unable to perform their natural function. He pointed out that what he said did not refer to the occasional chewing of gum, but to gum chewing "as a formed habit." Gardner also delivered a specific warning against gum chewing that was directed to females: "It spoils a girl's good looks, for the constant movement of the jaws strengthens the muscles of the jaws and causes them to become enlarged. The jaw will, after a time, protrude or will widen at the back so an unsightly condition is produced. If the girls who chew gum constantly knew how it is spoiling their looks they would not use it." Did you ever notice a room full of "shop girls" who were in the habit of chewing gum while they worked, keeping it in their mouths all the time, Gardner asked the reporter rhetorically. "They are nearly all pale and anemic and most of them have dyspepsia. Their digestion has been injured and gum chewing is the cause," the physician insisted.

One anonymous doctor did not agree with Wiley, claiming there was nothing injurious in the habit because before the salivary glands would suffer serious injury the chewer would become aware of it. Those glands would tell the chewer of their condition and the person would stop chewing. Another anonymous doctor said gum chewing certainly was not an aid to the system in any way but did no harm. Last word went to County Health Officer Dr. E. Van Buskirk, who was of the opinion that the moderate use of chewing gum did no harm. On the contrary, he thought a stick of gum used after meals aided digestion by stimulating the salivary glands. "I don't see what injury could result from the moderate use of chewing gum," he said. "If chewed to excess, of course, it will do harm, as any excess will, but the moderate use of chewing gum will do no harm."[42]

At around the same time, Dr. T. H. McClintock of the New York Hospital spoke to a reporter and stated it was all in the mind that gum chewing aided digestion, despite the fact that thousands of people were unshaken in the belief that it did that very thing, if it did nothing else. "To millions of our citizens, chewing gum spells tranquility and contentment," declared Dr. J. MacClellan. For him that process was as though one were ironing out the creases in the mind; as though one were brushing away dull care, not by means of drugs or drink but by a perfectly natural and harmless process.[43]

A lengthy article that touted the psychological effects of the product appeared in newspapers in March 1916. The journalist who wrote the piece began by stating; "Are you worried? Chew gum. Do you lie awake at night? Chew gum. Are you depressed? Is the world against you? Chew gum." In an analysis of the benefit and harm of gum chewing, Dr. Anna Dwyer, chief physician of the Morals Court of Chicago and member of the state charities commission, was cited as saying, "It is an invariable physical impossibility for worriment and depression to come upon an individual who is chewing gum." She said that the brain centers were so situated that when the act of mastication was begun all sense of depression and melancholia left the mind. From a purely mechanical standpoint, she insisted, "worriment is impossible while the jaws are moving rapidly. When an individual chews gum he, or more frequently she, has no concern or worry for the world." Dwyer explained that she prescribed chewing gum to those of her patients who were habitually depressed. "In doing so I have no illusion about the delicacy or good taste of the practice, but I advocate it on account of the undoubted benefits it brings to those who are threatened with nervous troubles." She insisted that one never saw a person who in the act of chewing gum was anything but cheerful and happy. It was her belief that it all had to do with the brain and its contributing blood and nervous systems. "A suggestion comes to the center of mastication and it relays the message," she declared. "The blood floods to meet the demand of the rapidly moving jaws and the nearby center of depression becomes inactive. As soon as the act of chewing is well under way the feeling of sadness leaves." In a similar fashion the center that governed concentration was quieted and "intensity of thought departs. The edge is taken off of the feelings. The human being becomes more reposeful." As well, for those people who had difficulty sleeping at night, Dwyer urged them to use chewing gum, as she had known the practice to stop insomnia, if followed diligently. And, "When women become hysterical it often helps them to chew gum. It produces a calm which robs them of much of their unreasonable fear." Dwyer claimed she never advised the use of chewing gum except from

It was said, in 1916, that baseball pitcher Christy Mathewson's "uncanny imperturbability" when he was on the pitcher's mound was due to his steady use of chewing gum.

a purely medical standpoint: "There is no doubt that its widespread use will make a better natured race of people, but it may also make a thoughtless, more or less inconsequential race."[44]

According to Dr. Walter Peet, in 1916, a wager had been made between a physician and an athletic director as to the relative endurance of two athletes training for an event requiring great stamina. A road walk lasting from sunrise to sunset was selected as the test of endurance. It was stipulated there would be no stops allowed for nourishment, but the two men were to be allowed to eat while walking. During the race the physician frequently gave his man a fresh piece of chewing gum while the athletic trainer gave his man food and "copious drink." For a long while the race was even, with the two contestants going along neck and neck until the doctor's man began to pull away—he won by a wide

The stenographer who works her jaws all day long is a standard joke. But, on the other hand, she never breaks down from nervous prostration.

The gum chewing stenographer was a standard joke everywhere in 1916 but, it was said, there was a benefit because the gum-chewing steno never broke down from nervous prostration.

margin and finished in better physical condition than his opponent and was also less tired. Two weeks later the same two men did then same race again. Only this time the physician's man was given food and water while the athletic trainer's man got only chewing gum. Once again the contestant receiving gum won the race, and won it easily. An unrelated anecdotal athletic account appeared in the same article, related to Christy Mathewson, then one of pro baseball's greatest pitchers. "Friends of the renowned baseball player Christy Mathewson assert that, at least some measure of his uncanny imperturbability in the pitcher's box is due to his steady use of chewing gum while playing," said the piece.[45]

Later in 1916 another medical person got on board the gum-makes-you-happy bandwagon. Dr. Frank Crane was also a newspaper columnist (apparently syndicated) who started his November 17, 1916, column by observing, "Chewing gum got in bad, as they say on the street. That is to say, it seems to be the proper attitude of the elect to view the practice with scorn ... and the upright and the au fait generally regard it as vulgar." Then he mentioned that gum made people happy, in the same sense that Dwyer described. Crane then went on to say the chewing of gum was also the habit of one class of people especially, namely "the Alert.... Those who have to be up to pitch physically every minute, ready for prompt, decisive action, take readily to gum." Then he reeled off a long list of groups of people who chewed gum: soldiers, baseball players, engineers, sailors, farm hands, steel workers, automobile racers, golfers, tennis players, and marathon runners. With respect to the habit of chewing gum, Crane wrote, "It is characteristically American. For the American excels all other races, not in beef or brain, but in nervous energy. American is a state of nerves. And gum chewing is peculiarly adapted to people of exuberant nervous force." Concluded Crane, "Let the children chew gum. Think of how many worse things they might be doing."[46]

Another article full of praise for the good effects of chewing gum appeared in the spring of 1920, written by journalist Frederic Haskin. His piece began by saying the teeth of civilized man were dropping out because they were not given enough work to do. The mouth of the average child of 1920 did not grow because the foods it ate required so little mastication that it was given almost no exercise. Haskin wrote that the mouth of an aboriginal (Native American) child increased .36 of an inch in width between the ages of three and eight while the mouth of the average American child of 1920 increased only .03 of an inch in width over the same period. As a result, the teeth in the latter case did not have sufficient space, could not grind properly, became loose, and the mouth was prone to pyorrhea. The result of all that, argued Haskin, was that the teeth of modern man had become the weak spot in his physique. Reportedly, dental researchers had come up with all that data from studying hundreds of skulls of primitive children in the National Museum at Washington. Researchers found that 90 percent of the sets of teeth of the primitive children were virtually perfect, while not five percent of the teeth of the "civilized" children were perfect. But the teeth of modern day Native Americans were no better than their white contemporaries, although teeth of ancient Indians were mostly perfect.

Haskin argued that the food eaten was responsible for the difference. A child of primitive man ground his own grain with his jaws and chewed his dried meat. In the case of the civilized child, it was fed soft, prepared foods such as soft vegetables and meat from which all resistance had been cooked out. There was, though, unanimity of opinion as to the cure. That is, the teeth had to be given more work and exercise. Haskin issued a call for a return to the good old days when the American household was familiar with a piece of beefsteak that was "normal and tough." Those unanimous experts also suggested a supply of not ground wheat be kept around the house, and that the children in those households get in the habit of chewing it. "They insist that the practice of chewing gum which is generally taboo, be made respectable and that it be given general encouragement. They urge gum manufacturers to make it tougher," concluded Haskin.[47]

A week later an editorial on Haskin's article appeared in a Connecticut newspaper. The editor commented, "The more you wear a pair of shoes, the sooner they wear out, the farther you drive an automobile, the sooner its tires go; but the more you use your teeth, the better they last." Following that, he added, "In fact, the American craving for chewing gum can be traced in large part to the fact that we may give ourselves sufficient exercise as talkers, but we don't give ourselves sufficient exercise as chewers, and there is a physiological need that finds expression in chewing gum."[48]

During a session of the U.S. Congress in the spring of 1921, Senator Lawrence Sherman of Illinois was speaking in favor of a bill to aid Amer-

ican meat packers. Pepsin, a much touted part of the chewing gum industry, was a byproduct that came out of the nation's packing houses, from
pigs. Said Sherman, "What under heaven would the gum chewers do if
pepsin could not be furnished now in commercial form.... Chewing
gum never could have reached its present magnitude if it had not been
for the pepsin taken from the packing plants of the country. The confirmed dyspeptic chews pepsin gum. No hurtful results follows." And,
"It is not like other bad habits. He has some excuse for it. It produces
no rosy blush upon any of his features, and no chronic habit results
except the working of the jaws, and that probably is a blessing, for while
we are working them that way we are not working them some other
way to the detriment of our neighbors." Concluded the senator, "So
out of that seemingly humble thing, has come a great industry. It is a
safety valve for the nervous and a minor activity to us all when under
stress."[49]

7

Employment and
the Courts

With so much media attention devoted to gum, it was not surprising that employers sometimes responded to the habit and its users, as did the courts. Judges always came down hard on users, when they addressed the matter, and employers did so as well, usually. Sometimes, though, the habit was encouraged by employers. For example, a very brief item in an Oakland, California, newspaper in 1875 claimed that girls who worked in millinery stores in that city were soon to be supplied with chewing gum on the job. Reportedly that was to be done so the girls would not "waste time in talking."[1]

An 1883 news account noted that in a Division Street (New York City) millinery, spruce gum was given to the employees by management. "There is a curious thing about this business. We can't get the girls to work well without it," explained a management spokesman. Those female employees all worked together in one large workroom and the bosses found that they talked so much that a good deal of time was lost from work, and when there was a rush of business it often delayed orders significantly. All that happened despite the fact the employees were paid on a piece work basis.

To correct the situation the forewoman suggested that an order be issued that the girls do no talking during work hours. "We put this into effect, but you might as well have tried to stop a flood with a bar of soap," said the spokesman. "To see the tricks they would resort to just to get a moment of gossip together was quite instructive." Next, the company tried a system of levying fines on the talkers, but this also proved to be unsuccessful, "They would lose their week's wages rather than not have their talk." Pondering the problem, management thought of constructing a lot of little work rooms—one for each employee—but decided not to proceed as they worried such a system would leave them with no employees at all.

Then management turned to what it called "bribery," bringing in some spruce gum to be given out. The forewoman announced that each girl would get one piece of the gum in the morning and another at night, on the condition they did not talk to each other during working hours. According to the spokesman, that plan worked admirably: "You can go up in the work-shop, and all the noise you will hear is that of a lot of jaws opening and closing. Hardly a word is spoken. The girls are contented. The problem is solved. A girl must move her mouth some way, and if it isn't chewing it is talking." It was also said that every workplace along that street had adopted the same plan.[2]

Agassiz Murphy was a guest at the Leland Hotel in Chicago in June 1890 and had been there for about one month. Each night as he returned to his hotel at about 6 p.m. he passed hundreds of girls who had just finished their shift at one of the big dry goods houses nearby and were homeward bound. For him, the remarkable thing about them was that every one was chewing gum "with the utmost velocity. So eagerly did they chew that rather than graduate the movement of their jaws to suit the words they poured into each other's ears they kept right on chewing, two chews to the second, cutting the words in the middle or toward the end, it all depended upon the length of the word." Murphy was not at all surprised that these girls should chew gum, as he found that to be "natural," but was only struck by the "ferociousness" of their chewing.

Becoming curious as to the reason for such an intensity of chewing, one afternoon he went into the workplace from which he had seen the young women exit. Inside the building Murphy reported he saw on one of the floors a big sign bearing the words; "Any clerk caught chewing gum between business hours will be discharged instanter." That sign allowed Murphy to say he then understood why the chewing he witnessed was so intense: "It was simply that they can't chew gum during the day, and when they get out they have to make up for lost time."[3]

At the Central Telephone Exchange in Detroit new rules came into effect in May 1891 that prohibited the chewing of gum by the employees during working hours, banned "flirtatious" conversation over the phones, and required those female operators to say "number" instead of "hello" when they took a call. Because of those rules the day shift girls—paid $16 a month—were said to be ready to strike. However, they were not organized and feared their chances of success would be small. As a result no action was taken, except perhaps grumbling. Much the same thing applied to the night girls—paid $20 a month. All the operators were reportedly mad and muttering over those rules, which went into effect around May 1. The mood of the girls was captured by a reporter who wrote, "Life without the soul-satisfying chewing gum is a bore."[4]

Because of an order issued by their foreman that they must refrain from chewing gum during working hours, 65 girls employed as band wrappers for the Samuel Cupples Envelope Company in St. Louis, Missouri, went out on strike in January 1903 and refused to return unless the order was withdrawn. Miss Geiseman, the forewoman, said she had no objection to the girls chewing gum during the noon hour but that it was necessary to prevent them from chewing gum during working hours. No outcome of the situation was reported.[5]

Later in 1903 it was reported that gum chewing by waitresses and maids in hotels was prohibited by the waiters' union and the Hotel Owners' Association of Chicago. Any woman found to be chewing gum was subject to discharge. The waitresses and chambermaids were furious at this new rule, demanding the right to chew gum if they wanted to. Industrial action was threatened. For their part, the proprietors objected to having wads of gum stuck all over the place. Finally the dispute was settled when it was agreed that if the girls received some increase in their wages they would not chew gum while on duty.[6]

Late in January 1904 it was reported that the Boston School Board was deep in a campaign against Boston school teachers who chewed gum. The matter was brought before a meeting of the school board by a member and was then subjected to vigorous discussion. Said a reporter, "The teachers one and all indignantly deny the accusation in language quite expressive, but scarcely as elegant as would be expected from a Boston teacher." A school official from Boston's Melrose School declared, "Melrose has never been troubled with such a heinous habit, and I know for positive fact that there is not one teacher in our entire corps who chews gum in public." And, "I cannot even think of such a practice among our teachers, and I am sure that if there was even one case it would have been brought to my attention."

Richard W. Nutter of the Malden Center Grammar School explained, "Malden teachers are dignified and never even think of chewing gum in public." Nutter added that during the years that he had taught school he had never seen a teacher chew gum: "It would be a bad example to the public and one which the children would readily acquire if they saw their teacher eating or chewing in class. If any one chews gum it is very probable that he or she would soon have an impediment in his speech, and in that way would be unable to properly articulate in speaking." He concluded, "Gum chewing in public should not be tolerated anywhere." With respect to this controversy in general, a reporter observed, "How humiliating must be such a plebian scandal in the heart of Boston's educational circles.... Boston, our modern Athens, whose teachers chew gum! Athens indeed! Imagine Plato, Aristotle, or Socrates chewing gum, or anything, indeed, but 'the rag.'"[7]

A different report on the controversy declared that a supposed canvass of the teachers revealed that "scores" of the teachers were gum chewers and it was learned that most of those came from Maine or New Hampshire—the spruce gum producing states—where they acquired the habit. Under consideration by the committee on hygiene of the school board was the advisability of issuing an order to prohibit Boston teachers from chewing gum. No outcome was reported.[8]

A partner in a prominent law firm in Syracuse, New York, declared, also in January 1904, "I don't suppose there is any real harm in gum chewing, but our stenographers are requested not to indulge in the habit, if we observe any signs of their doing so." He continued, "For one thing it makes me nervous to watch that continual movement of the jaws while a girl is at work. It seems to hypnotize me, and I can't pay attention to what I am doing myself."[9]

A 1908 letter to the editor of a Syracuse, New York, newspaper complained about gum-chewing clerks in retail outlets. With a state fair then underway in the city, the letter writer wondered why the manners of clerks had not been refurbished, as had the stores in anticipation of a retailing increase due to the fair. "The flagrant rudeness of which our clerks are guilty is gum chewing. Not only is gum chewing a rudeness in itself, but it breeds all indifference of speech and insolence of manner," he complained. He believed that no gum chewer actually engaged in "negotiations with the elastic quid" was ever truly courteous. "This is a proposition which we are prepared to defend to the uttermost and one which we respectfully urge upon the consideration of all employers." In conclusion, he urged the merchants of Syracuse to banish gum chewing from behind the counters and dreamed "what a boon it would be to the habitual shopper."[10]

A municipal reform movement that got underway in 1908 in Des Moines, Iowa, started off with a new commission form of city government. As a part of that a free municipal school was opened for the compulsory education of policemen. The school was held in a large room of the new city library. Faculty of the school taught subjects to the policemen such as criminal law and evidence, criminology, physical culture, first aid, mathematics, and civil government. Among the various forms of discipline imposed on those police pupils in class were no speaking aloud without permission, no eating apples, and no chewing gum.[11]

Newly added, in November 1911, to the list of things sailors in the U.S. Navy were not allowed to do was to chew gum. An official decree had been issued by the Navy Department stating that chewing gum would no longer form any part of ships' stores or of naval stocks ashore. Captain William P. Fullam, former commander of the *Mississippi*, was the party responsible for the prohibition of gum chewing and gave the following reason: "The habit of chewing gum at training stations and on board ship leads to constant reports for chewing gum in ranks, at quarters and at other times when it is highly improper and unmilitary." Fullam continued, "If men are encouraged to form this habit on board ship the navy deliberately invites them to do something one minute, for which they may be punished the next." The absolute prohibition of the habit was necessary to the enforcement of good discipline, argued the captain.[12]

In a different account about the U.S. Navy ban on gum, Fullam was quoted as having branded the chewing gum habit as "decidedly objectionable for obvious reasons."[13]

All that fuss by the U.S. Navy over gum caused the *Washington Post* to deliver an ironic and sarcastic editorial. "The news comes as a revelation and shock to the public, tempered, however, by a thank goodness that it is no worse," the editor wrote. "The further statement that thousands of the men behind the guns have been court-martialed and penalized for chewing gum at formations also gives us that staggering feeling that proceeds from breaking the news abruptly." He went on to say that until then little or nothing with respect to the methods employed to put an end to this "species of depravity" had been given publicity. Inasmuch as the practice of chewing gum was introduced in order to discourage or displace the use of tobacco in the Navy, the editor wondered just what substitute for the "vicious pepsin" was available. "That the men must have something to satisfy the demands of the maxillary glands is a fact as old as the history of navigation and is not to be ignored," he concluded.[14]

In the spring of 1915 coach Guy Nickalls of the Yale rowing crew put a ban on gum chewing. Nickalls declared chewing gum was injurious. Yale oarsmen in former years, it was reported, were noted for their consumption of gum.[15]

In 1917 Major-General John F. O'Ryan of the U.S. Army declared in Albany, New York, that it was up to the "real solider" to abstain from smoking on the streets, and chewing gum while in uniform. O'Ryan had a long talk with the New York State governor about his no smoking orders the day before. Later he announced, "There is no order prohibiting smoking by soldiers of the New York division." Explained O'Ryan, "Instructions were recently issued to all regional commanders to caution their men concerning military bearing and conduct generally during the period of mobilizations. These instructions referred incidentally to smoking and gum chewing when in uniform and on the city streets." O'Ryan added that it was up to the soldiers themselves to increase the public estimate of the guard. "It has been the unwritten rule for years in some of our units that soldiers in uniform should not smoke or chew gum on the streets."[16]

William Brady was a well-known medical doctor and syndicated columnist. The main focus of his column of April 28, 1919, was "Infection in Stores." Presumably a catalyst for the topic had been the major killer outbreak of influenza in 1918–1919. Much of the column was about how to treat new clothing purchased from a store—for example, always wash the item before wearing it for the first time. Another item discussed was whether or not taking clothing to a laundry, and retrieving same, posed an infection problem for the customers and the staff. Brady's answer was that it did not. Goods bought in stores in packages marked sterile should not be believed, said the doctor. When the customer took such a purchase home she should sterilized the item herself by boiling, baking or steaming. He gave the same advice for shaving brushes and all other brushes purchased at retail outlets. When purchased they were to be taken home and, at the very least, washed with soap and water and dried in direct sunlight for several hours, or, preferably, boiled. Clerks in stores afflicted with anything resembling an alleged "cold" should be required, he argued, to wear a suitable number (at least three) of layers of fine gauze as a mask. For a final piece of advice, Dr. Brady said, "Gum chewing in business hours should be prohibited."[17]

If messages about chewing gum delivered to employees by employers were sometimes mixed, the messages from judges to those who appeared in their courtrooms were unanimously negative. Justice Bradley put the district of Washington, D.C., on notice on January 7, 1897, when he announced that hereafter there would be no tobacco chewing or gum chewing allowed in his court.[18]

Some two years later, on June 2, 1899, Judge Baker interrupted the unintelligible testimony of a witness in his Chicago courtroom by saying, "Take that stuff out of your mouth. How do you expect me to hear what you are saying when your mouth is full of a wad of gum?" Baker continued, "The practice of gum-chewing on the witness stand must stop. If you talk as plainly as you can the jury will have trouble enough hearing you, without your making it worse by rolling that great wad under your tongue."[19]

Around August or September 1902 a judge in St. Louis, Missouri, fined a young woman for contempt of court for chewing gum in his courtroom. Just as the judge took his seat on the bench he spied the lady in question, who had been summoned as a witness in a case, busily engaged with a large wad of gum. The judge ordered her to cease. She obeyed temporarily but later resumed chewing, whereupon she was brought forward before the bar, severely lectured by the judge, and then fined $10 for contempt. As a result of that incident, an editor with the *Nashville Banner* newspaper was moved to comment, "One is sometimes constrained to wish that people who are addicted to the habit could be fined each time they put chewing um into their mouths, in and out of court. It is one of the ugliest of habits and while it is not so prevalent as at one time it is still far too common." In conclusion, this editor declared, "Perhaps in this matter one could not do better than follow the advice of an eminent Nashville educator, who used to advise his pupils, 'Chew gum if you will and have to, but first lock your door, turn out the gas and crawl under the bed.'"[20]

On September 23, 1903, an assault and battery case was being tried in the First Criminal Court in Jersey City, New Jersey. Isaac Goldhorn, counsel for the defendant, protested when one of the female witnesses was on the stand and permitted to chew gum and talk at the same time. The judge agreed with Goldhorn and so the witness was compelled to hold the gum in her hand until she finished giving testimony.[21]

From the New York *Evening Post* in March 1904 came another courtroom story. In an unidentified court a lawyer was summing up a case to a jury in which the jaws of several jurymen were chewing away. As the lawyer sat down, Judge Marean fixed his eyes on the jury box and said, with displeasure, "I have had occasion once before to speak of gum chewing in the jury box. I do not mean anything personal, but I wish to say that I think the habit unworthy of the position of a juryman. That is all." Reportedly, "The jaws stopped working and the case went on."[22]

When a San Francisco reporter discussed the chewing gum habit in his city, he remarked that the craze had passed from the telephone and shop girls and gone on to spread amazingly. He claimed that it all began locally with the jurors in the city's graft trials. Forced to sit through long hours for five or six days a week in the courtroom and deprived of the solace of cigar or tobacco, the jurors chewed gum. "The practice spread to the members of the juries which have followed, and now the casual visitor who drops in on one of the court rooms where any of the trials are in progress will see a roomful of slowly grinding jaws, jurors and court room habitués alike, chewing the produce of the chicle factories," he asserted.[23]

At a police court in Washington, D.C., in August 1909, Judge Kimball imposed a ban on chewing gum in his court. It was a ban that applied to witnesses and defendants.[24]

Magistrate Appleton stopped in the middle of a hearing in his courtroom at Yorkville Court in New York on February 11, 1911, and looked toward the center of the courtroom where several policemen were sitting, waiting for the cases they were involved in to be called. Suddenly the magistrate said, "Look at that officer. See his jaws wag. Fine spectacle he is making of himself. Gum-chewing is an accomplishment that does credit to the department, especially if indulged in at court." Following that rebuke the offending police officer removed his gum and Appleton went on with the hearing.[25]

When a man up on charges appeared before Judge McKinley in Chicago on March 15, 1912, and was in the act of chewing gum, he was rebuked by the judge. "Young man, one of the reasons we have so much crime in this country is that there are so many people in it like you, who have no respect for the law. You don't know how to behave yourself," McKinley told the defendant. "Anyone who had an atom of good manners wouldn't be standing up at the bar of this court in the predicament that you are in while chewing gum." A journalist with Chicago's *Daily Socialist* was sarcastic in his response, mocking the "majesty" of the law and the arbitrary fear it induced in people: "We shall look forward now to grand jury investigations of the men higher up in this gum-chewing incident. There is ground for action against the men who make gum and sell it to these anarchistic persons whom they persuade to chew it."[26]

When a well-publicized trial for white slavery opened in San Francisco in the summer of 1913, a newspaper article appeared outlining the details. Appearing alongside the article was a small boxed section that gum chewing was strictly forbidden in the courtroom, as it played havoc with the court's dignity. Bailiffs during the opening session of the Diggs white slavery trial were kept busy warning spectators, "especially girls," that such "violent mastication was strictly against the rules of the court and is extremely subversive of its dignity." Reportedly, a "score" of women were thus warned, "several leaving the room in high dudgeon."[27]

During her testimony in a court case in New York City in November 1915, Mrs. Gofoski was chewing vigorously, said a reporter, on a "generous mouthful" of gum. Presiding Judge John P. Kirby ordered her to stop. Gofoski, in an undertone, expressed the opinion that the court need not worry about her gum. For that observation Kirby declared Gofoski guilty of contempt of court and fined her $5. A witness fee of 70 cents was due her, and so she settled her account by paying the court $4.30.[28]

Gum Goes Abroad ... but Does Not Stick

Over the period covered by this book chewing gum was a distinctly and uniquely American habit, as drive-in theaters would be many decades later. Foreigners were often bemused by the practice of chewing gum and sometimes baffled and bewildered. American tourists and military personnel took the habit with them around the world but despite strong efforts, it never became very entrenched away from North America, although articles would sometimes dispute that idea. Canadians, though, took to it with about the same prevalence and enthusiasm as did Americans. Chewing gum was unknown outside of America in the 1870s but established everywhere, at least to a slight degree, by the end of the 1910s. England was the foreign country most heavily involved with chewing gum.

One of the earliest mentions of foreign nations came in a New England newspaper that remarked, in October 1882, "America is responsible for having introduced the vice of chewing gum into England. That is, it introduced chewing gum, and when the English girls began chewing gum the evil was established." Reportedly, one U.S. port shipped 50,000 pieces of spruce gum to England each week, enough to supply 10,000 moderate chewers with a day's allowance of the item.[1]

Enough inroads had been made by the habit into England by the spring of 1890 that a London newspaper, the *Pall Mall Gazette*, published an article (reprinted in America) on the subject. "One of the worst habits of American women is gum chewing," said the piece. "The habit seems so innocent and harmless that nothing much can be said against it from outside appearances; but, according to the medical men of America, it destroys the teeth, invites dyspepsia, and brings many small evils in its train that grow to be distinctly inconvenient and unhealthy." According to the piece, the practice of gum chewing was being introduced into England by the American Confectionary Company, which, of course, claimed the product to be full of advantages. To sort out the truth a reporter for the *Gazette* called at the Regent Street offices of American Confectionary to see if the habit was making any headway in England. Said company manager Miss Pope, "What smoking is to men gum chewing is to women in our country. Women chew gum all day. In the streets, in the tram cars, anywhere, they're never without their bit of gum. Some women have actually had their jaws paralyzed through working them too hard." When the reporter asked her if she thought her company could ever make chewing gum fashionable in London, Pope said, "Why not? There's a demand for it already among the men. We are introducing it to our customers by putting a small stick into every box of sweets. This kindles their curiosity. Of course the sale of gum among our American customers is immense. They are delighted at being able to get it in Europe." Pope went on to tell the reporter there were about 15 different types of gum with peppermint, licorice and spring-green being among the favorite flavors, although Adams' tutti frutti was cited as the most popular flavor. Some flavors were more costly, spring-green was sold in six-penny packets and ordinary flavors were bought in halfpenny and penny sticks. With regard to the lasting power of gum, Pope declared, "They will stand about four days' hard chewing. Casual chewers will make a stick last a month. The gum never wears out, but it gets sticky after a time and clings to the teeth."[2]

Just a couple of weeks later an English newspaper column, Eugene Fields' London Letter, remarked that gum chewing was an American vice exclusively and was likely to remain so due to the relatively high cost of the product. In the U.S. a small pack of the brand Yucatan cost five cents while in England, according to this source, the same item carried the "exorbitant" price tag of sixpence (12 cents American). "We cannot hope to introduce the vice into England so long as we accompany the vice with such flagrant extortion," he concluded.[3]

In 1891 there was a prosecution brought by the state over the sale of chewing gum, at the Hanley borough police court. It was a prosecution brought under the food and drug act, but it bogged down in court as no agreement could be reached on classifying gum as either a food or a drug. Consequently the case was ended with the imposition of a fine (of unstated amount) on the retailer of the chewing gum on the grounds the substance was sold to the prejudice of the purchaser, inasmuch as it was not in the nature of the substance and quality of the article demanded by the purchaser, "who asked for gum and got paraffine wax." With reference to that failed prosecution, the London publication the *Lancet* grumbled, "There is no room for doubting the inconvenience and danger which may arise from the accumulation of a mass of paraffine wax in the intestines; and yet when any legal interference with the sale of chewing gum, containing fifty percent of this substance, is attempted" it fails. A journalist putting this piece together came up with the following definition of chewing gum: "A substance of very variable composition, ignorantly employed by children, which, when containing paraffine wax, may lead to very grave dangers, and the sale of which should be prohibited."[4]

Regarding the status of gum abroad, a brief report in the summer of 1892 commented; "In England they do not chew gum, looking down on the habit as vulgar and even disgusting, but Australia seems to have taken it kindly, and is already making large demands on the resources of the American gum manufacturers."[5]

London's *Daily Mail* reprinted an article from the *British Medical Journal* in 1897 that raised the issue of whether there was any reason for supposing the practice of gum chewing, "so prevalent" in the U.S., was on the increase in England. "We have made some inquiries, and have ascertained that many young women—students, actresses, and others—appear to have acquired this disgusting habit, and are inveterate chewers," said the medical publication. "We have examined specimens of chewing gum obtained from various fashionable sweet shops in London, and find that, as a rule, it consists of rubber, flavored with aniseed or peppermint, or some other aromatic substance."[6]

The above article prompted an editorial response from the *Daily Mail* a few days later. Interviewed for the piece was Hubert Beaumont, managing director of the retailer Fuller's, who denied the "impeachment" of gum being made out of rubber. He explained that gum sold at Fuller's outlets was made from the sap of a Mexican tree. "It is a purely vegetable substance, and perfectly harmless." Beaumont took exception to the assertion of the medical journal that it was a "disgusting habit" and pointed out that for over 40 years the American public "have used chewing gum as a strength sustainer, an aid to digestion, and a thirst preventer." According to Beaumont there were other benefits from the habit, as it had lately been found to be of great use to cyclists and other athletes, and "it has also been adopted as a cure for the excessive tobacco habit." However, he did acknowledge that certain "inferior and cheap gums" were made from paraffin wax. "I understand that the manufacturers of paraffin wax gum are obliged by law to state on the labels of their article that it is not to be swallowed," he added. "This is a most proper precaution, but it does not apply to properly made chewing gum."[7]

A brief press report from London in September 1898 remarked that the health authorities in that city had issued a warning against the use of American chewing gum, which was reportedly becoming very popular among children in London's East End. According to the account, "The authorities consider it more dangerous than the ice cream which the Italians sell in the streets, and against which there has been a rigorous crusade." However, no other details were provided on the dangers of gum.[8]

When J. J. Amend, traveling representative of one of the largest chewing gum manufacturers in America (unnamed), was interviewed in New Orleans in late 1900, he was asked if his firm exported much chewing gum. He replied, "Only to England and Australia. None of the European nations take kindly to chewing gum. They won't have it at all in Germany, and there is absolutely no sale for it in France or, in fact, on the continent. England uses a great deal, but they don't care much for a variety of brands there."[9]

In the summer of 1901, U.S. journalist J. A. Morris wrote that the greatest portion of chewing gum was manufactured for home consumption, although the export trade was growing. Within recent years the gum habit had "invaded" Europe, Asia, Africa, Australia, and the South Sea Islands, he wrote. Reportedly, gum was used "a great deal" in South Africa, and during the late "unpleasantness" with Spain the sale of gum to the American soldiers was "enormous." Manila was said to then be a good market, as were Samoa and Honolulu. Markets were opening up in China, Japan and India, with "considerable consignments going to France and Scandinavia. Declared Morris, "Points at which nervous energy is tremendously expended are exactly those points where chewing gum finds its most ready sale."[10]

An overly melodramatic report about the spread of gum use appeared in a Kansas City newspaper in the spring of 1902. It argued that no matter whether the constitution followed the flag or not, it was certain that chewing gum did. From the United States, its real birthplace as an article of commerce, said the piece, it had moved with the soldiers into the new island possessions and moved into favor there almost from the start. "The tropics have taken kindly to it. There is yet hope for the civilization of the Filipino," wrote the journalist. "That hope lies in chewing gum. When every man, woman and child in the archipelago shall be chewing gum the flag will float tranquilly over a peaceable people. If we are a progressive nation and are leading the other countries of the world, it is so because, as a nation, we chew gum." And, "To bear this out is the fact that the United States has been rising in importance for the last half century—in other words, since the first production of chewing gum as we know it today."[11]

Five years later, in the summer of 1906 a reporter with the London *Express* came up with an unusual reason for the supposed increased consumption of gum in England. His account (reprinted in America) remarked on the fact that the adoption of the automobile as a means of transit meant the drivers and even passengers of autos could not smoke as they usually would have. Cars of the era, of course, were mostly completely exposed to the weather. Because "smoking is not consistent with comfort or careful driving ... the enjoyment of either pipe, cigar or cigarette is out of the question when speed exceeds six miles an hour," said the article. "Even the abstemious passenger finds it irksome, especially when called upon every few minutes to remove accumulations of tobacco dust from the region of the eyes." And, as a result, "they have resorted to American chewing gum in place of tobacco."

Prior to that, though, a number of odd and unsuccessful inventions had been tried in order to keep the tobacco habit going in a moving, open automobile. Inventions tried included a pipe with its own windshield and cigar and cigarette holders that were significantly tilted. Given that smoking was impossible in such situations, deciding on what to chew as a replacement had been, reportedly, something of a problem. Chewing tobacco was found to be wanting, for unspecified reasons. Drivers and passengers were in this quandary when an American chewing gum manufacturer arrived at the Hotel Cecil in London. Noticing the enforced abstemiousness of the drivers, he distributed packets of chewing gum among them "as a judicious advertisement." And from that moment on, declared the *Express* reporter, the problem was solved. "There are now dozens of men using the principal London garage to whom chewing gum appears indispensable. It is innocent and it is cheap. It is also popularized and guaranteed to cure indigestion."[12]

Two weeks later another report from London, commenting on the above, noted that while chewing gum had been known in the United Kingdom for several years, it had not done well until a year or so earlier when men who went driving in cars found they could not comfortably smoke while in a moving auto. "Chewing tobacco is undreamt of except among sailors, and so the motorist took to chewing gum," declared the account. Then the "lady of fashion"—who never took kindly to the gum habit before—picked up the practice from her male friends who were motorists.[13]

Toward the end of 1906, what was described as an "unusual" request from Germany was received by the U.S. Department of Commerce in Washington, D.C., which, said a reporter, showed "how the whole world is gradually becoming Americanized." That request was from a concern that wanted to be put in touch with manufacturers of chewing gum with a view to importing the item into Germany to sell to tourists and natives. It appeared from what the Germany inquiry said that the United States was "the only country in the world where such an article as chewing gum is made, and the American tourists have introduced it into Germany and caused the Germans themselves to set aside their steins long enough to try it. The result has been that they now relish and crave it."[14]

In the late spring of 1907 a reporter said Rome had "escaped the vice" of the chewing gum habit until recently when California sculptor Arthur Putnam arrived in Rome and brought the gum habit with him. He then introduced it to the locals. Putnam did not chew but he left the impression that all Americans did, and so the habit caught on and "now the faces of the aristocracy here are distorted at nearly all hours of the day beyond recognition." Chewing in public had become quite the thing, continued the reporter: "The Italian's long practice wrestling with unwilling macaroni has made him particularly fitted for a vigorous if not an extremely artistic attack on gum." Rome's American drug store was doing a big business in gum and new shipments had been ordered from the U.S.A.[15]

Many years after the court case against the retailer of gum had collapsed when the item could not be classified as food or drug, the issue seemed resolved. In 1910 a British court held pepsin chewing gum to be a drug under the English pure drug act and fined a druggist for selling some that contained less pepsin than was called for by the label.[16]

When 29 students and three professors from the University of Commerce in Cologne, Germany, were in America in October 1910, they found the gum chewing habit "looming large" among the wonders of the U.S.A. That caused a reporter to remark that there had been attempts to establish gum in Europe but the results had been "inconsiderable."[17]

Despite occasional articles that implied at least some popularity existed for gum in England, an equal number of articles seemed to contradict that idea. At the end of 1911 a news account stated that a group of American promoters had begun operations in London to make chewing gum a habit throughout the UK. "Tired of the refusal of the English people to buy American chewing gum, these promoters have arrived in town determined to force it down the British throats, figuratively speaking." Offices had been rented in the Strand and one of the largest makers of gum in America was in charge of the operations. The intention of that firm was to form a stock company with a capital of $750,000 for the manufacture and sale of gum in the UK. Already secured by that maker was the interest of one of the largest and richest London druggists with shops all over town. But, said the article, "Try an Englishman with a piece of gum and after rolling it about in his mouth he invariably swallows it. He knows nothing about its uses and apparently is dead to all its virtues."[18]

Two months later the respected British medical publication, *The Lancet* ascribed the popularity of gum chewing in America to "national nervousness" and other causes that included "most probably, the great dryness of the atmosphere."[19]

Leopold Kulka, trade investigator for the Hungarian government, was on an official visit to the United States in May 1912. While in Detroit he visited the R-C-H automobile plant. Kulka told plant sales manager F. R. Bump, "The Hungarians are American mad. They try and ape you at every opportunity. Their ideal of an American permits no mustache or beard." He added, "From somewhere they have got the idea that Americans are inveterate gum chewers, and about half of them are going about with big supplies of American gum."[20]

Another article on the supposed pervasiveness of gum chewing in the UK appeared in the summer of 1913. That story declared: "The English are chewing gum! No longer can John Bull make fun of Uncle Sam for the gum chewing habit. No longer can English cartoonists picture Americans with a wad of gum in their mouths, their faces distorted as they chew. The English short story writer has been robbed of another character—the gum chewing American tourist." Years ago, continued the article, only Americans chewed gum. When they chewed gum in England they were laughed at. English people nudged one another on the street when they saw a gum-chewing American. But that time was then all in the past. The U.S. journalist who wrote the piece admitted no one knew how the fad started there in the UK (one reason being that there was no evidence it had started) but went on to proclaim, "Be that as it may, the English nation is past taking from the States the title of the gum chewing nation, a title that Americans are only too glad to give up." It was a habit said to be increasing rapidly in England but, again, no supporting evidence was presented. Also, the practice was not confined to one class of people either, with typists, bookkeepers, office boys, and their employers all taking up the habit, along with English factory girls. "The nobility has not yet taken up the habit, and is not likely to do so; but the 'good middle class' has already gained great headway in gum chewing." In conclusion, said the reporter; "When a habit once fastens itself upon the English it is hard to break off, so by the time Americans have ceased gum chewing English people will still be chewing. And then it will be the American humorists' turn to make fun of the gum chewing habit of the British."[21]

Also in July 1913, a one-week campaign was waged in Frederick, Maryland, for contributions to a fund being raised for the benefit of the Greek soldiers who were engaged in a new war with the Bulgarians. That call to America for aid came from Queen Sophia of Greece. When a similar call for aid was made in Washington, D.C., it received $1,500 almost immediately, as that sum was raised in 10 minutes at a meeting at a Greek church in the nation's capital. It was hoped the week-long campaign in Frederick would raise $100. Money raised was mostly to aid the families of soldiers who were killed or wounded on the field of battle, with no part of the money going toward prosecuting the war. "It is understood, however, that a large part of the money from the Greeks in America will go to help buy chewing gum for the soldiers," said a journalist. "The American boys in the Greek Army have been given the credit for the discovery of the merits of chewing gum." They did not know much about chewing gum in Greece, wrote the journalist, until the approximately 55,000 American men returned home to Greece to fight for the mother country and brought the chewing gum habit with them. "Now the army officers say that thirst and hunger can be allayed for hours by the use of chewing gum, and the Queen has appealed for help in America. 200,000 sticks will be immediately brought, and given the soldiers."[22]

After a consignment of gum was shipped off to Greece, that American firm received, in due course, a letter of thanks from the Hon. Angelica Contostavcon, lady in waiting to her majesty Queen Sophia of Greece: "Dear Sirs: Her majesty the Queen desires to convey to you her sincerest thanks for your most generous gift of chewing gum for the use of our army. Her majesty fully appreciates your promptitude to offer such a liberal quantity of an article so useful to our soldiers in the field.[23]

An April 1914 article in the *Wall Street Journal* declared that although the English had long fought "that Yankee habit," chewing gum was then to be seen at most of the London confectioners, and many of the sweet shops in the provinces sold the well-known American gums. It was said that London dealers sold "large amounts" of it and English men and women "no longer look over their shoulders to see if any one is watching when they pay their two-pence for gum." An unnamed American who recently returned home from a trip to Europe predicted that within 10 years all Europe would be chewing gum and, as was the case with all converts, they would develop the habit to a stronger degree than it had been developed in the United States.[24]

When World War I was in full swing there was a flurry of articles about gum. A February 1917 piece in the Manchester *Guardian* (reprinted in the *Washington Post*) said that according to figures just published, the English had "suddenly" become a nation of gum chewers and the manufacturers stated that in the past six months they had increased their monthly sales in England from three million to 20 million sticks.

Declared the reporter, "It has been suggested that the habit has been introduced by the Canadian soldiers who, of course, share the Americans' fondness for chewing gum, but we are assured that they have nothing to do with it. The spread of the habit is purely a triumph of natural weakness and advertising." With respect to what groups were the most enthusiastic adherents to the habit, the reader was told they were not women clerks but were soldiers and then munitions workers, with the navy a fair third. For the previous four years chewing gum had been sold at army and navy canteens, but it had been only recently that the item was issued as an army ration: "The soldiers' theory is that it steadies his nerves to have something to chew on, and it certainly keeps his otherwise parched throat moist in times of stress."[25]

A month later an American reporter noted that for many years U.S. chewing gum manufacturers had tried to teach foreign countries to appreciate their product, advertising it assiduously in France, England, and Germany, but with "small success. The non–American couldn't understand it. He tried to swallow it, and when he couldn't he gave it up as incomprehensible nonsense," explained the newsman. "Over in London, where it was called 'American chewing candy,' many shops called attention to it, but the Britishers passed it by and went on buying toffee and lollipops and Turkish delights." Then "suddenly and without warning" the situation changed—cited was the increase mentioned in the above paragraph—and the English newspapers could not understand it. Mentioning the idea that gum steadied the nerves and kept thirst at bay, the reporter thought the explanation for the increase in sales was simple: "It is more than probable that the Canadian soldiers imported this information to the English Tommies—and experience did the rest." He concluded, "The chewing of gum by the British may now be added to the results of the 'American invasion' that we used to read so much about before the war."[26]

In May 1917 a U.S. reporter went so far as to declare, "American chewing gum has conquered the world. It has been a tedious process—extending over 20 years—but now the triumph is complete." It was a conclusion based on an announcement made by the U.S. Department of Commerce's bureau of foreign and domestic commerce. For the first nine months of the fiscal year exports of chewing gum had averaged a little over $100,000 a month, in spite of German interference with shipping lanes, with the result that America's export of chewing gum for the fiscal year would top $1 million, a figure never before reached. Trade in gum in 1917 was 500 times as large as in 1894, when American chewing gum started on its world "conquest." Increased exports of the item to Europe during the previous two years had generally been attributed to military demand. Statistics tended to bear out that view, as the European export shipments went mainly to England and France. In 1912 the value of U.S. chewing gum imported by England was $90,183; 1913, $81,042; 1914, $46,538; 1915, $92,075; 1916, $203,414; 1917 (first nine months), $582,294. In 1912 the value of U.S. chewing gum imported by France was $736; 1913, $198; 1914, $1,163; 1915, $2,573; 1916, $40,186; 1917 (first nine months), $90,201.[27]

Another May 1917 report said that French soldiers were to be supplied with one million packages of American chewing gum as a war measure. As recently as 1897 the value of U.S. gum exported to France had been zero. One confident prediction from an observer was, "When this war is over, France will retain at least two American contributions. The girls will be chewing gum and the boys will be playing baseball."[28]

Exports of chewing gum from the U.S. in 1894 has a total value of $2,658 for the entire world; in 1895, $1,709; 1896, $289; 1897, $0; 1915, $280,000; 1916, $574,423.[29]

In May 1917 a piece appeared in the London *Spectator* (reprinted in the U.S.) that tried to explain the popularity of gum chewing. "Sucking raises the blood pressure, and so gives a sense of well being. Hence gum chewing. The desire to suck something when one is engaged in deep thought, or taking action that calls for great concentration of mind, must have been noticed by many people." Examples cited were tobacco chewing, baby soothers, and the fact that in battle Marshal Saxe always sucked a lead bullet. Also added was the thought that Sir Thomas Browne would probably have said that we commemorated our nativities by the act of suction. The publication concluded, "In any case, gum chewing has come to stay. Our troops are taking to it already, and our alliance with America will make it virtually compulsory."[30]

Drawing a similar conclusion around the same time was an American journalist who said, "The gum-chewing habit will become firmly saddled on the British public when an American expedition comes over. Already the Canadians have introduced gum to their English brothers-in-arms." He added, "Medical folks, in weighty papers, find that the American chicle raises the blood-pressure and thereby imparts a sense of confidence in the attacking soldier."[31]

Another U.S. reporter was convinced, in June 1917, that one result of the war already in evidence—even though U.S. forces had not yet reached Europe—was the spread of two things "peculiarly American, baseball and chewing gum." Before the war, he explained, baseball was practically unknown outside of the United States and a small portion of Canada and, "As for chewing gum—well, its use was strictly American and vulgar." However, soldiers in the trenches had found that chewing gum was just what they wanted and vast quantities of the American product were being distributed. Canadians had probably introduced the habit, he thought, "but others were quick to take it up and the probability is that before very long men of most nations of the world will be experiencing the joys of masticating a bit of flavored and sweetened chicle."[32]

During the first nine months of the 1916–1917 fiscal year, the total exports of American chewing gum to the rest of the world had a value of $926,500. Of that total, over half ($509,049) went to Europe; $103,970 went to North America; $17,950 to South America; $14,538 to Asia; and $16,005 to Africa.[33]

At the very end of 1917 a report from London said the British government, on December 30, announced that it was allowing, under special license, the importation of large quantities of a brand new army ration—chewing gum. British soldiers were dependent almost entirely on America for it. Although before the war chewing gum was "practically unknown" in the UK, declared the report, it was then the article most in demand at canteens. London firms were supplying 15 million sticks of gum a month to the army and navy. In Palestine, Mesopotamia, and Egypt the British military personnel chewed it to ease thirst while in Belgium and France the native children competed with the canteens in selling it to the troops.[34]

A week later, a piece in the London *Weekly Dispatch* commented on the heavy use of chewing gum by the U.S. Army and went on to declare, "Practically every American chews gum all day and every day of his life."[35]

When an American reporter wrote a story about French soldiers and gum in August 1918 he started off with a humorous description of

He's Our Biggest Customer!

Millions of sticks of the Adams brands of chewing gum have gone to the boys in France. Millions are on the way. Millions more will go. Please remember this the next time you can't get your favorite brand of Adams gum. If Adams Black Jack is missing from the counter try Adams California Fruit, Adams Pepsin, Adams Yucatan or any Adams brand.

ADAMS
Pure Chewing Gum

Adams Black Jack		Adams California Fruit
Adams Chiclets		Adams Yucatan
Adams Pepsin	CHICLE	Adams Sen Sen
Adams Spearmint		Adams Clove

PUT 5 PACKAGES OF ADAMS GUM IN YOUR SOLDIER BOY'S CHRISTMAS BOX

This 1918 ad made use of the image of Uncle Sam and urged people to be patient if gum was scarce in their local communities. The reason was that so much of the product had been shipped overseas to U.S. troops then fighting in World War I.

the item. He called it a "well known vegetable product which may be found adhering to the underside of desks, to shoe soles, and to trouser seats throughout the United States. The self-same article that at once solaces the weary shop girl and the tired businessman who endeavors therewith to conceal the fume of the drinks that cheer." Then he related the tale of a storehouse in France that had been full of items such as chocolate, tobacco, canned goods, cookies, and a considerable quantity of chewing gum. As German troops advanced, the area was vacated by the French who attempted, before they left, to keep the supplies from falling into enemy hands. To that end they used what they could and destroyed the rest. With respect to the gum, he added that the poilus (French soldiers) that came upon the chewing gum—like most Frenchmen—were totally unfamiliar with it. They knew only that it looked like food, was wrapped like food and was stored with other things they knew to be food. They ventured further and tried it, stuffing the entire contents of a package into their mouths at one time. "It tasted like food, so after a brief period of mastication they essayed to swallow it. Too many of them succeeded," he wrote. "While no serious casualties resulted the Poilus were inspired with a remarkable regard for American digestive apparatuses and considerable awe for American edibles."[36]

Ford M. Jack, who with Johnny Evers (a pro baseball player) tried to teach the French baseball, returned to the U.S. in November 1918 and said the French were more interested in chewing gum than baseball. Jack thought they would have a hard time learning baseball because they had never had any previous exposure to it and they had no playgrounds and almost no parks, "but they certainly are crazy about chewing gum." He added, "I visited, all told, about 600 places in France where American troops are quartered and from the moment I got off the ship I was struck with the real need for gum over there." Jack also remarked, "I hadn't been in France three minutes when a group of little boys and girls crowded around me and shouted: 'Chewing gum, si'l vous plait?'" In the YMCA kiosks there, Jack discovered that cartons of Adams brands of gum were emptied as fast as they were put on display. "It certainly has been a great blessing for the little fellows of France to get a stick of gum, for there are two things they lack badly. One is a proper place in which to play and the other is sweets."[37]

Articles outlining the conquest of the world by American gum became more prominent and effusive in 1919. One, datelined Washington, D.C., said that from bathtubs to chewing gum, Europe was acquiring American habits. "The chewing proclivities of the Yanks—both as regards gum and tobacco—and their natural propensities toward bathing apparently have affected the French and the British," went the account. According to official trade figures some 3,500 miles of chewing gum had been exported from the U.S.A. between Armistice Day and April 1919. That translated into 735,000,000 sticks of gum. Over that same period of time America also sent abroad $1 million worth of plug (chewing) tobacco, and 1,183 bathtubs.[38]

At the same time a different account remarked that every year the U.S. shipped tons of chewing gum to China, Siam, and the Malay Islands, and then went on to speculate what could have created the demand for such a commodity in Hong Kong, Bangkok, and Singapore. For this journalist it all began with the missionaries, "good, resourceful people" who found that the nations whom they had come to "Christianize and civilize" had a "dreadful habit" of chewing betel nut. Betel nut was an item that contained small quantities of an injurious drug. Also, continued use of the item turned the teeth jet black. In order to counteract the effect of this "deleterious habit," the "ingenious" missionaries proceeded to cultivate in the natives a taste for Wrigley's Spearmint gum, and a corresponding disinclination for betel nut. "The natives came, they chewed, they were conquered, and much of America's chewing gum finds its final destiny in the mouths of Siam and Borneo," he wrote.

Next the article went on to suggest that perhaps the missionaries could find more worlds to conquer in the U.S.A., but different worlds. "Who has not been driven almost wild by the facial contortions of the reckless gum chewer? Who has not been repelled when the band plays 'The Star Spangled Banner' by a throng of people with patriotic jaws chewing in time to the music? What businessman has not found wads of gum plastered upon desk or typewriter by thrifty and prudent employees?" wondered the reporter. He went on to suggest "the comfort and spirituality of the people of this county would be much enhanced if the missionaries would labor her to curb the zeal and dexterity of the gum-chewers."[39]

Also in 1919, an American reporter noted the spread of the habit outside of North America and commented, "It has become virtually universal, due to the universality of moral waywardness because of the energy and ingenuity of American advertisers." For this journalist, England "resisted perpetual motion of the jaws for a long time, then fell; parts of Europe still held out bravely, but it is in the eastern hemisphere that chewing gum's greatest and most surprising ravages are to be found." If he was to be believed, the Chinese rickshaw coolie then had his gum, the Japanese geisha chewed in rhythm with her dancing feet, and there were similar manifestations of the growing popularity of gum in Burma, Siam, India, the Dutch East Indies, the Philippines, and Australia. In conclusion he declared, "Happily this token of civilization is not worse, but infinitely better, than the Orient's unwholesome betel nut, which it is to some degree supplanting."[40]

When a U.S. reporter surveyed the scene in France in January 1920, he declared there was then a rage in Paris for chewing gum, an "epidemic" as the habit caught on and took hold. He acknowledged that before the war, when the American soldiers had not yet come to Paris, chewing gum was all but unknown, mentioned only perhaps by an "exotic" novelist. Among the supplies that came when the American Army came to France were boxes full of gum: "And the little bit of perfumed gum became one of the instruments that the American boys used to attract the French girls." Despite the considerable use made of it, the stocks were so big that after the peace agreement had been signed there remained huge quantities of chewing gum, and that gave to many French people, he wrote, "the idea of civilizing the old Europe in making every one a gum chewer."[41]

Three months later a UK reporter told how a Frenchman by the name of M. Latzarus, writing in the *Avenir*, was perturbed by the craze among the French, and particularly among French girls, for chewing gum "in imitation of the American soldiers." Reportedly no fewer than 4,000 cases of gum had recently been landed at Rouen in the course of a fortnight and that gum was even more popular among well-brought-up girls than in the lower classes. Latzarus gave a graphic description of the facial contortions that accompanied the mastication of gum and remarked, "In the middle of a sentence a gum victim stops to ruminate and chew the cud."[42]

An article that appeared in March 1920 argued the practice of using gum had spread to Spain and that the young society girls and youths of

Madrid had taken to the American habit of chewing gum, and "their elders have been much exercised as a result." A Madrid conservative publication had recently devoted a column to that new practice, which "it denounced in strong terms." With respect to the reasons for the spread of the habit to Spain, the author of the piece declared gum chewing in Madrid was the result of people reading articles by Spanish writers who had recently visited America and to the Hollywood films exhibited in the Spanish cinemas.[43]

Yet another piece about the gum craze hitting Europe appeared in September 1920: "Efforts were made at different time to popularize chewing gum in the countries of Europe, but always without success until the American soldiers took some over there, after which the gum-chewing habit became a veritable craze." During the year 1919 chewing gum to the value of $2,164,200 was exported by the U.S.; England was the heaviest purchaser. "During the war chewing gum became very popular in the munitions factories of England, where it took the place of tobacco, smoking being banned," concluded the piece.[44]

And then suddenly articles about the craze spreading to Europe and other parts of the world stopped, replaced by something quite different. During the fiscal year ending June 30, 1921, "only" 1.5 billion sticks of gum were exported from the U.S. Until then exports had been double that number. According to this account, as soon as American soldiers were withdrawn from Europe after the war, exports of chewing gum began to fall off. However, exports of cars, jazz music, and the like, also made popular by the American Expeditionary Forces, showed little or no reduction in the quantities in which they flowed abroad. "But American chewing gum—tut! tut! Paris has dropped it. London scorns it, although London never took it to heart. But during the war London tolerated it. And Rome—well, Italy is barely mentioned in the list of those countries anxious to purchase American chewing gum."[45]

One month later, in October 1921, another American journalist reported there were then in France 16,540,200 sticks of chewing gum in perfectly good condition that nobody wanted to buy. Optimistically, the French had taken the gum, along with other things such as American tobacco, typewriters, mouse traps, and so forth. While all French tobacconists, cafes, bars, and street hawkers were supplied with stocks of chewing gum, it was said their only patrons had been American tourists and a few small boys who had picked up the habit from American soldiers during the war and had not managed to rid themselves of it. Since those boys tended not to pay for their gum (having little money, they relied on shoplifting), the revenue from gum sales was small. Monsieur Paisant, a minister in the French government, had the idea of reselling the gum to America. However, with the tariff barrier increased it was estimated each stick would cost twice as much in the U.S.A. as American gum that never left the home country. Advertising the gum in France had been tried with laudatory articles from eminent scientists appearing in the press, eulogizing the "sanitary" habit of gum chewing. Packs of gum (containing the standard five sticks) had sometimes been given away free to customers in the hope of starting the habit. But nothing had worked.[46]

The reason for the sudden shift in emphasis from the craze in Europe to gum being a drug on the market rested with the fact there had been no craze in the first place. Export of American chewing gum had indeed shot up dramatically in the last few years of the 1910s, but that was due to the presence abroad of large numbers of American soldiers. The vast majority of that exported gum was consumed by Americans abroad. However, many articles of the time chose to pretend the dramatic increase in gum exports meant the natives of various foreign countries had embraced the habit. It did not and they had not.

9

Wads, Novelties and Numbers

The chewing gum wad was the cause of much trouble and controversy. In today's more disease-conscious society, it is perhaps difficult to believe that people regularly used the same piece of gum over and over, taking it out of their mouths and sticking it to the nearest handy spot—such as under a table, or on a bed post—while they engaged in some activity that proscribed gum chewing, such as eating or sleeping. When the activity was completed the chewer would retrieve the piece and re-chew it. Even more extreme, by today's standards, was the not unusual habit of sharing the same wad between two or more people.

A reporter with an Illinois newspaper observed in 1872 that it was then considered the proper thing by young ladies of the progressive inclination there to take chewing gum with them when they went out calling. Supposedly, a "gum club" had been organized in town with a requirement of admission being the ability to chew on both sides of the mouth at once. It was also understood that when the club members wished to express sisterly feeling, they would "trade cuds."[1]

A man told a New York City newspaperman in 1883 that he and his wife, after they had gone to bed for the night, stuck their wads of chewing gum on the headboard of their bed where they remained until morning, when they were used again.[2]

An Oakland California boy by the name of Charles Thomas contracted diphtheria late in 1886. Reportedly, he caught the disease by trading chewing gum wads with a companion. That friend already had the disease and subsequently died from it.[3]

Another cautionary tale was present in the summer of 1890 when it was reported in a news account that diphtheria had broken out in a family that lived in East Des Moines, Iowa. After the family had all recovered they—parents and one child—visited some of their relatives in the country. Their child took along his chewing gum and when he arrived at the home of his relatives he shared his gum with the two children who lived there—his cousins. That is, all three children used the same wad of gum. Three or four days later those two cousins were simultaneously stricken with diphtheria.[4]

Writing in the New York *Herald* in 1893, a reporter remarked that it was not the gum chewing habit itself that he protested, but one of its offshoots. "This is the constantly growing habit of the chewer of this city to secrete her quid of gum on some article of furniture. A woman never throws away her gum. She hides it," he explained. "She sticks it under the mantelpiece, under the table top, on the headboard of the bed or on the back of the chair and leaves it there for future reference." Declaring such action to be an "unnice habit," he thought it was not a habit of economy to be encouraged either, because a fresh piece of gum could be purchased for no more than one cent. As well, he found it embarrassing to call at a house where a "gum girl" lived, as one was sure to find traces of her gum proclivities on every piece of furniture one touched. "Hard little knots of it are stuck in all sorts of places. When you find them, of course, you are surprised and say lots of things in a hurry that will probably 'queer' you with the girl forever."[5]

When an English woman wrote a letter to an English friend in 1894, she happened to mention the American habit of gum chewing and told her friend that when the chewer was finished with her gum the item was not to be swallowed but simply thrown away. Commenting on the latter, an American reporter declared that no American, not even a New York lady, however, would be guilty of such waste: "She would stick it under a table or chair until needed again," he wrote. "For, as the observant writer has noticed, chewing gum does not diminish in size; it may be retained for future occasions. In some parts of the country it is even kindly loaned out."[6]

A journalist with the New York *Sun* noted, also in 1894, that part of the daily duty of one of the girls in a Park Row, New York City, dairy restaurant consisted of removing from the undersides of the tables in the eatery the chewing gum that had been stuck there by customers. It took that girl a full hour every morning to accomplish the task; she removed it with a knife. "In any of the cheaper grades of restaurants the tables are decorated on their under sides in the same way," he said. "It is the men who practice this peculiar habit, and it goes to show how many of them use chewing gum."[7]

A death from unusual circumstances was said to have occurred in Fargo, North Dakota, on August 30, 1901. Two days earlier the family of J. E. McLaughlin moved to Fargo from Litchfield, Minnesota. On the next day the small son in the family, Roy Francis, was found to be eating something that made him very sick. An investigation revealed the young child had found several discarded wads of chewing gum stuck in different places around the house and he had picked them off and put them in his mouth. Doctors investigating were cited as having said, "The saliva on the partly chewed pieces had become rank poison and the chewing of them by the little one was the cause of the death."[8]

A Philadelphia reporter happened to be in a Chestnut Street restaurant in that city in December 1901 when he noticed a waiter going from table to table with a large kitchen knife, scraping the undersides of the tables not in use. When the curious journalist asked him what he was doing, the waiter explained he was removing wads of gum. "Well, you might not believe it, but at least every other day it is necessary to scrape those lumps off at every table. Sometimes we find as many as twenty of them under the edges of one table," the waiter explained. "They are chewing gum, left there by girls. At least one girl out of three takes a piece of chewing gum from her mouth and sticks it under the table when she sits down to luncheon or dinner."[9]

A Salt Lake City, Utah, journalist wrote, in February 1904, about a soda fountain in his city, a place where "the chewing gum girls" hang out. For the soda fountain jerk told, and showed, the reporter how many wads of gum were stuck in that establishment by girls. Wads were found all along the counter, under every chair in the place, under every table, and so forth. It was a big job for the employee to keep cleaning it up. "I've seen girls come in here a day or two after leaving their gum, and happening to think about it, reach under the counter and slip it in their mouths before going out," said the soda jerk. "Of course, they might get some other girl's, but what can I do under the circumstances? I couldn't say anything to them."[10]

An investigation of the tables at the recently defunct Booster Café in Des Moines, Iowa, was conducted in February 1907 by a reporter in that city. On the underside of one table were found 62 "intact" wads of chewing gum. And on that same table were many marks showing where wads had been at one time. In the restaurant were eight other tables. All of those had from 70 to 100 "clean spots" (marks where wads of gum had once been) on the underside, and they each had from 10 to 40 wads that were intact, that is, still stuck to the table. Explaining that people often took their gum back for more chewing on a day or a week later, the journalist observed that it was impossible for such people to accurately find their own old wad under a table. "It is declared by physicians that much disease is spread in this way. It is impossible to tell the extent in a case of this kind," he wrote. "Whether one got back his own gob would make little difference in the germ infection likely to result."[11]

A brief article in 1909 argued that since it was impossible to break women and children of the habit of chewing gum, placing it on the underside of a table and chewing it again later, their health demanded the invention of sanitary gum caps. When a woman stuck her gum to the underside of a table, went the piece, "it should be protected by a pure-air, carbolized, disinfected, deodorized gum cap, some sort of a covering that will keep out the germ-laden air. There is a fortune in this invention for some one."[12]

In 1911 a news account claimed that one could always tell a Houstonian by her reaching under the chair in search of something; that something being the piece of gum that is thus safely hidden during meal times, "And to be sure that one is always getting her own gum, the print of the teeth is left on it." As well, it was said that flirting by gum was well understood throughout Texas and that the courts in Texas had decided that the exchanging of one wad of gum between a man and a woman was "a proposal of marriage, and sufficient grounds on which to enter a suit for breach of promise."[13]

There was said to be a large commercial house in New York City in 1914 that employed about 200 girls and wherein there was a "chewing gum inspector." Part of that person's duties was to see that none of the gum used during the day by those employees ended up discarded on the floor, and a scrutiny of the desks and chairs, on the underside of which the girls were claimed to be prone to stick their gum when circumstances demanded its absence. A hotel owner in that city gave testimony to the fact that a considerable amount of gum was found on the undersides of the beds of some of the "smartest guests."[14]

9. Wads, Novelties and Numbers

A newspaper in Logansport, Indiana, presented a serious article on chewing gum wads in early 1919, an account that was also likely highly exaggerated for a humorous effect. An influenza scare rumor had been making the rounds in the city and one restaurant, in response, cut the ice cream soda and sundae service from its bill of fare. The center of that establishment was occupied by an array of tables and chairs, and when the ban went into effect, the chairs and tables were taken off the floor. They were relegated to the rear storage area of the store, turned upside down and piled together. It was estimated by the owner of that business that over the previous six months 20,000 people had sat at his ice cream tables. On the bottoms of those tables and chairs the owner, reportedly, found 9,133 wads of chewing gum that had been removed from the mouths of customers and stuck on the undersides of tables and chairs when their ice cream arrived. According to the account, chewing gum was so thick on the bottoms of chairs and tables that it required four wastebaskets to carry away the material.[15]

Famed boxer James J. Corbett had the 1920 byline for the bizarre article that put forward the idea that a wad of gum cost Johnny Dundee's featherweight crown. Johnny Montieth, former manager of Dundee, declared, "Five cents' worth of gum cost Johnny Dundee the featherweight championship of the world." Dundee was to fight Johnny Kilbane in 1913 with the match to take place on a Tuesday. On the Saturday prior to the fight Dundee, took the afternoon off from training to take part in some sort of benefit affair arranged by a local newspaper. It was held outdoors and conditions were dusty. When Dundee felt his throat getting dry he thought chewing gum would help, so he bought a five-cent pack and began chewing the whole pack—all five sticks at once. Later in the afternoon he had his shoes shined and as he was leaving the area the bootblack bumped against him and Dundee accidentally swallowed the entire wad of gum. He said nothing about it to his manager, Montieth, who did not learn about the gum until Monday.

On that Monday, Montieth thought something was wrong with his fighter, that Dundee was off his feed, somewhat hot and feverish. He seemed slow and sluggish but Montieth did not know why. Montieth continued to question his fighter as to his activities of the last few days until Dundee finally remembered to tell him about the gum. Said the manager, "Right away I knew what was wrong. The gum had 'gummed up' his innards." Montieth called in the doctor and the physician administered "drastic treatment," unspecified. Because of that, Dundee, on Tuesday morning, showed a lack of his usual pep and energy. Just before fight time, due to the boxer's lethargy, the manager decided it would be foolish to send Dundee into the ring at his usual whirlwind pace. So he told Dundee to just go easy for the first dozen rounds of the 20-round bout. Because of that change of strategy, Kilbane, by the end of the 13th round, had secured a lead of about three rounds on points. Then Montieth told Dundee to resume his usual whirlwind battling. He caught up with his opponent and even edged ahead on points, thought the manager, but the referee ruled it a draw. Since Kilbane was the reigning featherweight champion at the start of the fight, the draw allowed him to retain his title. "I know positively that if Johnny had not swallowed the gum and had not been forced to subject himself to violent medical handling twenty-four hours before the bout that he would have fought an entirely different fight," said Montieth. "I never would have let him hold back during the first dozen rounds. I'd have sent him out to win in a hurry and he would have secured such a tremendous lead on points that he would have won by a mile from Kilbane—if he didn't actually knock him out."[16]

In a cafeteria in Milwaukee a sign appeared in 1921 over a receptacle near the front of the eatery—"Park Gum Here." To add "insult to injury" a young female employee of the restaurant was stationed there to see that the gum was indeed parked. Waitresses at the place declared that the owners and staff were all fed up with gum chewers who made the undersides of chairs and table a parking place for gum, and this strategy was an attempt to deal with the problem.[17]

Novelties connected with chewing gum ranged from early advertising gimmicks to contests to strange inventions to original poetry. When a Jersey City, New Jersey, reporter wrote about the chewing gum mania in 1873, he remarked that the craze was not limited to New England or Philadelphia, with 1.5 million sticks recently shipped to the latter area. William Loft, of New Jersey, was said herein to be the originator of the prize gum business and was then shipping 3,000 boxes (450,000 sticks) weekly to Ohio, Indiana, Illinois, Wisconsin, and Missouri. Each box of 150 sticks contained a 25 cent baseball and 23 other prizes consisting of toys, cheap jewelry, and so on. Loft had just purchased $2,000 worth of French and German toys and jewelry to be used as prizes in his boxes of gum. From 12 to 15 girls were kept constantly employed in the Loft plant in packing the gum and prizes.[18]

When a New York City journalist interviewed the owner of a chewing gum factory in Brooklyn in 1887, he happened to ask the man if he'd ever heard of animals chewing gum. The manufacturer said he had heard of several dogs who indulged. One was a large dog in a town near Boston. When he saw a person chewing gum the animal would sit and beg for a piece until he got one and would then chew it quietly for 30 minutes or more. According to the reporter, a case of a pug dog that chewed gum had recently been reported in a Louisville paper.[19]

A St. Louis, Missouri, correspondent for the *Galveston Daily News* declared in April 1888 that among the latest fads taken up by the society ladies and leaders of St. Louis were the poodle, the tricycle, and certain types of elaborate dinner parties. Continuing on, the reporter added that it was thought at one time that the practice of gum chewing was confined exclusively to the plebian classes. However, of late the idea had been shown to be a popular fallacy. "Gum chewing is practiced in St. Louis by all indiscriminately, from the cook and maid servant to the grand ladies of coldest hauteur and beauty," said the article. "It can be seen everywhere. Hordes of women are constantly on the streets, chewing, talking, giggling and walking simultaneously. On the street cars it is the same." Also, it was said that "spectacle" could be seen at any hour and at almost any place in the city: "It appears to have taken a firm grip equally upon maidens and matrons, and they appear to derive exquisite pleasure from the practice."

In conjunction with the popularity of gum came a report of a new fad associated with the habit. The average St. Louis girl addicted to chewing gum was considered "of little consequence" if she did not carry a little silver "casket" to hold her gum when she went out. Those caskets were usually composed of chased silver and were shaped something like a canteen. When the gum chewing girl sallies out to the theater or any other place of amusement in St. Louis, she deftly hitches the casket, loaded with gum, to her girdle and feels thoroughly equipped. The case could be used to hold fresh gum or chewed wads—solving the problem of what to do with a wad. At the theater the proper St. Louis lady only chewed between acts or in the interludes and "invariably takes the gum out of her mouth when the curtain rises." As it used to be fashionable a few years ago, noted the reporter, for women to carry around a snuff box, so it is now to carry around a "neat little gum casket." Such items were bought at jewelry stores.[20]

A sight presented at a dime museum in Minneapolis in November 1888 consisted of 25 "gentle maidens, more or less beautiful" sitting upon high platforms and chewing gum to slow music. Supposedly this piece of entertainment would demonstrate whether it was better to bring the jaws together with a quick, steady movement, making a sound like the click of a telegraph instrument, or to bring them together like two freight trains in collision: "A decision can be made between the nervous, spasmodic chew, and the easy, graceful roll like a cow masticating hay." Concluded a reporter, "It will be a great week for gum chewers"—presumably sarcastically.[21]

So popular had chewing gum become in Logansport, Indiana, that it was said almost every girl in the city used it. Inspired by that fad, Arago Easton, described as a Logansport poet, wrote the following poem (titled simply, "Chewing Gum") specifically for a local newspaper, the Logansport *Pharos*.

> From two years old to ninety-nine,
> From sweet sixteen to baby mine,
> From palace cot, from elite to scum,
> Women are crazy for chewing gum.
> At home, in store, or on the street,
> With sweetest smile and bow, they greet,
> With joy caressing, face out of plumb,
> Then blow themselves on chewing gum.
> Rich and poor, high and low,
> Chew and chew where e'er they go,
> Old and young, blind, deaf and dumb,
> All have the craze of chewing gum.
> They chew and chew, it ain't no use,
> They are bound to chew and get the juice,
> You can't stop them, so give them some,
> And let them enjoy their chewing gum,
> I love the dear creatures, they don't me,
> I am getting too old, I plainly see,
> When I was young, they invited me to come,
> Spend the evening and chew their gum.
> I went, you bet, enjoyed it too,
> For I was young and loved to chew,

Please don't mention it the word is mum,
And I'll let you chew my chewing gum,
Girls, ain't you ashamed to chew and chew,
Do you think it's mine, and the thing to do?
To spoil a pretty mouth made to kiss and hum
Music sweet by chewing gum.[22]

The Gum Chewing Club of Yorkville, New York, held its annual reception and "grand chewing match" in October 1889. Reportedly, the club was an organization whose only object was "to encourage the act of chewing gum." To further that objective the group held a chewing match every now and then in which the person who chewed the biggest wad of gum got a prize. On the night in question the prize was a gold watch. Supposedly, 15,000 tickets for the event had been distributed and some 2,000 men and women came to the venue to see the match. As they entered the venue each spectator received a stick of tutti frutti gum. At 10:30 p.m. the five female contestants involved in the match took to the stage. They kept adding one stick of gum after the other to their mouths, after the previous stick had been properly "chewed in." When the reporter covering the event left the venue there were two contestants left, each one working at the time on a wad of 5.5 sticks. The all-time record was a wad of 9.5 sticks, set the previous year. In this particular contest, alas, the final outcome went unreported.[23]

Easton was not the only poet to write an ode to gum. A man by the name of Percy G. Mocatta had his offering, "My Chewing Gum," published in Ohio's *Sandusky Daily Register* on January 30, 1890.

I choose to chew my chewing gum,
For, chewing gum, you see
Is like an old and trusty chum,
It always sticks to me.
It sticks to me, what e'er betide,
It also sticks to you
To you, and all the world beside,
So, while we live, let's chew.
CHORUS My chewing gum, my chewing um,
          My sweet and sticky childhood's chum
          I'll quit the busy crowd and hum,
          In peace to chew my chewing gum.
Some live to sport a cigarette,
And some a stout cigar,

And some whatever they can get;
Such different men they are!
But I, I care not what may come,
Nor what my fate may be,
So I can chew my chewing gum,
My chewing gum for me.
CHORUS (repeats).[24]

During the spring of 1890 a chewing gum factory in Cleveland conceived a new idea for a brand of gum—wrapping it in imitation $5 greenbacks and calling it "Greenback Chewing Gum." It was put on the market in June or July of that year and was said to have been a hit. But then some government official from what a reporter described as "the effete east" came across the new brand, saw the imitation $5 bill and realized it was a violation of the laws of the United States. He notified the U.S. Treasury Department at Washington, D.C., which promptly sent the following telegram to all the district secret service officers, "Greenback chewing gum has a wrapper that is a violation of section 5,430. Suppress it." Upon receipt of the telegram Treasury Agent Carter of Indianapolis started out to look for the gum within his territory. In one wholesaler's place of business he found 500 boxes of the gum while in another he discovered 300 boxes. At each establishment he issued orders that the gum not be placed on the market.[25]

A Kentucky mathematician came up with some strange statistics about chewing gum. He declared the jaws of a "small-mouthed" young woman, who was "addicted" to the habit, moved 6,750,000 inches, or 103 miles a year, assuming a rate of 30 chews per minute for 10 hours a day.[26]

The Cleveland-based manufacturer of Yucatan chewing gum offered, in 1896, prizes for each state in the union, going to the contestant sending in the most Yucatan gum wrappers from each state. The winner from Iowa was a man named Elmer Maynard, who sent in 21,367 gum wrappers and was awarded the prize of a six-year old mare named Beatrice. In their letter of notification to Maynard, the Yucatan company told the winner that Beatrice was being held for him in Cleveland, awaiting his further instructions for delivery or pick-up. A reporter asked Maynard how he had secured such a large number of the little pink wrapper papers. The winner explained he had saved a number of them

5c   5c

MO-JO

WHAT IS MO-JO? **WHY IS MO-JO?** Two Questions Asked In Yesterday's World and Sun! -:-

MO-JO is no secret,—no DARK-CLOUDED HIDDEN MYSTERY, like the muddy colored chewing gums you have been chewing and are asked to believe are pure.

MO-JO is a PURE, delightfully flavored, chewing gum, absolutely free from dirt. It's the only pure white chewing gum—that's why it's clean.

WHY IS MO-JO?

For five years we have been experimenting on the manufacture of a cleaner, whiter, purer chewing gum; at a great expense we have discovered that the dark muddy colored gum, full of specks and grit can be made white, and free from dirt, through a refining process, filtered as it were. The result is our handsome refinery, built at an enormous expense, enabling us to give you a chewing gum, delightfully flavored, encased in the purest white granulated sugar, and at the same price as the inferior,—"Thus is MO-JO."

Where We Get Our Chewing Gum

Chicle is the product of the Sapodilla Tree in Mexico,—a creamy white sap, that is obtained by the natives hacking the bark of this tree in a trough like form, it flows and congeals—is gathered and sold to the shippers.

It is very sticky, catches everything that flies; the Tropics are full of bugs, flies, worms, moss, and like fly paper this chicle gets it's share. Then the natives down there are not well up on modern sanitary rules, never heard of a manicurist, and they sell this chicle by the pound, so even a little fly weighs something. After the biggest pieces of bark, moss, insects, etc., have been removed the gum makers hand out to you an attractive, highly flavored, but muddy colored chewing gum, and let you do the rest of the refining through your mouth.

Are you examining this muddy colored gum? Notice the black specks?—Yes, you are saving the gum makers thousands of dollars annually by chewing out and swallowing this filth.

Why not insist on a clean, pure chewing gum? Why not insist on MO-JO, the white chewing gum? It's the only pure gum.

Is MO-JO Chewing Gum Really Pure and Clean?

READ THIS CORRESPONDENCE

Fort Smith, Ark., July 10th, 1914.

Prof. Otto V. Martin, Analytical Chemist,
City Schools, Fort Smith, Ark.

Dear Sir:

We understand that several months ago you made a very thorough test and examination of the various Chewing Gums which are being sold in Fort Smith and that among them was "MO-JO." Will you kindly advise us of the result of your analysis in so far as it applied to MO-JO and greatly oblige.

Yours very truly,

The MO-JO Sales Co.,

Per E. S. LOCKETT, Secretary and Manager.

REPLY

Fort Smith, Ark., July 13th, 1914.

The MO-JO Sales Company,
Fort Smith, Ark.

Gentlemen:

Replying to yours of the 10th inst., I beg to state that in my analysis of the Gums sold on the local market, I found MO-JO to be entirely free from any foreign material and I also found that MO-JO ranked at the top in cleanliness, purity and quality.

Yours very truly,

(Signed) OTTO V. MARTIN.

Ask Your Dealer For MO-JO
The Clean White Chewing Gum

5c   5c

A long and wordy ad from 1914 for Mo-Jo chewing gum.

himself; he had all his friends saving them for him; he had bought a number of them from others who had also been saving them; and he had hired a number of small boys to gather them for him wherever they could find them. To those boys, Maynard paid 10 cents for every 100

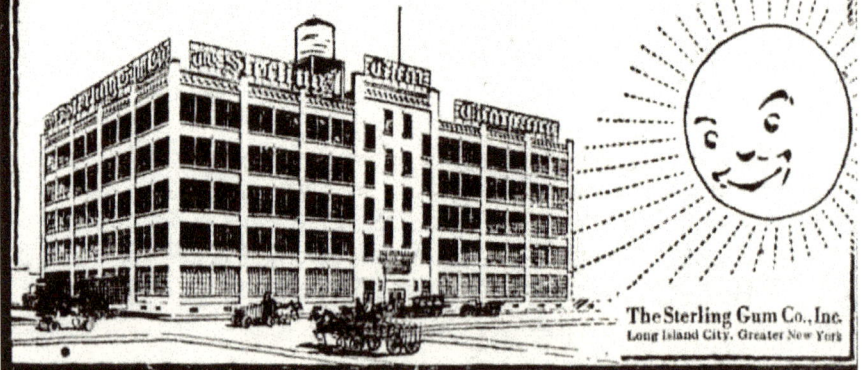

A 1915 ad for Sterling Gum touting cleanliness and purity and that it was produced in a daylight factory, with sunlight streaming in.

This 1916 ad for Yucatan urged consumers to get an early start with their chewing, right after breakfast.

wrappers they collected for him. When he sent all his wrappers to the Yucatan firm, he did so at one time in an express package that weighed nine pounds and cost $1 to send. Maynard estimated it cost him $20 in cash to win the prize.[27]

The manufacturer of an unnamed chewing gum put a coupon bearing one letter of the alphabet in each five-cent package of their gum, in 1897, and advertised that as soon as any one got the letters enabling them to spell certain specified words, the gum manufacturer would give that person a prize such as a watch or a bicycle. H. Smith, wagon driver for a wholesale grocery firm, was the first winner from the city of Ashtabula, Ohio. He acquired the letters that made the designated words and won a coupon allowing him to select from a retail outlet any bicycle that retailed for up to $100. So intense was the interest manifested by some of the gum chewers that one of the trolley car conductors in the city was said to have offered $25 for the letter "w"—the last one he needed to complete the designated words and win the prize.[28]

It was perhaps inevitable that someone would try and combine two of the "vices" of the era, tobacco and gum. An investigation by the Chicago Department of Education in 1901 resulted in the charge that an attempt had been made to bring school children into the tobacco habit through the distribution of packages of "gumbacco," a confection advertised as a "combination of the finest tobacco and chewing gum." Several children who had become addicted to the habit of chewing tobacco through the use of the gum had supposedly been reported.

At the Jenner School several children were reported to have been taken ill on a Friday. Principal Mary Lyons summoned medical assistance and the attending physician decided that the illnesses were due to narcotic poisoning. A search through the children's desks revealed sundry lumps of chewing gum, and further inspection revealed the fact that packages of gumbacco had been used by the children. Those children were said to have neglected to follow the directions found on the gumbacco wrappers: "Do not swallow; use as you would tobacco." Pupils told Principal Lyons they had bought the gum at a candy store at 115 Larrabee Street. Truant Officer Nuesse paid a visit to that store and threatened the dealer, L. D. Wolf, with arrest. Wolf declared his ignorance about the character of the product, but promptly destroyed his stock of gumbacco.[29]

An item from a Syracuse, New York, newspaper in 1904 stated the latest fad among young society people in that city, and elsewhere, was the chewing gum party. Each invited guest was provided upon arrival a package of chewing gum that was softened in the usual fashion (in the mouth) and was then used as a modeling material. There was reported to be practically no end to the shapes that the gum could be made to take, "This unique method of spending an evening has recently become very popular among some of the sororities at the university."[30]

Although the chewing gum locket was patented on January 1, 1889, by Christopher Robertson, of Somerville, Tennessee, it apparently received no attention from the media until 1913. The locket resembled the standard one that was used to carry a loved one's picture, but instead of a photograph it was lined with a porcelain glass interior. That allowed the chewer to place a used wad into the locket and have it handy and ready for future usage. Advantages of the locket were said to be to provide a place where chewing gum could be carried "attached to the person, as lockets are ordinarily worn," and "not left around carelessly to become dirty and fall into the hands of persons to whom it does not belong."[31]

On a day in March 1917, syndicated columnist Gene Ahern devoted his column to a humorous look at gum, describing it thusly: "Chewing gum is a piece of rubber tire without a backbone flavored with a smell." Expert gum chewers never threw away a wad of gum, but "each day they give it a different flavor, such as brass bed flavor, movie seat taste, office furniture flavor, etc." Ahearn declared, "The gum landscape on the under parts of movie seats and soda fountain chairs makes the Rocky Mountain scenery look flatter than Mexican beer."[32]

More weird numbers appeared in a January 1919 piece in the *San Antonio Light*. According to the article, the statistics came to the newspaper from the YMCA and concerned the chewing gum rations of the AEF (American Expeditionary Forces). It was observed that a one month's supply of chewing gum for the American soldiers in France weighed 77.5 tons. There were 16,320,000 sticks in those 77.5 tons and that meant that during one month U.S. soldiers in France used 48,960,000 inches of gum (one stick was three inches long). And that was 4,080,000 feet, or nearly 772 miles. As well, it was reported "the average man of phlegmatic temperament chews seventy times a minute, while an energetic, hard-working, ambitious young man will make eighty round trips with his jaws in the same length of time." Average life of a piece of chewing gum in the jaws of a soldier was five hours with the up-and-down stroke of the average gum chewer being one inch— half an inch each way. Reportedly the foregoing statistics came from "experiments," but no details were provided. If the chewing stroke was one inch and the life of a stick was five hours, then there were 1,750 jaw- feet in each stock. If there were 16,320,000 sticks of gum in 77.5 tons then U.S. soldiers in France traveled 5,409,000 jaw-miles in one month. If that was not enough "information," the reader was then told that in jaw-miles those soldiers circumnavigated the earth 216 times in one month or made 22.5 round trips to the moon.[33]

While bizarre statistics were occasionally put forward, most of the numbers presented were more coherent. As early as 1882 someone was already looking at the statistics, albeit vaguely. According to this account statistics of the chewing gum business had revealed that schoolgirls did not consume the majority of the product, as had been supposed; rather, that distinction went to factory girls.[34]

Another piece of anecdotal data collection could be seen in an 1889 article wherein it was stated that a man at one of the St. Paul, Minnesota, theaters had counted 97 people chewing gum in an audience of about 300. The journalist then extrapolated that figure to declare that one- third of the adult population of America was gum chewers.[35]

A report at the start of 1891 had it that Americans were spending $2.5 million annually on the penny-a-stick chewing gum. Every 24 hours, it was said, New Yorkers consumed 5,000 boxes (100 sticks per box): "It is no exaggeration to place the output of chewing gum in the United States at 3,500,00 pounds per annum, representing a total value of $2,500,000."[36]

A year later another reporter looked at the industry and observed the output from Chicago gum makers alone was about $1,500 a day, for every weekday of the year. He assumed about $1 million a year was spent on gum, using manufacturers' prices (wholesale, not retail). As the mak- ers sold their output to the jobbers at 35 cents a box, and the retailer sold the gum for $1 a box, he felt the public spent about $2.5 million a year on gum, "at the lowest estimate." As well, he pointed out that in one Ohio gum manufacturing plant the girls employed to wrap the finished product were paid a piece rate, one cent a box, and earned $2 to $3 a week.[37]

Late in 1895 it was reported that an estimated 30,000 to 35,000 people were engaged in the United States chewing gum business. American makers had introduced their product into China, Japan, Algiers, Egypt, Australia, and some parts of Europe. Some $20 million worth of gum was consumed annually in the U.S. (including exports), according to this account. One manufacturer alone was said to have sold $5 million worth of the item in one year.[38]

Six months later a Dr. Cyrus W. Edson was cited as having said the sum expended annually on gum was $20 million with the U.S. being home to five "immense" chewing gum factories, a dozen of moderate size, and "innumerable insignificant" firms. A journalist remarked that $20 million was greater by $9 million than the entire expense of running the prisons, courts, hospitals, and police forces of the city of New York. "The habit is increasing at such a rate that Americans bid fair to become a race of enormous facial development," he worried. "Chewing gum will be a national characteristic, as baseball is the national game, and clever slang is our native speech." By his estimate, "Twenty-five percent of the 75,000,000 people in the United States are already addicted to the habit, and not only do an ever-increasing multitude chew, but they chew openly, defiantly, on the public highways, at places of amusement, and at the clubs." What annoyed the reporter was the fact that the United States, "a nation of churches," spent $8 million more per year to purchase gum than it gave for the maintenance of the clergy of all denominations; it was a fact he considered to be "humiliating."[39]

Later in 1896, a different account repeated that people in America spent $20 million for chewing gum. For a comparison, this journalist said they spent $70 million a year for bicycles, but "the expenditure for these trifles is a bauble beside the amounts spent for beer, or for pleasuring at home and abroad." All of that caused a newspaper editor to conclude, "Can it be truly said of any nation, among whose population persons of moderate fortune are enabled to indulge themselves to such an extent in the purchase of things which cannot be classed as necessities, that is covered with calamity as with a shroud and that its classes are eating the vitals out of its masses?"[40]

By 1902 Chicago was reported to be the headquarters of the chewing gum trust. It was the main distribution point for the product and handled about half of the entire output of the gum trust, which annually then amounted to about 8,400,000 boxes, or a total of 840,000,000 individual pieces, or sticks, of gum. At a price of one cent a stick, that represented a payment of $8 million for gum made by the trust alone, about 4,000 tons in total. Still, the gum output of the trust was estimated to be less than half of the total chewing gum production of the United States. Cleveland was reported to be the greatest gum chewing city in America, with Chicago second and St. Louis ranked third.[41] The estimate was that the people of Chicago used approximately one ton of gum per day. That is, 2,000 boxes containing 200,000 pieces of chewing gum, and retailing for a total of $2,000.[42]

A reporter declared, in 1906, "The American man, woman and child, it appears, chews on average ten one-cent sticks of gum every year. The allowance would be somewhat larger if infants below the gum-chewing age be excluded." It was not explained how that number was determined. As well, this account declared that in the U.S. the net chewing gum bill was $8 million a year, much lower than most other estimates.[43]

An article in a 1906 newspaper, reprinted from the popular magazine *Review of Reviews*, also took a stab at estimating percentage of users. "The gum chewers are legion—one man of every two and one woman of every three will tell you that he or she delivers himself or herself so ardently and with such docile persistence to that exercise after every meal in order to facilitate digestion." As was usual, the data remained anecdotal.[44]

One report in 1908 stated that Americans spent $22 million for chewing gum in 1907 while a second one declared the production of chewing gum had increased 50 percent in 1908 over that of 1907.[45] A piece published in 1914 stated, without detail, that a conservative estimate of the number of gum chewers in the United States was 10 million, including habitual and occasional chewers.[46] That same year, 1914, statistics published by the U.S. Department of Commerce showed that during 1913 the U.S. imported 13,401,316 pounds of chicle, valued at $5,119,500. It was then estimated that 300,000,000 packages of gum were sold annually in America, containing an average of five sticks each.[47]

By 1915 an article remarked that the sale of chewing gum in America

A sweet child begging grandpa for another stick of gum, in 1917.

amounted to $120 million annually with the product containing just .17 percent chicle and 99.83 percent sugar.[48]

At the Kansas City meeting of the American Chemical Society in 1917, Dr. Frederick Dannerth of the research department of the Rubber Trade Laboratory presented some figures on gum. One pound of chicle made four pounds of gum. One pound of gum produced over 15.5 packages. In 1916 the U.S. exported 718,000 pounds of gum, about 11,129,000 packages. The total amount of chicle imported, processed and consumed in America in 1916 was 7,031,000 pounds, equivalent to 28,124,000 pounds of chewing gum. That represented a per capita consumption in the U.S. of about 3.5 pounds, or 55 packages per year.[49]

Figures from the U.S. Treasury Department revealed that for 1919, $1 billion was spent in America for candy, $350 million for soft drinks, and $50 million for chewing gum.[50]

Illustrating how uniquely American the chewing gum habit was, a 1920 article said that of

Wrigley's stressed its wax-wrapped, sealed package in this 1919 ad.

every 100 sticks of gum manufactured in the world, 99 came from American factories and 90 of those pieces of gum ended their existence between American teeth. According to this account, in 1919 Americans bought two billion packages of gum (at five cents each that would have been $100 million) and that amounted to 100 sticks for every man, woman and child in the country. If all that gum were spread out flat it would pave a road 10 feet wide running from New York to Seattle.[51]

Chapter Notes

Chapter 1

1. "Shoe blacking and cuff buttons." *Galveston Daily News*, May 28, 1907, p. 6.
2. "Pretty gum chewers." *Review* (Decatur, Illinois), October 27, 1886, p. 2.
3. "Chewing gum." *Decatur Daily Republican* (Illinois), December 26, 1888, p. 1.
4. "Feminine jaws chew tons of gum." *Logansport Journal* (Indiana), November 11, 1902, p. 7.
5. No title. *Hagerstown Mail* (Maryland), March 18, 1831, p. 1.
6. "The gum business." *Daily Free Democrat* (Milwaukee), February 12, 1851, p. 2.
7. Ad. *Janesville Gazette* (Wisconsin), September 4, 1851, p. 4.
8. "Rumination." *Milwaukee Daily Sentinel*, July 28, 1860, p. 1.
9. "Who chews gum." *Daily Miner* (Butte, Montana), January 14, 1882, p. 1.
10. "Chewing gum." *Bucks County Gazette* (Bristol, Pennsylvania), January 19, 1882, p. 1.
11. "The Maine girl's chewing gum." *Penn Yan Express* (Penn Yan, New York), May 14, 1884, p. 1.
12. "A great year for chewing gum." *Bucks County Gazette* (Bristol, Pennsylvania), April 16, 1885, p. 4.
13. "Spruce gum." *San Antonio Daily Express*, February 22, 1887, p. 8.
14. Ibid.
15. "Chewing gum." Reprinted in the *Decatur Daily Republican* (Illinois), December 26, 1888, p. 1.
16. "Chewing gum." *Times Democrat* (Lima, Ohio), September 1, 1896, p. 6.
17. "Spend holiday hunting gum." *Washington Post*, January 22, 1911, p. 40.
18. "For girls who chew gum." *Dubuque Daily Herald* (Iowa), September 27, 1867, p. 1.
19. "Chewing gum." *Freeborn County Standard* (Albert Lea, Minnesota), August 12, 1875, p. 4.
20. "All about chewing gum." *Salt Lake Daily Tribune*, January 5, 1879, p. 5.
21. "Thought chewing gum was rubber." *La Crosse Tribune and Leader-Press* (Wisconsin), August 9, 1917, p. 7.
22. "Chewing gum." *Daily Gazette* (Fort Wayne, Indiana), November 8, 1884, p. 5.
23. "Juice of the Sapota tree." *New York Times*, March 24, 1884, p. 8.
24. "Chapter on chewing gum." *Logansport Journal* (Indiana), January 14, 1880, p. 6.
25. Ibid.
26. "The chewing gum trade." *Sunday Herald* (Syracuse, New York), July 23, 1882, p. 3.
27. "Scraps." *Daily Journal* (Logansport, Indiana), September 4, 1883, p. 5.
28. "Petroleum chewing gum." *Janesville Daily Gazette* (Wisconsin), November 13, 1883, p. 3.
29. No title. *Davenport Daily Gazette* (Iowa), February 29, 1884, p. 1.
30. "Juice of the sapota tree." *New York Times*, March 24, 1884, p. 8.
31. "The uses of chewing gum." *Iowa State Reporter* (Waterloo), August 14, 1884, p. 8.
32. "Chewing gum." *Daily Gazette* (Fort Wayne, Indiana), November 8, 1884, p. 5.
33. "Making chewing gum of coal tar." *Weekly Reno Gazette*, April 30, 1885, p. 5.
34. "$9,000,000 worth of gum." *Oshkosh Record* (Wisconsin), December 10, 1887, p. 4.
35. "Chewing gum." *Oelwein Register* (Iowa), January 16, 1890, p. 3.
36. "A pernicious habit." *Salem Daily News* (Ohio), November 27, 1890, p. 3.
37. "How gum is made." *Logansport Reporter* (Indiana), July 2, 1892, p. 3.
38. "Gum! Gum!" *Lima Daily Times* (Ohio), July 9, 1892, p. 5.
39. "Chewing gum." *Delphos Daily Herald* (Ohio), January 9, 1895, p. 2.
40. "Chewing gum." *Times Democrat* (Lima, Ohio), September 1, 1896, p. 6.

41. "How chewing gum is made." *Nebraska State Journal* (Lincoln), June 29, 1897, p. 6.

42. "Chewing gum." *North Adams Transcript* (Massachusetts), September 9, 1897, p. 3.

43. "The gum America chews." *New York Times*, July 9, 1905, p. 29.

44. "Great horrors! Gum not pure?" *Waterloo Daily Courier* (Iowa), June 19, 1907, p. 6.

45. "With the interviewer." *Cedar Rapids Evening Gazette* (Iowa), June 20, 1907, p. 5.

46. "Chewing gum not classified." *Cedar Rapids Evening Gazette* (Iowa), June 24, 1907, p. 1.

47. "Reno maidens chew much gum." *Nevada State Journal* (Reno), July 14, 1908, p. 5.

48. Frederic J. Haskin. "Chewing gum industry." *Washington Post*, March 2, 1910, p. 5.

49. Russell Hastings Millward. "Chicle." *Oelwein Daily Register* (Iowa), May 20, 1910, p. 6.

50. Ibid.

51. "Horrors! War with Mexico might stop importation of chewing gum." *Wichita Daily Times* (Wichita Falls, Texas), May 4, 1914, p. 6.

52. "Tobacco co. to sell chewing gum." *Wall Street Journal*, May 11, 1914, p. 6; "United profit sharing." *Wall Street Journal*, July 11, 1914, p. 8.

53. "The referee." *Des Moines News* (Iowa), July 31, 1920, p. 1.

54. "Chewing gum strike." *Nevada State Journal* (Reno), March 18, 1888, p. 5.

55. "Chewing gum girls strike." *New York Times*, April 15, 1898, p. 12.

56. "Chewing gum war is over." *World* (New York, New York), April 16, 1898, p. 9.

57. "A curious strike." *Oshkosh Daly Northwestern* (Wisconsin), August 22, 1899, p. 4.

58. "Topics of the times." *New York Times*, August 24, 1899, p. 6.

59. "Chewing gum companies combine." *Middletown Daily Argus* (New York), January 13, 1899, p. 1.

60. J. A. Morris. "Facts about chewing gum." *Atlanta Constitution*, July 28, 1901, p. 33.

61. "American Chicle expansion." *New York Times*, December 15, 1901, p. WF5.

62. James Morrow. "George Heber Worthington tells of evolution of chewing gum trust." *Washington Post*, November 29, 1908, p. E1.

63. "Topics of the times." *New York Times*, April 30, 1897, p. 6.

64. "Small tax on chewing gum." *Washington Post*, March 9, 1897, p. 4.

65. No title. *Logansport Pharos* (Indiana), June 3, 1898, p. 4.

66. "The great chewing gum issue." *Syracuse Herald* (New York), October 16, 1921, p. 7.

67. "Taxation gummed-up." *Wisconsin Rapids Daily Tribune*, November 30, 1921, p. 5.

68. "The chewing gum trade." *Sunday Herald* (Syracuse, New York), July 23, 1882, p. 3.

69. "A nation of gum chewers." *Mansfield News* (Ohio), January 15, 1903, p. 8.

70. "$12,000 paid for single ad for spearmint." *Newark Advocate* (Ohio), March 27, 1914, p. 6.

71. "Chewing gum will conquer laziness." *New Castle News* (Pennsylvania), August 12, 1916, p. 6.

72. "George M. Cohan." *Muscatine Journal* (Iowa), June 18, 1917, p. 6.

73. Ad. *Winnipeg Free Press* (Manitoba), February 19, 1918, p. 4.

74. Ad. *Newark Advocate* (Ohio), November 13, 1918, p. 3.

75. Ad. *Reno Evening Gazette*, January 7, 1919, p. 8.

76. "$3,000,000 a year." *Oxnard Courier* (California), February 28, 1919, p. 2.

77. Ad. *Bridgeport Standard Telegram* (Connecticut), July 14, 1919, p. 3.

78. "Wrigley delivers gum by aeroplanes." *Daily Constitution* (Chillicothe, Missouri), August 26, 1919, p. 3.

79. "Sheboygan people thrilled as they make aerial flights over the city in Wrigley planes." *Sheboygan Journal* (Wisconsin), September 2, 1919, p. 1.

80. Ad. *Anniston Star* (Alabama), March 31, 1920, p. 8.

81. Ad. *Lethbridge Herald* (Alberta), December 9, 1919, p. 8.

82. "Adams, of chewing gum fame, dies in Brooklyn." *Trenton Times* (New Jersey), February 9, 1905, p. 6.

83. "An overlooked inventor." *Logansport Reporter* (Indiana), February 17, 1905, p. 4.

84. "How W. J. White made millions." *Newark Advocate* (Ohio), June 6, 1906, p. 2.

85. "New bride of the head of the chewing gum trust." *Fort Wayne Sentinel* (Indiana), October 6, 1906, p. 11.

86. "Shoe blacking and cuff buttons." *Galveston Daily News*, May 28, 1907, p. 6.

87. "Dr. Beeman dead, was from Lorain County." *Elyria Reporter* (Ohio), November 6, 1906, p. 4.

88. James Morrow. "George Heber Wor-

thington tells of evolution of chewing gum trust." *Washington Post*, November 29, 1908, p. E1.

89. Ibid.

90. "Every chew makes him more fame and fortune." *Indianapolis Star* (Indiana), May 18, 1919, p. 26.

91. Ibid.

Chapter 2

1. No title. *Dawson's Daily Times* (Fort Wayne, Indiana), February 21, 1860, p. 7.

2. "Daily Journal." *Daily Journal* (Racine, Wisconsin), March 13, 1860, p. 2.

3. "Rumination." *Milwaukee Daily Sentinel*, July 28, 1860, p. 1.

4. No title. *Rock County Recorder* (Janesville, Wisconsin), July 16, 1870, p. 4.

5. "About women." *Burlington Weekly Hawkeye*, March 2, 1876, p. 1.

6. No title. *Weekly Nevada State Journal* (Reno), April 29, 1876, p. 4.

7. "Femininities." *Milwaukee Daily News*, February 24, 1878, p. 3.

8. "The gum habit." *Standard* (Syracuse, New York), March 11, 1879, p. 2.

9. "Personal and political." *Petersburg Index-Appeal* (Virginia), March 3, 1880, p. 1.

10. No title. *Fort Wayne Daily Gazette* (Indiana), December 7, 1881, p. 4.

11. No title. *Davenport Daily Gazette* (Iowa). September 9, 1883, p. 8.

12. "The licorice craze." *Atchison Globe* (Kansas), May 15, 1885, p. 1.

13. "They all chew gum." *St. Joseph Herald* (Michigan), November 14, 1885, p. 1.

14. "Ugly gum chewers." *Stevens Point Daily Journal* (Wisconsin), December 5, 1891, p. 3.

15. "The chewing gum center." *Galveston Daily News*, October 27, 1891, p. 3.

16. Kate Dein. "The ethics of gum-chewing." *Salt Lake Tribune*, March 20, 1892, p. 13.

17. Ibid.

18. "The gum chewing habit." *Winnipeg Free Press* (Manitoba), February 24, 1893, p. 7.

19. "A habit that grows on one." *Standard* (Ogden, Utah), April 7, 1893, p. 11.

20. "Women and chewing gum." *Davenport Daily Leader* (Iowa), October 23, 1893, p. 2.

21. "Where gum chewers are caught." *Salt Lake Tribune*, February 7, 1904, p. 4.

22. "Gum chewing in vogue." *Independent* (Massillon, Ohio), July 16, 1906, p. 3.

23. "Reno maidens chew much gum." *Nevada State Journal* (Reno), July 14, 1908, p. 5.

24. "College girls are healthy, normal American girls." *New York Times*, November 17, 1912, p. SM12.

25. "Local." *Daily Patriot* (Madison, Wisconsin), February 16, 1860, p. 3.

26. "Flogging in schools." *Hagerstown Mail* (Maryland), November 25, 1870, p. 1.

27. "Jottings." *Janesville Gazette* (Wisconsin), December 1, 1870, p. 4.

28. "Our neighbors." *Daily Gazette* (Fort Wayne, Indiana), October 10, 1885, p. 6.

29. "The day's notations." *Daily Journal* (Freeport, Illinois), April 26, 1888, p. 4.

30. "Until he cried." *New Castle News* (Pennsylvania), October 17, 1894, p. 7.

31. "The teacher chewed gum." *Daily Kennebec Journal* (Maine), June 14, 1895, p. 8.

32. "Anti-gum chewing crusade." *New York Times*, May 22, 1903, p. 2.

33. "Gum chewers are punished." *Racine Daily Journal* (Wisconsin), March 8, 1907, p. 2.

34. "Known all over the country." *Racine Daily Journal* (Wisconsin), April 15, 1907, p. 8.

35. "Chewing gum barred." *Washington Post*, October 30, 1907, p. 5.

36. "Cure for chewing gum habit." *Galveston Daily News*, January 16, 1910, p. 2.

37. "Gum chewing by pupils not tolerated in Ohio." *New Castle News* (Pennsylvania), September 28, 1921, p. 5.

Chapter 3

1. No title. Reprinted in the *Iowa State Reporter* (Waterloo), June 10, 1886, p. 9.

2. "Gum chewing in Chicago." *Cambridge City Tribune* (Indiana), November 25, 1886, p. 1.

3. "Growth of a bad habit." *Alton Daily Telegraph* (Illinois), July 7, 1887, p. 2.

4. "The chewing gum habit." *Wisconsin State Journal* (Madison), January 27, 1888, p. 2.

5. "Gum chewing as an art." *Dunkirk Observer Journal* (New York), February 6, 1888, p. 3.

6. "The day's notations." *Daily Journal* (Freeport, Illinois), April 26, 1888, p. 4.

7. "A gum chewing fad." *Davenport Tribune* (Iowa), August 18, 1888, p. 3.

8. "All about chewing gum." *Huntingdon Globe* (Pennsylvania), October 4, 1888, p. 3.

9. "Chewing gum." *Decatur Daily Republican* (Illinois), December 26, 1888, p. 1.

10. "The gum chewing industry." *Washington Post*, July 24, 1889, p. 4.

11. "The gum chewers." *Trenton Times* (New Jersey), August 10, 1889, p. 3.

12. "For gum chewers." *Freeborn County Standard* (Albert Lea, Minnesota), August 22, 1889, p. 2.

13. "The look-about club." *Advance Argus* (Greenville, Pennsylvania), January 30, 1890, p. 1.

14. "The gum habit." *Oakland Daily Evening Tribune*, March 6, 1890, p. 5.

15. "A pernicious habit." *Salem Daily News* (Ohio), November 27, 1890, p. 3.

16. "The demand for gum." *Independent* (Massillon, Ohio), February 13, 1896, p. 5.

17. No title. *Spirit Lake Beacon* (Iowa), July 30, 1897, p. 2.

18. "Chewing gum machines." *Fort Wayne News* (Indiana), October 31, 1902, p. 10.

19. "The gum America chews." *New York Times*, July 9, 1905, p. 29.

20. "Reno maidens chew much gum." *Nevada State Journal* (Reno), July 14, 1908, p. 5.

21. "Win your gal with gum." *Washington Post*, August 25, 1911, p. 6.

22. Mabel Chadband. "Women habitual gum chewers." *Cedar Rapids Evening Gazette* (Iowa), September 26, 1914, p. 20.

23. "Much chewing gum used in Lower Valley." *Brownsville Herald* (Texas), April 1, 1918, p. 6.

24. "Some church members give more for chewing gum than they do to church." *New Castle News* (Pennsylvania), April 16, 1920, p. 20.

25. "The referee." *Des Moines News* (Iowa), July 31, 1920, p. 1.

26. "Candy and gum." *Oakland Tribune*, August 15, 1920, p. 36.

27. Molly Lee. "Molly Lee says today." *Sandusky Star Journal* (Ohio), May 2, 1921, p. 7.

28. "Americans losing ground as greatest gum chewers." *Woodland Daily Democrat* (California), June 9, 1921, p. 8.

Chapter 4

1. "The chewing gum trade." *Sunday Herald* (Syracuse, New York), July 23, 1882, p. 3.

2. "Girls who sigh for gum." *Oshkosh Daily Northwestern* (Wisconsin), September 22, 1883, p. 2.

3. "Chewing gum." *Daily Gazette* (Fort Wayne, Indiana), November 8, 1884, p. 5.

4. "A druggist's observations." *Bucks County Gazette* (Bristol, Pennsylvania), April 23, 1885, p. 1.

5. "Chewing gum." *Elyria Republican* (Ohio), October 29, 1885, p. 7.

6. "Special New York letter." *Galveston Daily News*, August 31, 1886, p. 7.

7. "Pretty gum chewers." *Review* (Decatur, Illinois), October 1886, p. 11.

8. "The Pacific coast gum chewer." *Titusville Herald* (Pennsylvania), November 12, 1886, p. 2.

9. "How St. Louis chews gum." *Washington Post*, November 23, 1887, p. 2.

10. "$9,000,000 worth of gum." *Oshkosh Record* (Wisconsin), December 10, 1887, p. 4.

11. "Prominent gum chewers." Reprinted in the *Pittsburgh Post*, June 18, 1889, p. 4.

12. "Gum chewing." *Reno Weekly and Stockman*, June 20, 1889, p. 2.

13. Ibid.

14. No title. *Hamilton Daily Democrat* (Ohio), January 27, 1894, p. 4.

15. "Men chew gum too." *Warren Ledger* (Pennsylvania), September 21, 1894, p. 8.

16. "Good gum chewing towns." Reprinted in the *Daily Kennebec Journal* (Maine), December 21, 1900, p. 6.

17. J. A. Morris. "Facts about chewing gum." *Atlanta Constitution*, July 28, 1901, p. 33.

18. "American soldiers are great gum chewers." *Indiana Democrat* (Pennsylvania), December 18, 1901, p. 3.

19. "Triumph of chewing gum." Reprinted in the *Atlanta Constitution*, April 13, 1902, p. 22.

20. "City of gum chewers." *Waterloo Daily Reporter* (Iowa), December 6, 1902, p. 3.

21. "The chewing season." *Perry Daily Chief* (Iowa), March 8, 1904, p. 4.

22. "Men chew gum, too." *New York Times*, October 16, 1904, p. 77.

23. "Autos develop gum habit." *Salt Lake Tribune*, October 29, 1905, p. 27.

24. "To back off bad habits." *Daily Free Press* (Carbondale, Illinois), October 15, 1906, p. 4.

25. "Vast army of gum chewers." *Hutchinson News* (Kansas), July 10, 1907, p. 6.

26. "The psychology of gum chewing." Reprinted in the *Fort Wayne Sentinel* (Indiana), December 31, 1910, p. 18.

27. Ibid.

28. "Gum chewing epidemic here." *New*

Castle News (Pennsylvania), April 12, 1911, p. 12.

29. "One view of chewing gum and love making." *Indianapolis Star*, March 22, 1914, p. 38.

30. "Chewing gum plays important part in keeping soldiers fit." *Logansport Pharos-Reporter* (Indiana), July 30, 1917, p. 2.

31. "Chewing gum thirst quencher." *Lincoln Sunday Star* (Nebraska), September 2, 1917, p. 12.

32. Ibid.

33. "Soldiers in the trenches must have chewing gum." *Elgin Echo* (Iowa), September 6, 1917, p. 2.

34. "Soldiers want chewing gum." *Oneonta Daily Star* (New York), December 25, 1917, p. 4.

35. "Soldiers want chewing gum." *Brownsville Herald* (Texas), December 27, 1917, p. 4.

36. Louis Ludlow. "Why chewing gum is needed by the army." *Fort Wayne News and Sentinel* (Indiana), September 10, 1918, p. 23.

37. "Can't send goodies to Yanks, but..." *Independent* (Helena, Montana), October 6, 1918, p. 6.

38. "Snap judgments." *Bridgeport Standard Telegram* (Connecticut), June 11, 1919, p. 24.

Chapter 5

1. "Local matters." *Independent* (Massillon, Ohio), August 3, 1870, p. 3.

2. "Things we like to see." *Greenville Argus* (Pennsylvania), May 31, 1873, p. 1.

3. "A bad habit." *Nevada State Journal* (Reno), June 14, 1873, p. 3.

4. No title. *Evening Gazette* (Port Jervis, New York), February 8, 1879, p. 2.

5. "Chewing gum." *Titusville Herald* (Pennsylvania), December 13, 1881, p. 2.

6. "The chewing gum habit." *Daily Huronite* (Huron, South Dakota), November 12, 1887, p. 2.

7. "Local correspondence." *Indiana Progress* (Indiana, Pennsylvania), December 11, 1889, p. 5.

8. "The place to chew gum." *Bismarck Daily Tribune* (North Dakota), November 4, 1890, p. 2.

9. "Why chewing gum is injurious." *Woodland Daily Democrat* (California), January 7, 1891, p. 1.

10. "Many thoughts." *Hawarden Independent* (Iowa), March 26, 1891, p. 4.

11. "Topics of the day." Reprinted in the *Evening News* (Mansfield, Ohio), May 10, 1891, p. 4.

12. "Queries and answers." *Sandusky Daily Register* (Ohio), May 18, 1891, p. 2.

13. "From my notebook." *Union Star* (Union, Iowa), January 26, 1894, p. 4.

14. "Shots here and there." *Middletown Daily Argus* (New York), September 8, 1894, p. 8.

15. "Chewing gum." *Newark Daily Advocate* (Ohio), May 18, 1897, p. 6.

16. "Fashion's caprices." *Iowa State Reporter* (Waterloo), December 16, 1897, p. 9.

17. "Gum and gum chewers." *Colorado Springs Gazette*, July 16, 1903, p. 11.

18. "Chew, sister, chew." *Titusville Herald* (Pennsylvania), August 25, 1904, p. 5.

19. "To the gum chewing girl." *Pella Chronicle* (Iowa), August 8, 1905, p. 7.

20. "Two innocent trusts." *Nevada State Journal* (Reno), July 26, 1906, p. 4.

21. "Gum-chewing." *New York Times*, August 12, 1906, p. 6.

22. "Gum chewing a necessity." *Des Moines Daily News* (Iowa), August 27, 1908, p. 4.

23. "Chewing gum famine." *Evening Independent* (Massillon, Ohio), November 19, 1909, p. 7.

24. "Edgerton's erudition." *Fort Wayne Weekly Gazette* (Indiana), June 18, 1885, p. 6.

25. No title. *Tyrone Daily Herald* (Pennsylvania), July 20, 1888, p. 4.

26. "The look-about club." *Advance Argus* (Greenville, Pennsylvania), January 30, 1890, p. 1.

27. "Letters from the people." *Portsmouth Herald* (New Hampshire), June 8, 1903, p. 1.

28. Enid Lid. "Timely topics." *Fort Wayne News* (Indiana), October 2, 1903, p. 10.

29. Ibid.

30. Mikkel Vip. "Just jottings." *Racine Daily Journal* (Wisconsin), August 23, 1906, p. 7.

31. "Effect of chewing gum." *Washington Post*, August 20, 1907, p. 6.

32. "Normal notes." *Gazette* (Stevens Point, Wisconsin), March 18, 1908, p. 3.

33. Blanche Bruce. "Many girls have chewing gum habit." *Sheboygan Journal* (Wisconsin), October 14, 1911, p. 6.

34. Lillian Russell. "The habit of chewing gum." *Oakland Tribune*, February 12, 1912, p. 8.

35. "A knock at chewing gum." *Oshkosh Daily Northwestern* (Wisconsin), February 24, 1913, p. 6.

36. Elizabeth Thompson. "Heart and beauty problems." *Eau Claire Leader* (Wisconsin), October 18, 1917, p. 6.
37. Molly Lee. "Molly Lee says today." *Sandusky Star Journal* (Ohio), May 2, 1921, p. 7.
38. Annie Laurie. "Advice to girls." *Hamilton Evening Journal* (Ohio), August 26, 1921, p. 6.
39. No title. *San Antonio Light*, August 28, 1883, p. 2.
40. "Gum and candy lotteries." *New York Times*, March 3, 1884, p. 3.
41. Ibid.
42. No title. *Evening Gazette* (Cedar Rapids, Iowa), April 9, 1886, p. 3.
43. "Chewing gum, too." *New York Times*, June 8, 1888, p. 3.
44. "The gum-chewer's fate." *Northern Vindicator* (Estherville, Iowa), August 17, 1888, p. 6.
45. "The state press." *Galveston Daily News*, January 26, 1891, p. 7.
46. "A new reform started." *Kokomo Daily Tribune* (Indiana), October 6, 1894, p. 2.
47. "Gum chewing." *Daily Review* (Decatur, Illinois), November 10, 1902, p. 2.
48. "Gum chewing vulgar?" *Racine Daily Journal* (Wisconsin), December 1, 1903, p. 8.
49. "Put ban on gum chewing." *Racine Daily Journal* (Wisconsin), September 26, 1905, p. 6.
50. "Richfield girls stop chewing." *Ogden Standard* (Utah), March 8, 1907, p. 2.
51. "War on child gum sellers." *Washington Post*, November 19, 1910, p. 16.
52. "Hawk-Eyetems." *Mountain Democrat* (Placerville, California), June 7, 1879, p. 6.
53. No title. *Decatur Weekly Republican* (Illinois), June 1, 1882, p. 7.
54. No title. *Sandusky Daily Register* (Ohio), February 28, 1890, p. 2.
55. "Charged with chewing gum." *New York Times*, September 28, 1890, p. 8.
56. "Gum chewing, too." *Middletown Daily Press* (New York), October 4, 1890, p. 2.
57. "Advanced woman upheld." *New York Times*, September 2, 1895, p. 5.
58. "Horrid gum chewing." *Daily Republican* (Decatur, Illinois), December 28, 1895, p. 4.
59. "Gum chewing denounced." *Logansport Pharos* (Indiana), February 4, 1898, p. 3.
60. "Chewing gum." *Bedford Free Press* (Iowa), February 10, 1898, p. 7.
61. "The gum chewing habit." *Hedrick Journal* (Iowa), May 4, 1898, p. 4.
62. "No gum at Ocean Grove." *New York Times*, July 7, 1907, p. X2.
63. "His choir chewed gum." *Logansport Pharos* (Indiana), November 17, 1907, p. 1.
64. "Low neck dressed and chewing gum habit on taboo in Zion City." *Lima News* (Ohio), December 19, 1920, p. 1.

Chapter 6

1. "Chewing gum." *Daily State Journal* (Madison, Wisconsin), December 6, 1859, p. 1.
2. "Chewing gum." *Nevada State Journal* (Reno), June 10, 1871, p. 1.
3. No title. *Dixon Telegraph* (Illinois), December 25, 1872, p. 1.
4. "A warning to gum-chewers." *Iowa State Reporter* (Waterloo), May 10, 1876, p. 3.
5. "All about chewing gum." *Salt Lake Daily Tribune*, January 5, 1879, p. 5.
6. "The gum habit." *Standard* (Syracuse, New York), March 11, 1879, p. 2.
7. No title. *Athens Messenger* (Ohio), July 12, 1883, p. 7.
8. "Girls who sigh for gum." *Oshkosh Daily Northwestern* (Wisconsin), September 22, 1883, p. 2.
9. "The gum cure for dyspepsia." *Weekly Wisconsin* (Milwaukee), October 17, 1883, p. 6.
10. "The uses of chewing gum. *Iowa State Reporter* (Waterloo), August 14, 1884, p. 8.
11. "Gum and mathematics." Reprinted in the *Iowa State Reporter* (Waterloo), January 22, 1885, p. 8.
12. "Evil effects of chewing gum." *Mitchell Daily Republican* (South Dakota), February 9, 1886, p. 4.
13. "As to chewing gum." *Critic* (Logansport, Indiana), February 14, 1886, p. 6.
14. No title. *Iowa State Reporter* (Waterloo), June 10, 1886, p. 9.
15. "What chewing gum does." *Galveston Daily News*, August 13, 1886, p. 12.
16. No title. *Xenia Daily Gazette* (Ohio), September 24, 1886, p. 3.
17. "Pretty gum chewers." *Review* (Decatur, Illinois), October 27, 1886, p. 2.
18. No title. *Iowa State Reporter* (Waterloo), November 25, 1886, p. 4.
19. "Gum chewing in Chicago." *Cambridge City Tribune* (Indiana), November 25, 1886, p. 1.
20. "Growth of a bad habit." *Alton Daily Telegraph* (Illinois), July 7, 1887, p. 2.

21. "Stop chewing gum." *Daily Journal* (Freeport, Illinois), September 27, 1888, p. 4.
22. Ibid.
23. "All about chewing gum." *Huntingdon Globe* (Kansas), October 4, 1888, p. 3.
24. "Excessive gum chewing." *Cambridge City Tribune* (Indiana), November 22, 1888, p. 4.
25. "Chewing gum." *Decatur Daily Republican* (Illinois), December 26, 1888, p. 1.
26. "Talks here and there." *Washington Post*, August 26, 1889, p. 5.
27. "A pernicious habit." Reprinted in the *Salem Daily News* (Ohio), November 27, 1890, p. 3.
28. "A blinding habit." *Iowa State Reporter* (Waterloo), April 2, 1891, p. 6.
29. "Chewing gum for sea sickness." *News* (Frederick, Maryland), February 5, 1894, p. 4.
30. No title. *Trenton Evening Times* (New Jersey), December 26, 1895, p. 2.
31. "The chewing gum face." *Morning Telegram* (Eau Claire, Wisconsin), February 2, 1896, p. 2.
32. "Gum makes wrinkles." *Logansport Journal* (Indiana), December 23, 1896, p. 5.
33. "Teeth and chewing gum." *Mountain Democrat* (Placerville, California), September 11, 1897, p. 6.
34. "The danger of chewing gum." *Fort Wayne Journal* (Indiana), November 28, 1897, p. 4.
35. "Old gum man." *Waterloo Daily Reporter* (Iowa), August 21, 1900, p. 7.
36. "Found at last." *Anaconda Standard* (Montana), October 17, 1903, p. 6.
37. "Children and chewing gum." *Waterloo Daily Reporter* (Iowa), July 9, 1904, p. 10.
38. "Thinks gum chewing good." *Racine Daily Journal* (Wisconsin), November 15, 1906, p. 12.
39. "Gum a destroyer." *Lebanon Daily News* (Pennsylvania), December 20, 1910, p. 1.
40. "Immoderate chewing of gum injurious." *Salt Lake Tribune*, January 31, 1913, p. 8.
41. "Local doctors tell what they think of Dr. Wiley's tirade against gum chewing." *Fort Wayne News* (Indiana), March 14, 1914, p. 12.
42. Ibid.
43. "One view on chewing gum and lovemaking." *Indianapolis Star*, March 22, 1914, p. 38.
44. "How science has found that chewing gum is worry's greatest foe." *Fort Wayne Sentinel* (Indiana), March 28, 1916, p. 14.
45. Ibid.

46. Frank Crane. "Gum." *Syracuse Herald* (New York), November 27, 1916, p. 16.
47. Frederic J. Haskin. "Exercise for the teeth." *Janesville Daily Gazette* (Wisconsin), May 5, 1920, p. 6.
48. "Making teeth work." *Bridgeport Telegram* (Connecticut), May 12, 1920, p. 31.
49. "Thoughts on men and things." *Hamilton Daily News* (Ohio), April 6, 1921, p. 6.

Chapter 7

1. "A novelty." *Daily Evening Tribune* (Oakland, California), January 12, 1875, p. 3.
2. "Girls who sigh for gum." *Oshkosh Daily Northwestern* (Wisconsin), September 22, 1883, p. 2.
3. "Chewing gum against time." *Washington Post*, June 8, 1890, p. 16.
4. "Telephone girls mad." *Decatur Morning Review* (Illinois), May 6, 1891, p. 1.
5. "Refuses to stop chewing gum." *Naugatuck Daily News* (Connecticut), January 17, 1903, p. 4.
6. "Gum must go." *Logansport Reporter* (Indiana), July 27, 1903, p. 5.
7. "They don't chew gum." *Washington Post*, January 28, 1904, p. 6.
8. "Teachers to lose gum." *Burlington Hawk-Eye* (Iowa), January 9, 1904, p. 1.
9. "The American girl and her chewing gum." *Sunday Herald* (Syracuse, New York), January 31, 1904, p. 27.
10. "Gum chewing clerks." *Syracuse Herald* (New York), September 4, 1908, p. 4.
11. "Police must not chew gum." *Washington Post*, October 8, 1908, p. 6.
12. "Tars mayn't chaw gum." *Centralia Weekly Chronicle* (Washington), December 27, 1911, p. 6.
13. "Gum chewing under ban." *Sheboygan Journal* (Wisconsin), January 22, 1912, p. 3.
14. "Navy's ban on gum-chewing." *Washington Post*, November 22, 1911, p. 6.
15. "Cigarets and gum are bumped hard." *Janesville Daily Gazette* (Wisconsin), April 1, 1915, p. 3.
16. "Street smoking up to guardsmen." *Orange County Times-Press* (Middletown, New York), July 13, 1917, p. 1.
17. William Brady. "Health talks." *Janesville Daily Gazette* (Wisconsin), April 28, 1919, p. 7.
18. "Will have more time to talk." *Washington Post*, January 8, 1897, p. 10.
19. "Made a witness stop chewing gum." *New York Times*, June 3, 1899, p. 8.

20. "Fined for chewing gum." Reprinted in the *Portsmouth Herald* (New Hampshire), September 9, 1902, p. 4.
21. "Court told woman to stop chewing the gum." *Trenton Times* (New Jersey), September 24, 1903, p. 1.
22. "Gum chewers rebuked." Reprinted in the *Cedar Rapids Evening Gazette* (Iowa), March 4, 1904, p. 2.
23. "Chew gum in court." *New Castle News* (Pennsylvania), December 23, 1907, p. 4.
24. "No gum in the court." *Washington Post*, August 3, 1909, p. 14.
25. "No gum chewing in court." *New York Times*, February 12, 1911, p. 3.
26. "Gum chewing and law." *Indianapolis Star* (Indiana), March 15, 1912, p. 7.
27. "Looks bad for Diggs and Drew Caminetti." *Fort Wayne News* (Indiana), August 8, 1913, p. 12.
28. "Woman chews gum; fined." *Washington Post*, November 18, 1915, p. 4.

Chapter 8

1. "Random notes." *Weekly Hawk-Eye* (Burlington, Vermont), October 19, 1882, p. 6.
2. "Gum chewing in England." *Weekly Wisconsin* (Milwaukee), March 29, 1890, p. 3.
3. "American chewing gum in London." *Mitchell Daily Republican* (South Dakota), April 9, 1890, p. 2.
4. "Concerning chewing gum." *Logansport Reporter* (Indiana), June 15, 1891, p. 2.
5. "How gum is made." *Logansport Reporter* (Indiana), July 2, 1892, p. 3.
6. "Gum chewing in London." *London Daily Mail* (UK), October 15, 1897, p. 4.
7. "In defence of chewing gum." *London Daily Mail* (UK), October 21, 1897, p. 6.
8. "Against American chewing gum." *New York Times*, September 11, 1898, p. 17.
9. "Good gum chewing towns." *Daily Kennebec Journal* (Maine), December 21, 1908, p. 6.
10. J. A. Morris. "Facts about chewing gum." *Atlanta Constitution*, July 28, 1901, p. 33.
11. "Triumph of chewing gum." Reprinted in the *Atlanta Constitution*, April 13, 1902, p. 22.
12. "Their windscreen pipes." *Hutchinson News* (Kansas), July 21, 1906, p. 2.
13. "More chewing gum abroad." *Logansport Journal* (Indiana), August 1, 1906, p. 2.

14. "Germany wants our chewing gum." *Logansport Reporter* (Indiana), November 10, 1906, p. 4.
15. "All smack in chorus." *Oakland Tribune*, June 23, 1907, p. 8.
16. Frederic J. Haskin. "Chewing gum industry." *Washington Post*, March 2, 1910, p. 5.
17. "Gum chewing in America." *Oelwein Daily Register* (Iowa), October 14, 1910, p. 3.
18. "Hopes Britons may learn to chew gum." *Indianapolis Star* (Indiana), December 24, 1911, p. 32.
19. "Why we chew gum." *New York Times*, February 23, 1912, p. 4.
20. "Hungarians are Americans." *Washington Post*, May 19, 1912, p. 13.
21. "English people becoming champion gum chewers." *Fairbanks Daily News-Miner* (Alaska), July 14, 1913, p. 3.
22. "Greeks here get appeal for funds." *News* (Frederick, Maryland), July 19, 1913, p. 3.
23. "Chewing gum used in Army." *Washington Post*, October 22, 1914, p. 6.
24. "All the world chewing gum." *Wall Street Journal*, April 27, 1914, p. 2.
25. "Chewing gum wins English." *Washington Post*, February 10, 1917, p. 6.
26. "Chewing gum quiets nerves of soldiers in British line." *Galveston Daily News*, March 18, 1917, p. 21.
27. "U.S. chewing gum conquering the world." *New Castle News* (Pennsylvania), May 21, 1917, p. 12.
28. "Gum and baseball in France." *Ogden Standard* (Utah), May 21, 1917, p. 4.
29. "Chewing gum exports are on increase." *Lebanon Daily News* (Pennsylvania), May 23, 1917, p. 3.
30. "Take to chewing gum." *San Antonio Light*, May 25, 1917, p. 8.
31. "United States big figure." *Commerce Journal* (Texas), June 1, 1917, p. 4.
32. "Baseball and gum." *Sandusky Star-Journal* (Ohio), June 9, 1917, p. 4.
33. "American chewing gum in trenches." *San Antonio Light*, June 10, 1917, p. 3.
34. "Import chewing gum for British troops." *Lincoln Daily Star* (Nebraska), December 30, 1917, p. 11.
35. "They like gum." *Daily Gazette* (Xenia, Ohio), January 5, 1918, p. 1.
36. "Poilu tackles gum." *Tyrone Daily Herald* (Pennsylvania), August 26, 1918, p. 5.
37. "Gum, that interest French, not baseball." *Oakland Tribune*, November 16, 1918, p. 5.
38. "Gum, prunes and bathtubs sent Eu-

rope by U.S." *Sheboygan Journal* (Wisconsin), April 17, 1919, p. 4.

39. "A missionary enterprise." *Glenwood Opinion* (Iowa), April 17, 1919, p. 2.

40. "Gum chewing popular in Far East." *Lake Park News* (Iowa), August 7, 1919, p. 6.

41. "Paris is busy chewing gum it gets from U.S." *Anniston Star* (Alabama), January 12, 1920, p. 4.

42. "French chewing-gum girls." *London Daily Mail* (UK), April 8, 1920, p. 5.

43. "Young society folds of Madrid have taken up habit of chewing gum." *Galveston Daily News*, March 4, 1920, p. 1.

44. "Europe takes to chewing gum." *Gazette* (Stevens Point, Wisconsin), September 9, 1920, p. 4.

45. "Foreigners care less for U.S. chewing gum." *Moberly Democrat* (Missouri), September 4, 1921, p. 13.

46. "American chewing gum in France continues to be drug on market." *Salt Lake Tribune*, October 2, 1921, p. 12.

Chapter 9

1. No title. *Dixon Telegraph* (Illinois), December 25, 1872, p. 1.

2. No title. *Athens Messenger* (Ohio), July 12, 1883, p. 7.

3. "The world over." *Indiana Weekly Progress* (Indiana, Pennsylvania), November 11, 1886, p. 2.

4. "Infection in chewing gum." *Daily Huronite* (Huron, South Dakota), July 15, 1890, p. 3.

5. "The gum chewing habit." Reprinted in the *Winnipeg Free Press* (Manitoba), February 24, 1893, p. 7.

6. "Chewing gum for seasickness." *News* (Frederick, Maryland), February 5, 1894, p. 4.

7. "Table decorations." *San Antonio Daily Light*, April 4, 1894, p. 8.

8. "Killed by chewing gum." *Waterloo Semi-Weekly Courier* (Iowa), September 3, 1901, p. 2.

9. "The lumps under the table." *Racine Daily Journal* (Wisconsin), December 2, 1901, p. 7.

10. "Where gum chewers are caught." *Salt Lake Tribune*, February 7, 1904, p. 4.

11. "Has been wads of gum unearthed." *Des Moines Daily News* (Iowa), February 5, 1907, p. 8.

12. "Chewing gum protection." *Oakland Tribune*, September 17, 1909, p. 6.

13. "Win your girl with gum." *Washington Post*, August 25, 1911, p. 6.

14. "One view of chewing gum and love making." *Indianapolis Star* (Indiana), March 22, 1914, p. 38.

15. "Lack of affinity." *Logansport Pharos-Reporter* (Indiana), January 17, 1919, p. 6.

16. James J. Corbett. "Wad of gum cost Johnny Dundee featherweight crown." *Des Moines Capital* (Iowa), February 29, 1920, p. 32.

17. "Check your gum lady." *Evening Independent* (Massillon, Ohio), June 9, 1921, p. 14.

18. "Chewing gum statistics." *Northern Vindicator* (Estherville, Iowa), September 13, 1873, p. 3.

19. "$9,000,000 worth of gum." *Oshkosh Record* (Wisconsin), December 10, 1887, p. 4.

20. "Latest fads in St. Louis." *Galveston Daily News*, April 22, 1888, p. 11.

21. "Chewing gum for a prize." *Washington Post*, November 23, 1888, p. 7.

22. "Chewing gum." *Logansport Pharos* (Indiana), August 31, 1889, p. 3.

23. "Gum chewing for prizes." *New Era* (Humeston, Iowa), October 2, 1889, p. 3.

24. "My chewing gum." *Sandusky Daily Register* (Ohio), January 30, 1890, p. 4.

25. "Indiana news." *Logansport Daily Pharos* (Indiana), July 24, 1890, p. 1.

26. "Daughters of Eve." *Daily Gazette* (Janesville, Wisconsin), July 18, 1894, p. 4.

27. No title. *Daily Iowa Capital* (Des Moines), November 2, 1896, p. 6.

28. "A gum game in Ohio." *Mills County Tribune* (Glenwood, Iowa), August 12, 1887, p. 4.

29. "Tobacco in chewing gum." *Davenport Daily Republican* (Iowa), January 30, 1901, p. 2.

30. "The American girl and her chewing gum." *Sunday Herald* (Syracuse, New York), January 31, 1904, p. 27.

31. "Many freak inventions." *Washington Post*, March 2, 1913, p. M2.

32. Gene Ahern. "Ain't nature wonderful." *Fort Wayne Sentinel* (Indiana), March 24, 1917, p. 4.

33. "Our Army's jaw-power." *San Antonio Light*, January 8, 1919, p. 4.

34. "Who chews gum." *Daily Miner* (Butte, Montana), January 14, 1882, p. 1.

35. "St. Paul gum chewers." *San Antonio Daily Light*, March 7, 1889, p. 11.

36. "Millions spent for chewing gum." *Davenport Daily Gazette* (Iowa), January 9, 1891, p. 3.

37. "About chewing gum." *Titusville Herald* (Pennsylvania), March 10, 1892, p. 3.

38. No title. *Trenton Evening Times* (New Jersey), December 26, 1895, p. 2.

39. "A gum chewing nation." *Homestead* (Des Moines, Iowa), June 5, 1896, p. 21.

40. "Chewing gum in politics." *Washington Post*, September 24, 1896, p. 6.

41. "Feminine jaws chew tons of gum." *Logansport Journal* (Indiana), November 11, 1902, p. 7.

42. "Chew tons of gum." *Elgin Echo* (Iowa), December 31, 1903, p. 12.

43. "Gum chewing statistics." *Oelwein Daily Register* (Iowa), October 29, 1906, p. 2.

44. "Thinks gum chewing good." *Racine Daily Journal* (Wisconsin), November 15, 1906, p. 12.

45. "For chewing gum." *Decatur Review* (Illinois), February 12, 1908, p. 3; "Reno maidens chew much gum." *Nevada State Journal* (Reno), July 14, 1908, p. 5.

46. "Horrors! War with Mexico might stop importation of chewing gum." *Wichita Daily Times* (Wichita Falls, Kansas), May 4, 1914, p. 6.

47. "Chicle and chewing gum." *Wall Street Journal*, May 2, 1914, p. 5.

48. "Wealth of romance compressed into package of chewing-gum." *San Antonio Light*, August 9, 1915, p. 3.

49. "Chewing gum popular pastime." *Galveston Daily News*, April 30, 1917, p. 5.

50. "Bits of information." *Des Moines Daily News* (Iowa), July 6, 1920, p. 4.

51. "The referee." *Des Moines News* (Iowa), July 31, 1920, p. 1.

Bibliography

"About chewing gum." *Titusville Herald* (Pennsylvania), March 10, 1892, p. 3.

"About women." *Burlington Weekly Hawkeye*, March 2, 1876, p. 1.

Ad. *Anniston Star* (Alabama), March 31, 1920, p. 8.

Ad. *Bridgeport Standard Telegram* (Connecticut), July 14, 1919, p. 3.

Ad. *Janesville Gazette* (Wisconsin), September 4, 1851, p. 4.

Ad. *Lethbridge Herald* (Alberta), December 9, 1919, p. 8.

Ad. *Newark Advocate* (Ohio), November 13, 1918, p. 3.

Ad. *Reno Evening Gazette*, January 7, 1919, p. 8.

Ad. *Winnipeg Free Press* (Manitoba), February 19, 1918, p. 4.

"Adams, of chewing gum fame, dies in Brooklyn." *Trenton Times* (New Jersey), February 9, 1905, p. 6.

"Advanced woman upheld." *New York Times*, September 2, 1895, p. 5.

"Against American chewing gum." *New York Times*, September 11, 1898, p. 17.

Ahern, Gene. "Ain't nature wonderful." *Fort Wayne Sentinel* (Indiana), March 24, 1917, p. 4.

"All about chewing gum." *Huntingdon Globe* (Pennsylvania), October 4, 1888, p. 3.

"All about chewing gum." *Salt Lake Daily Tribune*, January 5, 1879, p. 5.

"All smack in chorus." *Oakland Tribune*, June 23, 1907, p. 8.

"All the world chewing gum." *Wall Street Journal*, April 27, 1914, p. 2.

"American chewing gum in France continues to be drug on market." *Salt Lake Tribune*, October 2, 1921, p. 12.

"American chewing gum in London." *Mitchell Daily Republican* (South Dakota), April 9, 1890, p. 2.

"American chewing gum in trenches." *San Antonio Light*, June 10, 1917, p. 3.

"American Chicle expansion." *New York Times*, December 15, 1901, p. WF5.

"The American girl and her chewing gum." *Sunday Herald* (Syracuse, New York), January 31, 1904, p. 27.

"American soldiers are great gum chewers." *Indiana Democrat* (Indiana, Pennsylvania), December 18, 1901, p. 3.

"Americans losing ground as greatest gum chewers." *Woodland Daily Democrat* (California), June 9, 1921, p. 8.

"Anti-gum chewing crusade." *New York Times*, May 22, 1903, p. 2.

"As to chewing gum." *Critic* (Logansport, Indiana), February 14, 1886, p. 6.

"Autos develop gum habit." *Salt Lake Tribune*, October 29, 1905, p. 27.

"A bad habit." *Nevada State Journal* (Reno), June 14, 1873, p. 3.

"Baseball and gum." *Sandusky Star-Journal* (Ohio), June 9, 1917, p. 4.

"Bits of information." *Des Moines Daily News* (Iowa), July 6, 1920, p. 4.

"A blinding habit." *Iowa State Reporter* (Waterloo), April 2, 1891, p. 6.

Brady, William. "Health talks." *Janesville Daily Gazette* (Wisconsin), April 28, 1919, p. 7.

Bruce, Blanche. "Many girls have chewing gum habit." *Sheboygan Journal* (Wisconsin), October 14, 1911, p. 6.

"Candy and gum." *Oakland Tribune*, August 15, 1920, p. 36.

"Can't send goodies to Yanks, but..." *Independent* (Helena, Montana), October 6, 1918, p. 6.

Chadband, Mabel. "Women habitual gum chewers." *Cedar Rapids Evening Gazette* (Iowa), September 26, 1914, p. 20.

"Chapter on chewing gum." *Logansport Journal* (Indiana), January 14, 1880, p. 6.

"Charged with chewing gum." *New York Times*, September 28, 1890, p. 8.

"Check your gum lady." *Evening Independent* (Massillon, Ohio), June 9, 1921, p. 14.

Bibliography

"Chew gum in court." *New Castle News* (Pennsylvania), December 23, 1907, p. 4.

"Chew, sister, chew." *Titusville Herald* (Pennsylvania), August 25, 1904, p. 5.

"Chew tons of gum." *Elgin Echo* (Iowa), December 31, 1903, p. 12.

"Chewing gum." *Bedford Free Press* (Iowa), February 10, 1898, p. 7.

"Chewing gum." *Bucks County Gazette* (Bristol, Pennsylvania), January 19, 1882, p. 1.

"Chewing gum." *Daily Gazette* (Fort Wayne, Indiana), November 8, 1884, p. 5.

"Chewing gum." *Daily State Journal* (Madison, Wisconsin), December 6, 1859, p. 1.

"Chewing gum." *Decatur Daily Republican* (Illinois), December 26, 1888, p. 1.

"Chewing gum." *Delphos Daily Herald* (Ohio), January 9, 1895, p. 2.

"Chewing gum." *Elyria Republican* (Ohio), October 29, 1885, p. 7.

"Chewing gum." *Freeborn County Standard* (Albert Lea, Minnesota), August 12, 1875, p. 4.

"Chewing gum." *Logansport Pharos* (Indiana), August 31, 1889, p. 3.

"Chewing gum." *Nevada State Journal* (Reno), June 10, 1871, p. 1.

"Chewing gum." *Newark Daily Advocate* (Ohio), May 18, 1897, p. 6.

"Chewing gum." *North Adams Transcript* (Massachusetts), September 9, 1897, p. 3.

"Chewing gum." *Oelwein Register* (Iowa), January 16, 1890, p. 3.

"Chewing gum." *Times Democrat* (Lima, Ohio), September 1, 1896, p. 6.

"Chewing gum." *Titusville Herald* (Pennsylvania), December 13, 1881, p. 2.

"Chewing gum a thirst quencher." *Lincoln Sunday Star* (Nebraska), September 2, 1917, p. 12.

"Chewing gum against time." *Washington Post*, June 8, 1890, p. 16.

"Chewing gum barred." *Washington Post*, October 30, 1907, p. 5.

"The chewing gum center." *Galveston Daily News*, October 27, 1891, p. 3.

"Chewing gum companies combine." *Middletown Daily Argus* (New York), January 13, 1899, p. 1.

"Chewing gum exports are on increase." *Lebanon Daily News* (Pennsylvania), May 23, 1917, p. 3.

"The chewing gum face." *Morning Telegram* (Eau Claire, Wisconsin), February 2, 1896, p. 2.

"Chewing gum famine." *Evening Independent* (Massillon, Ohio), November 19, 1909, p. 7.

"Chewing gum for a prize." *Washington Post*, November 23, 1888, p. 7.

"Chewing gum for sea sickness." *News* (Frederick, Maryland), February 5, 1894, p. 4.

"Chewing gum girls strike." *New York Times*, April 15, 1898, p. 12.

"Chewing gum habit." *Daily Huronite* (Huron, South Dakota), November 12, 1887, p. 2.

"Chewing gum habit." *Wisconsin State Journal* (Madison), January 27, 1888, p. 2.

"Chewing gum in politics." *Washington Post*, September 24, 1896, p. 6.

"Chewing gum machines." *Fort Wayne News* (Indiana), October 31, 1902, p. 10.

"Chewing gum not classified." *Cedar Rapids Evening Gazette* (Iowa), June 24, 1907, p. 1.

"Chewing gum plays important part in keeping soldiers fit." *Logansport Pharos-Reporter* (Indiana), July 30, 1917, p. 2.

"Chewing gum popular pastime." *Galveston Daily News*, April 30, 1917, p. 5.

"Chewing gum quiets nerves of soldiers in British line." *Galveston Daily News*, March 18, 1917, p. 21.

"Chewing gum statistics." *Northern Vindicator* (Estherville, Iowa), September 13, 1873, p. 3.

"Chewing gum strike." *Nevada State Journal* (Reno), March 18, 1888, p. 5.

"Chewing gum, too." *New York Times*, June 8, 1888, p. 3.

"The chewing gum trade." *Sunday Herald* (Syracuse, New York), July 23, 1882, p. 3.

"Chewing gum used in Army." *Washington Post*, October 22, 1914, p. 6.

"Chewing gum war is over." *World* (New York, New York), April 16, 1898, p. 9.

"Chewing gum will conquer laziness." *New Castle News* (Pennsylvania), August 12, 1916, p. 6.

"Chewing gum wins English." *Washington Post*, February 10, 1917, p. 6.

"The chewing season." *Perry Daily Chief* (Iowa), March 8, 1904, p. 4.

"Chicle and chewing gum." *Wall Street Journal*, May 2, 1914, p. 5.

"Children and chewing gum." *Waterloo Daily Reporter* (Iowa), July 9, 1904, p. 10.

"Cigarets and gum are bumped hard." *Janesville Daily Gazette* (Wisconsin), April 1, 1915, p. 3.

"City of gum chewers." *Waterloo Daily Reporter* (Iowa), December 6, 1902, p. 2.

"College girls are healthy, normal American girls." *New York Times*, November 17, 1912, p. SM12.

"Concerning chewing gum." *Logansport Reporter* (Indiana), June 15, 1891, p. 2.

Corbett, James J. "Wad of gum cost Johnny Dundee featherweight crown." *Des Moines Capital* (Iowa), February 29, 1920, p. 32.

"Court told woman to stop chewing gum." *Trenton Times* (New Jersey), September 24, 1903, p. 1.

Crane, Frank. "Gum." *Syracuse Herald* (New York), November 27, 1916, p. 16.

"Cure for chewing gum habit." *Galveston Daily News*, January 16, 1910, p. 25.

"A curious strike." *Oshkosh Daily Northwestern* (Wisconsin), August 22, 1899, p. 4.

"Daily journal." *Daily Journal* (Racine, Wisconsin), March 13, 1860, p. 2.

"The danger of chewing gum." *Fort Wayne Journal* (Indiana), November 28, 1897, p. 4.

"Daughters of Eve." *Daily Gazette* (Janesville, Wisconsin), July 18, 1894, p. 4.

"The day's notations." *Daily Journal* (Freeport, Illinois), April 26, 1888, p. 4.

Dein, Kate. "The ethics of gum-chewing." *Salt Lake Tribune*, March 20, 1892, p. 13.

"The demand for gum." *Independent* (Massillon, Ohio), February 13, 1896, p. 5.

"Dr. Beeman dead, was from Lorain County." *Elyria Reporter* (Ohio), November 6, 1906, p. 4.

"A druggist's observations." *Bucks County Gazette* (Bristol, Pennsylvania), April 23, 1885, p. 1.

"Edgerton's erudition." *Fort Wayne Weekly Gazette* (Indiana), June 18, 1885, p. 6.

"Effect of chewing gum." *Washington Post*, August 20, 1907, p. 6.

"English people becoming champion gum chewers." *Fairbanks Daily News-Miner* (Alaska), July 14, 1913, p. 3.

"Europe takes to chewing gum." *Gazette* (Stevens Point, Wisconsin), September 9, 1920, p. 4.

"Every chew makes him more fame and fortune." *Indianapolis Star* (Indiana), May 18, 1919, p. 26.

"Evil effects of chewing gum." *Mitchell Daily Republican* (South Dakota), February 9, 1886, p. 4.

"Excessive gum chewing." *Cambridge City Tribune* (Indiana), November 22, 1888, p. 4.

"Fashion caprices." *Iowa State Reporter* (Waterloo), December 16, 1897, p. 9.

"Feminine jaws chew tons of gum." *Logansport Journal* (Indiana), November 11, 1902, p. 7.

"Femininities." *Milwaukee Daily News*, February 24, 1878, p. 3.

"Fined for chewing gum." *Portsmouth Herald* (New Hampshire), September 9, 1902, p. 4.

"Flogging in schools." *Hagerstown Mail* (Maryland), November 25, 1870, p. 1.

"For chewing gum." *Decatur Review* (Illinois), February 12, 1908, p. 3.

"For girls who chew gum." *Dubuque Herald* (Iowa), September 27, 1867, p. 1.

"For gum chewers." *Freeborn County Standard* (Albert Lea, Minnesota), August 22, 1889, p. 2.

"Foreigners care less for U.S. chewing gum." *Moberly Democrat* (Missouri), September 4, 1921, p. 13.

"Found at last." *Anaconda Standard* (Montana), October 17, 1903, p. 6.

"French chewing-gum girls." *London Daily Mail* (UK), April 8, 1920, p. 5.

"From my notebook." *Union Star* (Union, Iowa), January 26, 1894, p. 4.

"George M. Cohan." *Muscatine Journal* (Iowa), June 18, 1917, p. 6.

"Germany wants our chewing gum." *Logansport Reporter* (Indiana), November 10, 1906, p. 4.

"Girls who sigh for gum." *Oshkosh Daily Northwestern* (Wisconsin), September 22, 1883, p. 2.

"Good gum chewing towns." *Daily Kennebec Journal* (Maine), December 21, 1900, p. 6.

"The great chewing-gum issue." *Syracuse Herald* (New York), October 16, 1921, p. 7.

"Great horrors! Gum not pure?" *Waterloo Daily Courier* (Iowa), June 19, 1907, p. 6.

"A great year for chewing gum." *Bucks County Gazette* (Bristol, Pennsylvania), April 16, 1885, p. 4.

"Greeks here get appeal for funds." *News* (Frederick, Maryland), July 19, 1913, p. 3.

"Growth of a bad habit." *Alton Daily Telegraph* (Illinois), July 7, 1887, p. 2.

"Gum! Gum!" *Lima Daily Times* (Ohio), July 9, 1892, p. 5.

"The gum America chews." *New York Times*, July 9, 1905, p. 29.

"Gum and baseball in France." *Ogden Standard* (Utah), May 21, 1917, p. 4.

"Gum and candy lotteries." *New York Times*, March 3, 1884, p. 3.

"Gum and gum chewers." *Colorado Springs Gazette*, July 16, 1903, p. 11.

"Gum and mathematics." *Iowa State Reporter* (Waterloo), January 22, 1885, p. 8.

"The gum business." *Daily Free Democrat* (Milwaukee), February 12, 1851, p. 2.

"The gum chewers." *Trenton Times* (New Jersey), August 10, 1889, p. 3.

"Gum chewers are punished." *Racine Daily Journal* (Wisconsin), March 8, 1907, p. 2.

Bibliography

"The gum-chewer's fate." *Northern Vindicator* (Estherville, Iowa), August 17, 1888, p. 6.

"Gum chewers rebuked." *Cedar Rapids Evening Gazette* (Iowa), March 4, 1904, p. 2.

"Gum chewing." *Reno Weekly and Stockman*, June 20, 1889, p. 2.

"Gum chewing." *New York Times*, August 12, 1906, p. 6.

"Gum chewing a necessity." *Des Moines Daily News* (Iowa), August 27, 1908, p. 4.

"Gum chewing and law." *Indianapolis Star* (Indiana), March 15, 1912, p. 7.

"Gum chewing as an art." *Dunkirk Observer Journal* (New York), February 6, 1888, p. 3.

"Gum chewing by pupils not tolerated in Ohio." *New Castle News* (Pennsylvania), September 28, 1921, p. 5.

"Gum chewing clerks." *Syracuse Herald* (New York), September 4, 1908, p. 4.

"Gum chewing denounced." *Logansport Pharos* (Indiana), February 4, 1898, p. 3.

"Gum chewing epidemic here." *New Castle News* (Pennsylvania), April 12, 1911, p. 12.

"A gum chewing fad." *Davenport Tribune* (Iowa), August 18, 1888, p. 3.

"Gum chewing for prizes." *New Era* (Humeston, Iowa), October 2, 1889, p. 3.

"The gum chewing habit." *Hedrick Journal* (Iowa), May 4, 1898, p. 4.

"The gum chewing habit." *Winnipeg Free Press*, February 24, 1893, p. 7.

"Gum chewing in America." *Oelwein Daily Register* (Iowa), October 14, 1910, p. 3.

"Gum chewing in Chicago." *Cambridge City Tribune* (Indiana), November 25, 1886, p. 1.

"Gum chewing in England." *Weekly Wisconsin* (Milwaukee), March 29, 1890, p. 3.

"Gum chewing in London." *London Daily Mail* (UK), October 15, 1897, p. 4.

"Gum chewing in vogue." *Independent* (Massillon, Ohio), July 16, 1906, p. 3.

"The gum chewing industry." *Washington Post*, July 24, 1889, p. 4.

"A gum chewing nation." *Homestead* (Des Moines, Iowa), June 5, 1896, p. 21.

"Gum chewing now under ban." *Sheboygan Journal* (Wisconsin), January 22, 1912, p. 3.

"Gum chewing popular in Far East." *Lake Park News* (Iowa), August 7, 1919, p. 6.

"Gum chewing statistics." *Oelwein Daily Register* (Iowa), October 29, 1906, p. 2.

"Gum chewing, too." *Middletown Daily Press* (New York), October 4, 1890, p. 2.

"Gum chewing vulgar?" *Racine Daily Journal* (Wisconsin), December 1, 1903, p. 8.

"The gum cure for dyspepsia." *Weekly Wisconsin* (Milwaukee), October 17, 1883, p. 6.

"A gum game in Ohio." *Mills County Tribune* (Glenwood, Iowa), August 12, 1897, p. 4.

"The gum habit." *Oakland Daily Evening Tribune*, March 6, 1890, p. 5.

"The gum habit." *Standard* (Syracuse, New York), March 11, 1879, p. 2.

"Gum makes wrinkles." *Logansport Journal* (Indiana), December 23, 1896, p. 5.

"Gum must go." *Logansport Reporter* (Indiana), July 27, 1903, p. 5.

"Gum, prunes and bathtubs sent Europe by U.S." *Sheboygan Journal* (Wisconsin), April 17, 1919, p. 4.

"Gum, that interests French, not baseball." *Oakland Tribune*, November 16, 1918, p. 5.

"A habit that grows on one." *Standard* (Ogden, Utah), April 9, 1893, p. 11.

"Has been wads of gum unearthed." *Des Moines Daily News* (Iowa), February 5, 1907, p. 8.

Haskin, Frederic J. "Chewing gum industry." *Washington Post*, March 2, 1910, p. 5.

Haskin, Frederic J. "Exercise for the teeth." *Janesville Daily Gazette* (Wisconsin), May 5, 1920, p. 6.

"Hawk-Eyetems." *Mountain Democrat* (Placerville, California), June 7, 1879, p. 6.

"His choir chewed gum." *Logansport Pharos* (Indiana), November 11, 1907, p. 1.

"Hopes Britons may learn to chew gum." *Indianapolis Star* (Indiana), December 24, 1911, p. 32.

"Horrid gum chewing." *Daily Republican* (Decatur, Illinois), December 28, 1895, p. 4.

"Horrors! War with Mexico might stop importation of chewing gum." *Wichita Daily Times* (Wichita Falls, Texas), May 4, 1914, p. 6.

"How chewing gum is made." *Nebraska State Journal* (Lincoln), June 29, 1897, p. 6.

"How gum is made." *Logansport Reporter* (Indiana), July 2, 1892, p. 3.

"How science has found that chewing gum is worry's greatest foe." *Fort Wayne Sentinel* (Indiana), March 28, 1916, p. 14.

"How St. Louis chews gum." *Washington Post*, November 23, 1887, p. 2.

"How W. J. White made millions." *Newark Advocate* (Ohio), June 6, 1906, p. 2.

"Hungarians are Americans." *Washington Post*, May 19, 1912, p. 13.

"Immoderate chewing of gum injurious." *Salt Lake Tribune*, January 31, 1913, p. 8.

"Import chewing gum for British troops." *Lin-*

coln *Daily Star* (Nebraska), December 30, 1917, p. 11.

"In defence of chewing gum." *London Daily Mail* (UK), October 21, 1897, p. 6.

"Indiana news." *Logansport Daily Pharos* (Indiana), July 24, 1890, p. 1.

"Infection in chewing gum." *Daily Huronite* (Huron, South Dakota), July 15, 1890, p. 3.

"Jottings." *Janesville Gazette* (Wisconsin), December 1, 1870, p. 4.

"Juice of the Sapota tree." *New York Times*, March 24, 1884, p. 8.

"Killed by chewing gum." *Waterloo Semi-Weekly Courier* (Iowa), September 3, 1901, p. 2.

"A knock at chewing gum." *Oshkosh Daily Northwestern* (Wisconsin), February 24, 1913, p. 6.

"Known all over country." *Racine Daily Journal* (Wisconsin), April 15, 1907, p. 8.

"Lack of affinity." *Logansport Pharos-Reporter* (Indiana), January 17, 1919, p. 6.

"Latest fads in St. Louis." *Galveston Daily News*, April 22, 1888, p. 11.

Laurie, Annie. "Advice to girls." *Hamilton Evening Journal* (Ohio), August 26, 1921, p. 6.

Lee, Molly. "Molly Lee says today." *Sandusky Star Journal* (Ohio), May 2, 1921, p. 7.

"Letters from the people." *Portsmouth Herald* (New Hampshire), June 8, 1903, p. 1.

"The licorice craze." *Atchison Globe* (Kansas), May 15, 1885, p. 1.

Lid, Enid. "Timely topics." *Fort Wayne News* (Indiana), October 2, 1903, p. 10.

"Local." *Daily Patriot* (Madison, Wisconsin), February 16, 1860, p. 3.

"Local correspondence." *Indiana Progress* (Indiana, Pennsylvania), December 11, 1889, p. 5.

"Local doctors tell what they think of Dr. Wiley's tirade against chewing gum." *Fort Wayne News* (Indiana), March 14, 1914, p. 12.

"Local matters." *Independent* (Massillon, Ohio), August 3, 1870, p. 3.

"The look-about club." *Advance Argus* (Greenville, Pennsylvania), January 30, 1890, p. 1.

"Looks bad for Diggs and Drew Caminetti." *Fort Wayne News* (Indiana), August 8, 1913, p. 12.

"Low neck dresses and chewing gum habit on taboo in Zion City." *Lima News* (Ohio), December 19, 1920, p. 1.

Ludlow, Louis. "Why chewing gum is needed by the army." *Fort Wayne News and Sentinel* (Indiana), September 10, 1918, p. 23.

"The lumps under the table." *Racine Daily Journal* (Wisconsin), December 2, 1901, p. 7.

"Made a witness stop chewing gum." *New York Times*, June 3, 1899, p. 8.

"The Maine girl's chewing gum." *Penn Yan Express* (Penn Yan, New York), May 14, 1884, p. 1.

"Making chewing gum of coal tar." *Weekly Reno Gazette*, April 30, 1885, p. 5.

"Making teeth work." *Bridgeport Telegram* (Connecticut), May 12, 1920, p. 31.

"Many freak inventions." *Washington Post*, March 2, 1913, p. M2.

"Many thoughts." *Hawarden Independent* (Iowa), March 26, 1891, p. 4.

"Men chew gum, too." *New York Times*, October 16, 1904, p. 77.

"Men chew gum too." *Warren Ledger* (Pennsylvania), September 21, 1894, p. 8.

"Millions spent for chewing gum." *Davenport Daily Gazette* (Iowa), January 9, 1891, p. 3.

Millward, Russell Hastings. "Chicle." Oelwein *Daily Register* (Iowa), May 20, 1910, p. 6.

"A missionary enterprise." *Glenwood Opinion* (Iowa), April 17, 1919, p. 2.

"More gum chewing abroad." *Logansport Journal* (Indiana), August 1, 1906, p. 2.

Morris, J. A. "Facts about chewing gum." *Atlanta Constitution*, July 28, 1901, p. 33.

Morrow, James. "George Heber Worthington tells of evolution of chewing gum trust." *Washington Post*, November 29, 1908, p. E1.

"Much chewing gum used in Lower Valley." *Brownsville Herald* (Texas), April 1, 1918, p. 6.

"My chewing gum." *Sandusky Daily Register* (Ohio), January 30, 1890, p. 4.

"A nation of gum chewers." *Mansfield News* (Ohio), January 15, 1903, p. 8.

"Navy's ban on gum-chewing." *Washington Post*, November 22, 1911, p. 6.

"New bride of the head of the chewing gum trust." *Fort Wayne Sentinel* (Indiana), October 6, 1906, p. 11.

"A new reform started." *Kokomo Daily Tribune* (Indiana), October 6, 1894, p. 2.

"$9,000,000 worth of gum." *Oshkosh Record* (Wisconsin), December 10, 1887, p. 4.

"No gum at Ocean Grove." *New York Times*, July 7, 1907, p. X2.

"No gum chewing in court." *New York Times*, February 12, 1911, p. 3.

"No gum in the court." *Washington Post*, August 3, 1909, p. 14.

No title. *Athens Messenger* (Ohio), July 12, 1883, p. 7.

Bibliography

No title. *Daily Iowa Capital* (Des Moines), November 2, 1896, p. 6.

No title. *Davenport Daily Gazette* (Iowa), February 29, 1884, p. 1.

No title. *Davenport Daily Gazette* (Iowa), September 9, 1883, p. 8.

No title. *Dawson's Daily Times* (Fort Wayne, Indiana), February 21, 1860, p. 7.

No title. *Decatur Weekly Republican* (Illinois), June 1, 1882, p. 7.

No title. *Dixon Telegraph* (Illinois), December 25, 1872, p. 1.

No title. *Evening Gazette* (Cedar Rapids, Iowa), April 9, 1886, p. 3.

No title. *Evening Gazette* (Port Jervis, New York), February 8, 1879, p. 2.

No title. *Fort Wayne Daily Gazette* (Indiana), December 7, 1881, p. 4.

No title. *Hagerstown Mail* (Maryland), March 18, 1831, p. 1.

No title. *Hamilton Daily Democrat* (Ohio), January 27, 1894, p. 4.

No title. *Iowa State Reporter* (Waterloo), June 10, 1886, p. 9.

No title. *Iowa State Reporter* (Waterloo), November 25, 1886, p. 4.

No title. *Logansport Pharos* (Indiana), June 3, 1898, p. 4.

No title. *Rock County Recorder* (Janesville, Wisconsin), July 16, 1870, p. 4.

No title. *San Antonio Light*, August 28, 1883, p. 2.

No title. *Sandusky Daily Register* (Ohio), February 28, 1890, p. 2.

No title. *Spirit Lake Beacon* (Iowa), July 30, 1897, p. 2.

No title. *Trenton Evening Times* (New Jersey), December 26, 1895, p. 2.

No title. *Tyrone Daily Herald* (Pennsylvania), July 20, 1888, p. 4.

No title. *Weekly Nevada State Journal* (Reno), April 29, 1876, p. 4.

No title. *Xenia Daily Gazette* (Ohio), September 24, 1886, p. 3.

"Normal notes." *Gazette* (Stevens Point, Wisconsin), March 18, 1908, p. 3.

"A novelty." *Daily Evening Tribune* (Oakland), January 12, 1875, p. 3.

"Old gum man." *Waterloo Daily Reporter* (Iowa), August 21, 1900, p. 7.

"One view of chewing gum and love making." *Indianapolis Star* (Indiana), March 22, 1914, p. 38.

"Our Army's jaw-power." *San Antonio Light*, January 8, 1919, p. 4.

"Our neighbors." *Daily Gazette* (Fort Wayne, Indiana), October 10, 1885, p. 6.

"An overlooked inventor." *Logansport Reporter* (Indiana), February 17, 1905, p. 4.

"The Pacific Coast gum chewer." *Titusville Herald* (Pennsylvania), November 12, 1886, p. 2.

"Paris is busy chewing gum it gets from U.S." *Anniston Star* (Alabama), January 12, 1920, p. 4.

"A pernicious habit." *Salem Daily News* (Ohio), November 27, 1890, p. 3.

"Personal and political." *Petersburg Index-Appeal* (Virginia), March 3, 1880, p. 1.

"Petroleum chewing gum." *Janesville Daily Gazette* (Wisconsin), November 13, 1883, p. 3.

"The place to chew gum." *Bismarck Daily Tribune* (North Dakota), November 4, 1890, p. 2.

"Poilu tackles gum." *Tyrone Daily Herald* (Pennsylvania), August 26, 1918, p. 5.

"Police must not chew gum." *Washington Post*, October 8, 1908, p. 6.

"Pretty gum chewers." *Review* (Decatur, Illinois), October 27, 1886, p. 2.

"Prominent gum chewers." *Pittsburgh Post*, June 18, 1889, p. 4.

"The psychology of gum chewing." *Fort Wayne Sentinel* (Indiana), December 31, 1910, p. 18.

"Put ban on gum chewing." *Racine Daily Journal* (Wisconsin), September 26, 1905, p. 6.

"Queries and answers." *Sandusky Daily Register* (Ohio), May 18, 1891, p. 2.

"Random notes." *Weekly Hawk-Eye* (Burlington, Vermont), October 19, 1882, p. 6.

"The referee." *Des Moines News* (Iowa), July 31, 1920, p. 1.

"Refuses to stop chewing gum." *Naugatuck Daily News* (Connecticut), January 17, 1903, p. 4.

"Reno maidens chew much gum." *Nevada State Journal* (Reno), July 14, 1908, p. 5.

"Richfield girls stop chewing." *Ogden Standard* (Utah), February 14, 1907, p. 2.

"Rumination." *Milwaukee Daily Sentinel*, July 28, 1860, p. 1.

Russell, Lillian. "The habit of chewing gum." *Oakland Tribune*, February 12, 1912, p. 8.

"Scraps." *Daily Journal* (Logansport, Indiana), September 4, 1883, p. 5.

"Sheboygan people thrilled as they make aerial flights over city in Wrigley planes." *Sheboygan Journal* (Wisconsin), September 2, 1919, p. 1.

"Shoe blacking and cuff buttons." *Galveston Daily News*, May 28, 1907, p. 6.

"Shots here and there." *Middletown Daily Argus* (New York), September 8, 1894, p. 8.

"Small tax on chewing gum." *Washington Post*, March 9, 1897, p. 4.

"Snap judgments." *Bridgeport Standard Telegram* (Connecticut), June 11, 1919, p. 24.

"Soldiers in the trenches must have chewing gum." *Elgin Echo* (Iowa), September 6, 1917, p. 2.

"Soldiers want chewing gum." *Brownsville Herald* (Texas), December 27, 1917, p. 4.

"Soldiers want chewing gum." *Oneonta Daily Star* (New York), December 25, 1917, p. 4.

"Some church members give more for chewing gum than they do to church." *New Castle News* (Pennsylvania), April 16, 1920, p. 20.

"Special New York letter." *Galveston Daily News*, August 31, 1886, p. 11.

"Spend holidays hunting gum." *Washington Post*, January 22, 1911, p. 40.

"Spruce gum." *San Antonio Daily Express*, February 22, 1887, p. 8.

"St. Paul gum chewers." *San Antonio Daily Light*, March 7, 1889, p. 11.

"The state press." *Galveston Daily News*, January 26, 1891, p. 7.

"Stop chewing gum." *Daily Journal* (Freeport, Illinois), September 27, 1888, p. 4.

"Street smoking up to guardsmen." *Orange County Times-Press* (Middletown, New York), July 13, 1917, p. 1.

"Table decorations." *San Antonio Daily Light*, April 4, 1894, p. 8.

"Take to chewing gum." *San Antonio Light*, May 25, 1917, p. 8.

"Talks here and there." *Washington Post*, August 26, 1889, p. 5.

"Tars mayn't chaw gum." *Centralia Weekly Chronicle* (Washington), December 27, 1911, p. 6.

"Taxation gummed-up." *Wisconsin Rapids Daily Tribune* (Wisconsin), November 30, 1921, p. 5.

"The teacher chewed gum." *Daily Kennebec Journal* (Maine), June 14, 1895, p. 8.

"Teachers to lose gum." *Burlington Hawk-Eye* (Iowa), January 9, 1904, p. 1.

"Teeth and chewing gum." *Mountain Democrat* (Placerville, California), September 11, 1897, p. 6.

"Telephone girls mad." *Decatur Morning Review* (Illinois), May 6, 1891, p. 1.

"Their windscreen pipes." *Hutchinson News* (Kansas), July 21, 1906, p. 1.

"They all chew gum." *St. Joseph Herald* (Michigan), November 14, 1885, p. 1.

"They don't chew gum." *Washington Post*, January 28, 1904, p. 6.

"They like gum." *Daily Gazette* (Xenia, Ohio), January 5, 1918, p. 1.

"Things we like to see." *Greenville Argus* (Pennsylvania), May 31, 1873, p. 1.

"Thinks gum chewing good." *Racine Daily Journal* (Wisconsin), November 15, 1906, p. 12.

Thompson, Elizabeth. "Heart and beauty problems." *Eau Claire Leader* (Wisconsin), October 18, 1917, p. 6.

"Thought chewing gum was rubber." *La Crosse Tribune and Leader-Press* (Wisconsin), August 9, 1917, p. 7.

"Thoughts on men and things." *Hamilton Daily News* (Ohio), April 6, 1921, p. 6.

"$3,000,000 a year." *Oxnard Courier* (California), February 28, 1919, p. 2.

"To break off bad habits." *Daily Free Press* (Carbondale, Illinois), October 15, 1906, p. 4.

"To the gum chewing girl." *Pella Chronicle* (Iowa), August 8, 1905, p. 7.

"Tobacco Co. to sell chewing gum." *Wall Street Journal*, May 11, 1914, p. 6.

"Tobacco in chewing gum." *Davenport Daily Republican* (Iowa), January 30, 1901, p. 2.

"Topics of the day." *Evening News* (Mansfield, Ohio), May 10, 1891, p. 4.

"Topics of the times." *New York Times*, April 30, 1897, p. 6.

"Topics of the times." *New York Times*, August 24, 1899, p. 6.

"Triumph of chewing gum." *Atlanta Constitution*, April 13, 1902, p. 22.

"$12,000 paid for single ad for spearmint." *Newark Advocate* (Ohio), March 27, 1914, p. 6.

"Two innocent trusts." *Nevada State Journal* (Reno), July 26, 1906, p. 4.

"Ugly gum chewers." *Stevens Point Daily Journal* (Wisconsin), December 5, 1891, p. 3.

"United profit sharing." *Wall Street Journal*, July 11, 1914, p. 8.

"United States big figure." *Commerce Journal* (Texas), June 1, 1917, p. 4.

"U.S. chewing gum conquering the world." *New Castle News* (Pennsylvania), May 21, 1917, p. 12.

"Until he cried." *New Castle News* (Pennsylvania), October 17, 1894, p. 7.

"The uses of chewing gum." *Iowa State Reporter* (Waterloo), August 14, 1884, p. 8.

"Vast army of gum chewers." *Hutchinson News* (Kansas), July 10, 1907, p. 10.

Bibliography

Vip, Mikkel. "Just jottings." *Racine Daily Journal* (Wisconsin), August 23, 1906, p. 7.

"War on child gum sellers." *Washington Post*, November 19, 1910, p. 16.

"A warning to gum-chewers." *Iowa State Reporter* (Waterloo), May 10, 1876, p. 3.

"Wealth of romance compressed into package of chewing gum." *San Antonio Light*, August 9, 1915, p. 3.

"What chewing gum does." *Galveston Daily News*, August 13, 1886, p. 12.

"Where gum chewers are caught." *Salt Lake Tribune*, February 7, 1904, p. 4.

"Who chews gum." *Daily Miner* (Butte, Montana), January 14, 1882, p. 1.

"Why gum chewing is injurious." *Woodland Daily Democrat* (California), January 7, 1891, p. 1.

"Why we chew gum." *New York Times*, February 23, 1912, p. 4.

"Will have more time to talk." *Washington Post*, January 8, 1897, p. 10.

"Win your girl with gum." *Washington Post*, August 25, 1911, p. 6.

"With the interviewer." *Cedar Rapids Evening Gazette* (Iowa), June 20, 1907, p. 5.

"Woman chews gum; fined." *Washington Post*, November 8, 1915, p. 4.

"Women and chewing gum." *Davenport Daily Leader* (Iowa), October 23, 1893, p. 2.

"The world over." *Indiana Weekly Progress* (Indiana, Pennsylvania), November 11, 1886, p. 2.

"Wrigley delivers gum by aeroplanes." *Daily Constitution* (Chillicothe, Missouri), August 26, 1919, p. 3.

"Young society folks of Madrid have taken up habit of chewing gum." *Galveston Daily News*, March 4, 1920, p. 1.

Index

Index

Index

Index

www.ingramcontent.com/pod-product-compliance
Lightning Source LLC
Chambersburg PA
CBHW031130270326
41929CB00011B/1571